COED
REVOLUTION

ASIA-PACIFIC: CULTURE, POLITICS, AND SOCIETY

Edited by Rey Chow, Harry Harootunian, Michael Dutton, and Rosalind Morris

COED REVOLUTION

THE FEMALE STUDENT IN THE JAPANESE NEW LEFT

CHELSEA SZENDI SCHIEDER

DUKE UNIVERSITY PRESS · DURHAM AND LONDON · 2021

© 2021 DUKE UNIVERSITY PRESS
All rights reserved
Designed by Matthew Tauch
Typeset in Arno Pro and Quadratt Sans by Copperline
Book Services.

Library of Congress Cataloging-in-Publication Data

Cover art: A woman throwing a rock at police in Kanda,
Tokyo, September 12, 1969. Source: *Mainichi News*.

Duke University Press gratefully acknowledges the support
of the Association for Asian Studies, which provided funds
toward the publication of this book.

This one's for Miriam.

CONTENTS

ix   *Acknowledgments*

1   Introduction: Gendering the Japanese New Left

21   1   Naive Politics: A Maiden Sacrifice for Postwar Democracy

49   2   "My Love and Rebellion": The Politics of Nurturing, the Logic of Capital, and the Rationalization of Coeducation

78   3   Is the Personal Political? Everyday Life as a Site of Struggle in the Campus New Left

104   4   "When You Fuck a Vanguard Girl . . . ": The Spectacle of New Left Masculinity

132   5   "Gewalt Rosas": The Creation of the Terrifying, Titillating Female Student Activist

158   Conclusion: Revolutionary Desire

169   *Notes*
191   *Bibliography*
205   *Index*

ACKNOWLEDGMENTS

This is a poor and incomplete acknowledgment of the debts I have accrued in framing, researching, writing, and revising the following pages over a decade. The project began at Columbia University, and I will begin by thanking the mentors who encouraged me there: Gregory Pflugfelder, Kim Brandt, and Carol Gluck. While I was technically never his responsibility, Harry Harootunian has always made time for me and has continued to support this work. Comments from Eugenia Lean and Eric Zolov and coursework with Marilyn Ivy and Guobin Yang shaped this project in profound ways. I would not have chosen to become a historian without having the good fortune to have many impassioned history teachers along the way: Mark Hallam at Folsom High School and the history faculty at the University of California, Los Angeles. I want to thank Teofilo Ruiz, Hermann Ooms, Janice Reiff, and Miriam Silverberg in particular for recommending a demanding, often lonely, and endlessly fascinating path. Miriam, I have missed you.

Many organizations made possible the travel necessary to research this book. Fellowships from the Japan Foundation and the Japan American Association of New York–Honjo Foundation enabled me to spend over a year conducting research in Tokyo while in graduate school. Summer funding from the Weatherhead East Asian Institute and Columbia University's Department of East Asian Languages and Cultures allowed me two summers at the Takazawa Collection at the University of Hawai'i at Mānoa. Triangle Center for Japan Studies Travel Grants facilitated work in the Masaki Motoi Collection at Duke University. I was able to consult the Pacific Film Archive at the University of California, Berkeley, with a Pacific Film Archive Research Fellowship. Brebner Travel Awards and research funds from Meiji University and Aoyama Gakuin University made it possible for me to present my ideas and get feedback at conferences and workshops throughout my graduate studies career and after. The Weatherhead East Asian Institute Junior Fellowship in Japan Studies supported me in my final writing year, and a Japan Society for the Promotion of Science grant made research possible after graduate school.

At each of these sites and in each of these moments, several people facilitated this research. In Tokyo my advisor at Waseda University, Umemori Naoyuki, invited me into his seminar group. I am grateful to him and his students for our many conversations. I must also thank Kano Akihiro, Kano Tatsuko, and Kosaka Fumiko for their warm hospitality and openness to my many questions. Through Kano Akihiro, I was able to meet several members of Project Inoshishikai, and I am indebted to all those who agreed to speak with me about their lives. Particular thanks go to Tarōra Jōji and Mihashi Toshiaki. At the Takazawa Collection, Patricia Steinhoff and Tokiko Bazzel took wonderful care of me, and Kristina Troost assisted me at Duke University. I thank also the staff at Columbia University's Department of East Asian Languages and Cultures for their tireless support. I thank also Laura Warne and Mary The Trieu at the Weatherhead East Asian Institute for their work and kindness. A research university is nothing without its libraries and librarians, and I wish to acknowledge the efforts of those at the C. V. Starr East Asian Library who made my research possible: Kenneth Harlin, Rongxiang Zhang, Rich Jandovitz, and Dave Levkoff, thank you for managing all those stacks of books and patiently guiding each new generation of graduate students. At Butler Library, Bob Scott and Nancy Friedland demystified various aspects of digital humanities for me, ushering me into the archives of the twenty-first century. At Duke University Press, I want to thank everyone and particularly Nina Foster, Joshua Tranen, and Kate Herman. Thank you, Ken Wissoker, for believing in this project enough to take it on as a book.

The greatest joy I've experienced throughout this process has been the forging of new friendships based on intellectual engagement. I will fail in naming everyone here, but I must thank Ariel Acosta, Westenley Alcenat, Takemasa Ando, George Aumoithe, Joshua Batts, Buyun Chen, Kaijun Chen, Ryan Cook, Andre Deckrow, Anatoly Detwyler, James Gerien-Chen, Arunabh Ghosh, Robert Goree, Yukiko Hanawa, Mamiko Ito, Iwasaki Minoru, Colin Jones, Thai Jones, Nick Juravich, Ana Isabel Keilson, Kim Eunae, Naoko Koda, Andy Liu, Shi-Lin Loh, David Marcus, Anne McKnight, Jenny Wang Medina, Takashi Miyamoto, Mariko Naito, Odawara Rin, Kristen Roebuck, Joshua Schlachet, Shimada Yoshiko, Shinoda Toru, Nate Shockey, Joanna Sturiano, Grace Ting, Zeb Tortorici, Stacey Van Vleet,

Maja Vodopivec, Max Ward, Dustin Wright, Tim Yang, Yurou Zhong, and Ran Zwigenberg. Readings from the following friends helped shape this book: Ramona Bajema, Nathen Clerici, Alisa Freedman, Reto Hofmann, Nathan Hopson, Kim Icreverzi, John Leisure, Bill Marotti, Setsu Shigematsu, Wakako Suzuki, Akiko Takenaka, and Gavin Walker. The work also benefited from opportunities to present offered by David Slater, Phoebe Holdgrün, Youngran Ko, Aleksandra Kobiljiski, Christophe Thouny, and Kazuyuki "Ikko" Takahashi. I want to give a special thanks to the scholar-moms Sayaka Chatani, H. Yumi Kim, Gal Gvili, Liza Lawrence, and Mi-Ryong Shim who help me navigate the shifting terrain of scholarship and parenting. Everyone named here has made this work not only (one hopes) a better piece of scholarship but also work that feels worthwhile.

Several communities outside of academe have provided the support I needed as well: thank you to my fellow staff at Bozu and Momo Sushi Shack, my fellow founders and organizers of the Student + Activist + Community Coalition at Columbia University, my fellow faculty and staff at Meiji University and at Aoyama Gakuin University, and the daycare workers who make it possible for me to shower and do academic work. Thank you always to my kin: the chosen family that keeps growing and giving.

I have accrued a huge debt with my Japanese kinship network, most particularly the Yamaguchi family, who opened their homes to me many times over the years and opened my mind as well. It was the stories of Toshiaki and Hiromi—of the Zengakuren and Zenkyōtō generations respectively—that prompted the curiosity that became a vocation.

Thanks and apologies are due to my parents and my brother for this project that seems to take so much and give so little. "Thank you" is a poor reward for everything you have done for me. I also apologize to Josey for how this project siphoned off your mother's attention.

The most thanks goes, as ever, to ZDRM, my partner in all things. Every day with you is a radical praxis.

Introduction

Gendering the Japanese New Left

In April 1970, at an event attended by antiwar activists, students, vagabonds, and other assorted left-leaning young Japanese in Tokyo, four
young women stormed the stage. They wore the helmets then in vogue
among radical street fighters, but in place of the names of existing factions,
they had adorned their black helmets with the white letters S-E-X. The four
women, student activists at Tama Arts University, had planned this de-
but for their new Thought Group S.E.X. as a challenge to the masculinist
culture of the New Left. Their confrontation went awry, however, when
someone turned up the volume on the ten TV screens at the venue and
drowned out their voices, and the crowd turned to watch a teenage girl
perform a nonsensical game of dancing rock, paper, and scissors. When the
young woman began to strip, the men in the audience demanded that the
helmeted women strip as well. They slunk off the stage, ashamed. In their
reflections on this failed intervention, the women of Thought Group S.E.X.
expressed anger at how male activists had isolated women and their concerns in the movement yet again.[1]

The young women of Thought Group S.E.X. described how the campus
struggles and barricades of the late 1960s had seemed like a place where relations between men and women could be rebuilt, how a coeducational revolution might have been possible in newly coeducational spaces. They too
had shared in formulating a leftist critique of the world in which they lived,
in challenging the state and capital. Hadn't they also built the barricades

and faced the shields of the riot police alongside male student activists? However, they noted in retrospect, "That struggle was certainly our struggle, but at the same time it wasn't."[2] This is the story of "that struggle"— the campus-based New Left in Japan. Here I explore the meanings created by the participation of female university students in radical protest in the 1960s, as young men and women battled police in the streets, challenged political institutions, and paralyzed the higher education system.

The leftist student movement in postwar Japan criticized how the Japanese state and economy benefited from a capitalist geopolitical order maintained through U.S.-led military might and also implicated them and their education in that system. But what made this movement a "new" Left was its break from the "old" establishment Left of the Japanese Communist Party and Japanese Socialist Party. What I identify as the campus-based New Left in Japan demanded a more expansive definition of politics and applied leftist insights about economic oppression to a broader range of dynamics. In the context of the civil rights movement in the United States, popular challenges to Stalinism in the Eastern Bloc, and third world nationalist liberation struggles—of which the Vietnam War became the most influential—activists began to consider how racism and imperialism intersected with the economics of capitalism, for example. This expansive idea of liberation struggles would inspire women's liberation activists in the 1970s. Student activists' sweeping critiques of power in postwar Japan promised to completely dismantle the hierarchies that undergirded various forms of domination and intimated a more radical call to reformulate various relationships: economic, social, political, and intimate.

Young women in particular often found that New Left activism offered them opportunities to formulate a revolutionary sensibility that could transcend social expectations based on sex. In the late 1950s, when the left-leaning student movement broke from the Japanese Communist Party, part of what marked this New Left as new for many observers was precisely the participation of female students. Along with gaining new access to the political realm through enfranchisement, women also entered formerly all-male spaces of higher education in the postwar period, as previously men-only universities were forced to become coeducational. Shifting definitions of politics and violence associated with the New Left map onto changes in popular representations of the female student activist and illuminate the potential of and limits to the movement's politics.

While many women's movements in modern Japan framed activism around assumptions about women's domestic role, the New Left's radical understanding of politics promised to subvert the most basic assumptions about society.[3] Young women involved in the campus-based New Left also thought it would offer them a rare chance to engage in activism away from gendered expectations and spaces, such as the home, and to participate as full equals with young men.

And yet various dynamics—within the movement and in the interpretation of the movement within the mass media—often foreclosed that opportunity. Portrayals of the New Left by activists and journalists alike applied a gendered script to postwar student activism, defining how women could participate in radical politics. The movement was unable to address, in a meaningful way, the critiques brought up by young female participants about continued exclusion based on sexual difference, and it came to celebrate a masculine ideal of political action. There is a tension within this history: the campus-based New Left in Japan was a radical movement that in many ways prompted its participants to consider how lived daily life intersected with larger political and economic structures, and thus it opened up spaces for consideration of the often invisible role of female labor within modern capitalism, while dynamics within the movement also foreclosed such discussions.

There is also a tension within the historiography of the 1960s, inasmuch as it often memorializes the New Left as primarily male. This is particularly pronounced in the Japanese case, but it is not exclusive to Japan. Susana Draper, writing on "the women of 1968" in Mexico, also identified a "masculine monopoly over the memory of the moment." This does a great disservice to the profoundly unsettling nature of the radical New Left in the global 1960s. As Draper noted, "One gets the impression that, instead of actualizing a moment profoundly open to the destabilization of conventional roles, the liberatory potential of the moment was superseded by a memory that was consummated in reproducing the same system of hierarchy that they had previously contested, in terms of both social class and sexual difference."[4] Such a masculinist memorialization reproduces some of the strains of a masculinist culture that in many ways undermined the student movement in Japan and elsewhere. We could, instead, examine the expansive vision of politics that mobilized a generation of not only young men but also young women to recover a profoundly radical feminist genealogy from within the New Left, as young people questioned the status quo and sought a space to radically reconceptualize their relationships with all social expectations. On the level of the daily lived negotiations within radical movements in the 1960s, we can see how women and men organizing together often revealed tensions about sexism but also troubled received notions about the proper social roles of women.

Not only have women's participation in and contributions to the New Left in Japan been ignored, but a great deal of energy has been expended to ignore them, and that process requires attention. Female participation in student activism was quickly and persistently policed both from within the movement and from without, through the actions of male activists and of the mass media. One of my goals here is to understand female contributions to the radical student movement and the contemporaneous operations by which these contributions were undermined, in order to uncover a dynamic tension within radical politics in postwar Japan. Emancipatory, radical, anticapitalist politics was at the heart of the global 1960s, and while activists may have had their own oversights and failings, it was a moment in which revolution against the status quo was on the agenda, and people were not afraid to point out the contradictions at the heart of their everyday lives.

But why write a history of the female student in the Japanese New Left when one of the fascinating things about the 1960s as a political moment was the way in which conventional roles were destabilized? One risks reifying the category of "woman" while narrating a kind of herstory of the postwar student movement. Rather than understand all female students as sharing the same experience of activism, however, I try to understand women within a relational system of social expectations attached to sex-based differences (following Joan Scott) and thus use gender as a tool to analyze status quo expectations.[5] Not only is the category of woman relative, but it is also defined within hierarchies of power and intersects with other vectors of power and access in a society. This study touches on the gendered language and symbols available in postwar Japan to interpret political activism, and how individuals related to these symbols, by focusing on moments of contested politics and considering a movement that demanded a more expansive definition of politics. In that sense, what I am doing is a gendered history that attempts to understand how women—a category that actually contains a wide diversity of experiences—were configured in regard to labor and care in postwar Japan.

While I understand "women" as a social concept based on a constellation of expectations, I also understand that speaking of gender in the 1960s can be an anachronistic framing, since people living at the time did not use the term. For that reason, even while illuminating what I see as gendered dynamics at work in postwar Japanese society and in the student New Left,

I also try to reflect the vocabulary employed at the time, hence the employment of the term *coed* to refer to the female student.

The title of my study, *Coed Revolution*, emphasizes the newly coeducational character of many universities and of student activism in 1960s Japan, while also underlining that the female coed represented a potentially revolutionary figure. The English word *coed* also carries reactionary valences that make it my favored translation for the Japanese term *joshigakusei* (female student).[6] This literally means "girl student," which I translate as *coed* to emphasize the secondary status this term implies in contrast to "student," or *gakusei*, which, because maleness is the assumed norm, was unburdened by the gendered qualifier. The postwar student movement in Japan was coed inasmuch as postwar higher education reforms encouraged integration of young women into formerly all-male institutions. This experience often tested the radical politics of student activists and exposed moments of persistent exclusion.

WHY FOCUS ON THE FEMALE STUDENT?

The female university student tested the radical politics of student activists at the same time as she was challenging general social and economic divisions that insisted on separate spheres for men and women. She was a middle-class identity in a time when the middle class was expanding and bolstering a myth of a classless, ethnically homogeneous nation in Japan.[7] As Tessa Morris-Suzuki has pointed out, the postwar definition of the post-empire citizen "narrowed possible *ethnic* meanings" and thus excluded former colonial subjects from postwar citizenship. But it also "broadened the *political* meaning of nationality" by including previously oppositional political positions and also women.[8] In this context, middle-class Japanese women, particularly politically radical middle-class women, tested the limits of access to citizen subjectivity from within.

My use of the English *New Left*, following Takemasa Ando, is not a literal translation of the Japanese term *shinsayoku*, which refers strictly to factions that splintered from the establishment Left of the Japanese Communist Party from the late 1950s onward and that demanded a high degree of commitment, organization, and adherence to a specific dogma.[9] The term *shinsayoku* implies strict hierarchies and militancy and has become a loaded term in Japanese, implying almost sociopathic fanaticism. Many participants in the student movement in postwar Japan would reject the label of *shinsayoku*, but their leftist activism reflected many concerns that can be identified as characteristic of a global New Left at the time, as university-based radicalism shaped its identity and concerns in reaction to liberal democracy, global capital, and the established Left. There was overlap in participants and in campaigns between New Left factions and more self-consciously nonhierarchical groups such as the loosely organized Zenkyōtō (short for Zengaku kyōtō kaigi, or All-Campus Joint Struggle Committees) and students who defined themselves as "nonpolitical" (*nonpori*) but still participated in activism. Using the term *New Left* highlights this global phenomenon, even as I detail here the specific genealogy and strategies of the postwar student movement in Japan, which responded to a distinct historical and political context.

Although it is possible, as Ando has done, to expand the definition of the New Left in Japan to include citizens' and workers' groups, I limit my project to the student movement.[10] I seek to uncover a dynamic history in which a student movement shaped by postwar policies of coeducation negotiated rapidly changing—and gendered—ideals of political participation. Not only did the phrase *student power* become a powerful rallying cry among the growing university student population worldwide by the late 1960s, but examining a postwar student New Left across generations of activists and causes between 1957 and 1972 reveals significant shifts in the social meaning of activism as a whole.

Work on the mass demonstrations of 1960 often focuses on a paradigm shift away from ideologies of class struggle toward a new ethos of citizen activism. While female participants often contributed to these new social movements, such a focus de-emphasizes both the New Left's radical challenge to postwar ideals of liberal citizenship and also the challenge New Left women posed to social expectations regarding female political participation.[11] Many women involved in civic activism participated in protests as wives and mothers.[12] Workers' groups also often kept women's units separate in the same period.[13] In postwar Japan it was the student New Left that offered a real experiment in coed revolution.

Placing the experiences, interpretations, and representations of female student activists at the center of a history of the postwar student movement also insists on the challenges posed by female participation to the internal dynamics of the New Left in Japan. Works that mention the existence of sexism in the student New Left often treat that dynamic as a subcategory.[14] I understand the meanings created by female student activist participation as critical to the larger context in which a coed New Left was interpreted and also to the internal dynamics of the student movement.

Violent events involving female students symbolized the rise and fall of the New Left in Japan, from the 1960 death of Kanba Michiko in a mass demonstration to the 1972 murders committed under the leadership of Nagata Hiroko in a sectarian purge. Kanba became a kind of "maiden sacrifice" for Japan's fragile postwar democracy in 1960, whereas Nagata came to represent the violent excesses of youth radicalism in the early 1970s. The same arc frames current narratives of the postwar student movement in Japan: from vulnerable to dangerous in the course of a decade. The female student coed as a radical activist played a distinct role in mass media reportage on the student movement; the media portrayed her as a figure of particular vulnerability or particular violence, a character to inspire sympathy or fear.

The expanding mass media of the 1960s in many ways defined the social meaning of the student movement, and the press was not a neutral observer. Particularly in a time of rapidly changing social expectations, the cultural debates that circulated in print media played a critical role in representing the New Left, often obscuring the debates most important to the participants themselves.[15] Activists in postwar Japan often tried to counter the narratives of the mass media through their own *minikomi*—their shorthand for their minicommunications, in the form of mimeographed fliers and hand-stenciled posters countering the vested powers of mass communications and the mass media. Although I listen also for the voices of student activists, and female student activists in particular, my analysis devotes sustained attention to the mass media as an actor creating social meaning. The pervasive influence of mass media in the 1960s resulted also in an acute sense of the synchronicity of student power, particularly during the late 1960s as campus-based protests erupted worldwide and images of street demonstrations flew across the globe via print media as well as the moving images of television.

Another mass phenomenon traced in this study is the rise of mass higher education. By the late 1960s, not only had the postwar baby boom generation come of age, but they were also attending higher education institutions at an unprecedented rate.[16] Being a university student remained a relatively privileged socioeconomic position, but in a society that increasingly defined itself as middle-class, it also became a critical part of the definition of the ideal Japanese citizen.[17] In 1963 Japan was already third in the world in the number of higher education institutions, behind only the United States and the Soviet Union.[18] While women's rate of continuing on to higher education lagged behind that of men in the postwar period, in 1969 women and men went on to tertiary institutions at almost the same rate: 22.3 percent of women and 24.1 percent of men continued their education beyond secondary school.[19]

It is difficult to estimate precisely how many young women participated in the leftist student movement, but it is clear that female students were active across factions and campuses in the late 1960s New Left. They joined for reasons similar to those of their male comrades: they felt compelled by the global situation and the paradoxes they saw in their society, and they understood activism as a natural part of being a student and a member of their campus community. One survey conducted in the early 1990s published the results of 529 questionnaires filled out by people who self-identified as part of the late 1960s student New Left at eighty-one higher education institutions across Japan. That publication included the testimonies of forty-three female respondents from twenty-four universities, each involved in a diverse range of activist activities with varying levels of commitment at the time and afterward.[20] As mentioned previously, histories of the New Left in Japan often characterize the New Left as male, which further obscures the complex legacy of female participation in the postwar student movement.

Even when considering how women within the New Left came to criticize the movement from 1970 onward, thus fueling a post–New Left women-only women's liberation movement, many scholars overemphasize a Left-to-lib break. Even when a women's movement is cited as a reaction to New Left male chauvinism, the arguments articulated by feminists do not seem to actually penetrate many of the influential analyses by male academics. Oguma Eiji offers an oft-cited and voluminous social history of the late 1960s New Left but in many cases seems intent on listing characteristics of the movement rather than engaging with the intellectual challenges and critiques launched by student activism. While drawing extensively on contemporary journalism, his history remains unconcerned with the nonneutral position of the mass media's reports, particularly when it came to female activists. In listing what he saw as the motivations for female students' participation in the New Left—along with "[the] same as the male students, a sense of dissatisfaction with the present conditions of the university and society and a sense of justice"—Oguma includes that, "as reported in the news at the time, 'having just discovered a wonderful boyfriend, they "without theory" ran to his sect.'"[21] To suggest that only women chose their political affiliations based on interpersonal relationships is historically false, and Oguma's failure to read against the grain of the contemporary mass media reports replicates the sexist logic that tended to interpret all female political participation as irrational (unlike the male students, who ostensibly acted *only* according to their grievances and theoretical considerations). Further, as women's lib activist Tanaka Mitsu pointed out in an article that originated in a blistering review on Japan's Amazon site, Oguma described feminists like Tanaka in precisely the same terms as the tabloid media of the 1960s did, undermining their political positions by regurgitating sexist mass media rumors about eating disorders or sexual promiscuity or even their unbecoming fashion choices.[22]

In contrast, coming from a leftist position, Suga Hidemi demands a more serious engagement with the theories of the 1960s—in particular, the late 1960s—and points out that discourses about women's rights and also minorities' rights and ecology, which emerged in the New Left at its dissolution, have in many ways come to serve neoliberal political goals and obscure a true reckoning with the New Left critique of capitalism.[23] Suga is particularly impatient with what he sees as the "insufficient" attention paid to economic angles by women writers associated with women's liberation (Tanaka Mitsu) and even an earlier postwar generation of feminist writers (Morisaki Kazue).[24] He largely dismisses feminism in Japan throughout the 1970s and 1980s as a movement limited to demanding women's increased access to a prosperous consumer society. What Suga does not do is engage critically with the writings and critiques of the women of the post–New Left women's liberation movement, and he thus fails to see how feminism in Japan in the 1970s and 1980s made it possible to open up new questions precisely about the role of women—as producers and reproducers—in the projects of nation, empire, and global capital.[25]

Both Oguma, from a "melancholy liberal" position, and Suga, from the left, replicate the coed logic in which female activists' experiences in and analyses of the New Left are marginalized, regarded as somehow supplementary to the more rational and focused activism of New Left men. Oguma and Suga thereby reinforce what Draper dubbed the "masculine monopoly over the memory of the moment." In their analyses, the two narratives—that of the campus-based New Left and that of the post–New Left women's liberation movement—tend to be held separate, in constant tension, even as many activists involved in the 1970s women's liberation movement have written and spoken about the New Left genealogy of the post–New Left feminist movement, which included sexist marginalization but also many influences in terms of the framings of debates and strategies.[26]

What would it mean to actually investigate how women figured in the radical postwar student movement? Ueno Chizuko, Japan's most well-known feminist scholar who also attended university in the late 1960s, has declared that women in the student movement in Japan had only two roles available to them: to act the part of a "cutie" and seek male affection or to internalize male values and become an aggressive female leader.[27] These gendered patterns of political activism certainly existed. But to dismiss all female participation in the New Left as mindless conforming to standards imposed by a sexist movement obscures the many negotiations among the movement's coed members and those between the movement and the mass media. Rather than dismiss women's participation in the New Left or dismiss the New Left altogether as irredeemably sexist, what would it mean to incorporate women's experiences and critiques of leftist activism *into* a radical leftist critique of global capitalism as it organized society in Japan in a period of unprecedented economic growth? The answer requires situating the New Left and its gendered politics in a broader political and social context.

THE "WOMAN QUESTION" IN RADICAL POLITICS

There is a longer conflicted history of women's participation in leftist social movements in Japan and elsewhere. A lingering question for many female socialists in modern Japan has been, which comes first: freedom from exploitation based on class difference or freedom from exploitation based on sexual difference? This question has come up in several movements that fought to expand the political and social rights of various groups throughout the process of modernization. Many activists—identifying variously as Christian reformers, anarchists, socialists, or imperialists—reflected the influence of the political ideas then shaking up the world and advocated for female access to education and political rights in the early twentieth century in Japan.[28] Women were active in organizations associated with leftist thought—the socialist Heiminsha (Commoners' Society) and labor groups—from their inception in the early twentieth century.[29] Their participation reflected the new social reality in which women were incorporated into the industrial workforce, particularly as cheap labor for Japan's modern textile industry, on which the state founded its new export economy.[30] However, women were often relegated to support positions within the socialist movement throughout the prewar period.[31] Women writers involved in socialist and leftist communities, such as Hirabayashi Taiko, who was active from the 1920s, penned critiques of the sexism women faced in those circles.[32] While engaging in deep analyses of the state and political practices, the socialist movement in Japan often re-created the gendered divisions of labor seen in society at large and advocated by the state.

These debates occurred in a broader global context. Within leftist thought from the late nineteenth century onward, debates on the proper social role of women, and particularly the character of some future equality between men and women, occupied anarchists and socialists alike. Equality between men and women was ostensibly a goal of the radical social programs envisioned by modern revolutionary thinkers on the left. Anarchist thinker Emma Goldman considered sexuality alongside radical politics but encountered criticism from fellow anarchists, most famously from Pyotr Kropotkin, who insisted that sexuality was personal and not a suitable aspect of political discussion.[33] Many in the nineteenth century assumed that once a revolution in economic and political relations among all people came about, relations between men and women would become equal as well.

The achievement of an ostensible workers' paradise on earth with the creation of the Soviet Union precluded many open discussions about potentially modifying intimate relations and also eventually closed down discussions about continuing patriarchal attitudes and structures. Cinzia Arruzza has recently written of how the unified front presented by global Communism under the Third International following the success of the Russian Revolution in the early twentieth century contributed to an authoritarian orthodoxy that negated socialist women's contributions to politics and theory.[34] Although many socialists had been optimistic that restructuring economic relations between the sexes and educating young men and women alongside each other would resolve inequalities based on sexual difference, discussions of intimate relationships—the family, romantic love, domestic chores—were often dismissed as outside the realm of the political. This history influenced how national Communist parties in various countries defined "politics" and handled (or, more often, dismissed) inequalities among activists rooted in received ideas about gender.

New Left activism promised, but never delivered, a more expansive socialist politics than the orthodoxy of the established Left in the mid-twentieth century. However, many female activists' experiences in the New Left made them skeptical that prioritizing the revolution would improve their lives. Young women who came to activism through the postwar New Left in Japan found that their marginalization within the movement echoed similar exclusions in modern theories of capital and labor.[35] These young women who had become sensitive to analyses of labor, everyday life, and alienation found that the New Left still cut them out of the revolution. One of the young women who went on to be active in the women's liberation movement recalled male activists leaning on leftist theory to exclude her: "One boy said, 'haven't you read Marx? Women's labor in the home isn't labor.'"[36] Female activists countered such limited interpretations of labor and production, insisting that childbirth was also production and was far from a personal, private matter.[37] They concluded their observations on the supplementary and exceptional role played by women in the student movement and modern revolutionary movements with a call to reconnect the political struggle with private issues.

WHAT'S SO NEW ABOUT THE NEW LEFT?

Following the example of other scholars of the 1960s, I try to understand how New Left activists in Japan attempted to expand the notion of what constituted political action. In writing about art-based activism in the 1960s in Japan, William Marotti—drawing on the work of Jacques Rancière and Kristen Ross—points to how the radical political engagement of the period actually challenged the very definitions of what was considered political.[38] Carl Boggs Jr. coined the term *prefigurative politics* in a 1977 piece on what he identified as "one of the most troublesome dilemmas encountered by Marxist movements and regimes": how could they wage a battle for political power while also integrating what ought to be the "ultimate ends of the revolutionary process itself: popular self-emancipation, collective social and authority relations, socialist democracy"? Boggs dubbed negotiations over the internal dynamics and processes of a movement *prefigurative politics*, while he categorized the strategies employed to obtain political power itself *instrumental politics*.[39] Wini Breines, writing about the U.S. New Left, employed the term prefigurative politics to indicate how radicals in the 1960s insisted upon formulating their own counterinstitutions and alternatives rather than operating within the existing political system to change it.[40] This attention to *how* one participated in politics drew on older political and faith traditions, and has sometimes been dismissed as simply expressive politics, defined only as opposition and limited to personal or cultural change.

The New Left emphasis on democratic participation wove together many people's very political concerns about class struggle and anti-imperialism with the observation that many of the contemporary organizations that claimed to fight such fights—namely, the established Left—did not necessarily present a real alternative in terms of political practices. As Francesca Polletta notes in the cases of many organizations in contemporary U.S. history, a focus on the process of radical democracy was not simply about fostering a more expressive style but also about understanding the politics of an organization's practices. They thus emphasized debate, encouraged the consensus necessary for radical actions, and attracted many people who would not otherwise have participated in a social movement.[41] It is easy to dismiss youth activism as too idealistic or even reactionary, but youth in modern societies are often uniquely positioned to feel the pressures of socialization as they are subjected to them in economic, political, and educational situations. We can get a sense of the larger political stakes by listening to the voices of student activists and the ways they were interpreted and misinterpreted.

From within the Japanese New Left, Tokoro Mitsuko, a graduate student in biology and an activist leader, argued that it was absurd to employ the logic of capitalist rationalization to facilitate a movement against capitalism. In her analysis of the established Left of the Japanese Communist Party, she noted that in its rigid maintenance of hierarchy and rationalization of its members' activities, it "has not avoided the logic of capitalism: ranking humans by their production value."[42] Many student activists, particularly female students who felt close to the everyday labor of caring for their families and friends, framed their activism in terms of a set of intimate practices, and I see this as an invitation to pay close attention to how the daily life operations of the student movement related to the movement's theories and larger social context.

At the same time, because many activists within the coed revolution of the campus-based New Left—both male and female—saw their political movement as transcending what they saw as the narrow bourgeois concerns of the usual women's issues groups, such as those involved in consumers' movements and the peace movement, I risk betraying their intentions in insisting on a distinctly "female student activist" experience of the movement. Women within the New Left in Japan also often understood their work, which might be stereotypically "women's labor," as something qualitatively different when in the movement. As Katō Mitsuko, a female student activist at the University of Tokyo in the late 1960s, described it, she felt that the construction of the student-run barricades broke with the logic of the everyday world of society at large, thus allowing her to engage in nurturing and cooking for her comrades in their "commune" free from the historical and social gendered baggage attendant on care work in Japanese society outside of the barricaded campus.[43] Katō herself noted that this assessment may have been a bit premature, since the student barricades did not escape the larger logic of society, but if we dismiss the experiences and words of these women as self-deluded and complicit in their own exploitation, as some post–New Left feminists did, we replicate the gendered hierarchy of leadership as authentic activism and of "support work" as somehow less important.

Considering the way that women had figured in the unpaid labor structures undergirding modern capitalist societies, it should not surprise us that a political movement that attempted to occupy and liberate spaces to generate a more authentic set of everyday political practices would find that negotiating those spaces entailed confronting gendered ideas about labor. Again, this is not limited to Japan but is an issue of how women fit into larger, global structures of labor at the time. When Deborah Cohen and Lessie Jo Frazier discuss the barricades created and maintained by student activists in Mexico, they could also be writing about Japan:

> When students occupied the universities, campus spaces were transformed into their political and physical home. In the classrooms, libraries, and cafeterias where men and women had studied economics, philosophy, and mathematics, they ate, slept, crafted propaganda, and held meetings. The new transformation of former classrooms into semidomestic spaces also required new logistical arrangements; women's labor underpinned these reconfigurations. Both men and women took turns guarding the school buildings against the police; they maintained the sanctity of the movement's home and fragile borders. In so doing, they drew on a pervasive twentieth-century war rhetoric of protecting hearth and home. In this sense, women's presence in the occupied university was not anomalous, but rather necessary in order to regender this space as an embattled home front.[44]

To return to Katō's words, "We can't talk about solving the problems concerning 'being woman' [*onna de aru koto*] without linking it to a big movement demanding revolution. But it's not a simple matter of extending a political movement, nor can we have a real revolution without solving those problems."[45] That is to say, a political movement that stopped short of complete socioeconomic revolution could not actually resolve the many contradictions women faced, as producers and reproducers of paid and unpaid labor. And the necessary socioeconomic revolution would need to grapple with the uneven distribution of not only resources but also voice and agency based on class and also gender.

That male chauvinism proved a defining characteristic of many women's experiences of New Left activism around the world undermines arguments that Japanese sexism is some kind of immutable and ahistorical feudal remnant handed down to the present unchanged over time. I understand female students as occupying a position in the New Left that exposed the unexamined categories of an otherwise wide-ranging critique of the often unseen operations of authority that undergirded Japan's economic miracle. In many ways, a very modern idea of the proper place of female labor within gendered hierarchies defined the New Left's sexism. Masculinist definitions of the ideal movement activist often colored the dynamics of the New Left and its commemoration in Japan and beyond.

In the United States, Marge Piercy's 1969 outraged takedown of the sexist New Left, *The Grand Coolie Damn*, described a momentary liberation within "the Movement" that nevertheless lapsed into a situation in which men continued to understand their status as defined by "the people whose labor one can possess and direct in one's projects"—people who often ended up being women as sexual partners, as "domestic-servants-mother-surrogates," and "constantly as economic producers." While Piercy acknowledged that too much "introspection and fascination with the wriggles of the psyche"—that is, constant consciousness-raising—can obstruct activism, she also noted that "there is also a point beyond which cutting off sensitivity to others and honesty to what one is doing does not produce a more efficient revolutionary, but only a more efficient son of a bitch." Piercy described how the men in the movement gained prominence, while "the real basis is the largely unpaid, largely female labor force that does the daily work. Reflecting the values of the larger capitalist society, there is no prestige whatsoever attached to actually working. Workers are invisible."[46]

Piercy's account is interesting inasmuch as she very much kept her eyes on the larger economic picture of how women's labor figured in the New Left while she also pointed out a romantic, erotic economy that valued certain forms of not only action but also thinking in a way that privileged access for masculine voice and activities, as well as male sexual access to women. The catch for women in the campus-based leftist activism in the United States, as Piercy saw it, was that "by definition women are bourgeois: they are housewives and domesticators."[47] In a movement that sought to defeat bourgeois economics alongside the bourgeois family and moral codes, women became a target for revolutionary scorn. This is the case in the Japanese New Left as well, in which female labor reproduced much of the menial day-to-day organization of the movement—mimeographing fliers, cooking and cleaning in the barricades, providing jail support—and was often rendered invisible. Activists also came to reject what they saw as the bourgeois morality that underpinned such care work, as represented by the scorn they expressed for the figure of the mother and their attraction to a particularly aggressive manifestation of masculinity. The liberatory potential of "free sex" was also mitigated by the actual practices, which often defined free sex as unrestricted male access to female bodies.

The contested role of the female student activist in the New Left in Japan, then, is also part of a global story. Women-only radical movements emerged from many New Lefts in the late 1960s. This was also the case in Japan. There remains a need to understand what within the New Left—its theories and practices—convinced radical women who participated in campus-based activism that they needed to form a separatist movement. The contemporaneity of the New Left and the subsequent women's lib movement in Japan aligns it with similar movements at other sites, which actually requires bringing Japan's history of protest into a larger global history. Since there is a tendency to isolate Japanese national history along national borders, examining the history of a moment in which dissent took inspiration from global social movements offers a chance to frame events that occurred in Japan more broadly. There is something about the way that women figure into modern capitalist societies that defines women's labor—in both formal and informal economies—and that is shared across national borders. But the various negotiations and resistances to those formulations, and the extent to which they consider not only gendered divisions of labor but also racial, ethnic, and class-based oppressions, can be very different. Sara M. Evans has already noted the "interesting lacuna" in the historiography of the global "1968 generation," which has left out gender analyses even as "feminism and dramatic challenges to gender relations were among the primary legacies of activism."[48]

In discussions of how such hierarchies based on gender can develop in ostensibly liberatory and radically democratic movements, however, it is also worth bearing in mind that, as studies of women-only movements have detailed, some power dynamics that existed in the New Left were also at work in ostensibly nonhierarchical women's liberation movements, even as they became disconnected from sexual difference. Jo Freeman noted the potential for structurelessness within a group of activists to actually become "a way of masking power, and within the women's movement it is usually most strongly advocated by those who are the most powerful (whether they are conscious of their power or not)."[49] Such conflicts emerged in various groups that organized explicitly to confront patriarchy: Kimberly Springer has noted the tendency for women who wrote in the Combahee River Collective (and other radical black feminist organizations) to gain prominence over those who did not; Setsu Shigematsu analyzes the same trend among the women's lib activists who ran the collective Shinjuku Lib Center in the 1970s in Japan.[50] Post–New Left women's liberation activists in Japan often spoke of the difficulty of undoing their own internalized disdain for forms of expression and types of labor coded feminine, and in many instances, care work—the invisible, daily labor of a movement—went unappreciated. So while a coed movement brought to the fore many previously underappreciated issues regarding how gender defined power and labor, the solution to such problems was not as simple as launching a women-only movement, even as women-only movements provided spaces in which women could better articulate how larger structures of social injustice intervened into daily life practices.

I am studying the roles and receptions of women in the Japanese postwar student movement to understand the possibilities and limits they faced in making radical, revolutionary demands on the society in which they lived. I employ three broader analytic categories: vulnerability, violence, and voice. These interact in various ways throughout the chapters. None is a fixed category, but all frame political action by student activists, and female student activists in particular. While the growing violence of the late 1960s student movement has been attributed to, among other factors, an "excess of ethics" that made student radicals feel justified in carrying out intensified attacks on police, university property, and each other, I track shifts in popular support of student activism to reveal a gendered dynamic of violence and vulnerability.[51] The way violence and vulnerability intersected with gendered expectations in the student New Left defined the movement's relationship to its members and to the public at large, as communicated in the expanding mass media of the time, which amplified certain voices and obscured others. For female student activists, as we will see, there was never a moment when their voices, as mediated by newspapers, magazines, and other activists, were free from expectations about feminine vulnerability or violence.

Chapter 1 explores the meaning created by the 1960 death of Kanba Michiko, a female student activist leader killed in mass demonstrations against the U.S.-Japan Security Treaty (Anpo). With her death, Kanba fit into a narrative forged in the mass media, of young, middle-class women as particularly vulnerable to state violence in the postwar period. Popular sympathy for Kanba as a maiden sacrifice for postwar democracy emerged in a context that encompassed broader discourses about legitimate forms of political expression, including what I call "naive politics." Various attempts to speak on her behalf and fit her death into shared frames of popular empathy silenced Kanba's own radical politics. While Kanba became representative of the fragility of postwar democracy, her writings underscore the discrepancy between her public significance and her personal relationship to radical politics. Kanba's case demonstrates how a gendered political discourse about vulnerability and victimization, while mobilizing popular sympathy for a New Left cause, also reinforced existing values and emotional standards at the time of the 1960 Anpo demonstrations.

Chapter 2 introduces the writings of Tokoro Mitsuko, a young woman who participated in the 1960 Anpo protests as an undergraduate student and continued to write on political themes as a graduate student. Her theoretical pieces on how to create a horizontal style of organization in a political movement, written in reaction to the strong hierarchical system of the traditional Left in Japan, influenced the organizational ideals of the late-1960s student New Left. Tokoro's analyses drew on her personal experiences in leftist activism and also on ideas about "women's logic" as a potential source of opposition to the rationalist logic of economic efficiency and war. Tokoro's articulation of women's logic forces us to consider both how a female student's ideas influenced the Japanese New Left and also how "women's issues" were erased in the course of the movement. While replicating many essentialist discourses about women as basically vulnerable and nurturing, Tokoro attempted to understand how a gendered subjectivity created meaning in society and how one could listen to those excluded from hierarchies of power.

Her writings on how the student Left ought to relate to both violence and its imagined (and likewise gendered) opposite, nurturing, proposed bringing nonviolent and nurturing feminine values to the student movement as a whole to challenge what she identified as the violence of postwar efforts to rationalize society, education, and the workforce. And although Tokoro and other female students rejected these rationalizations of labor, particularly the conservative division between male work in the public sphere and female labor in the private sphere of the home, such a gendered rationalization was in many ways based on the same gendered understandings of nurturing embraced by Tokoro, and it also influenced understandings of how women ought to configure in postwar education and work.

Although the student movement imagined itself as immune to the logic of the state and the mass media, the practices of the late 1960s campus-based student movement, examined in chapter 3, illustrate how larger societal assumptions about gender roles informed the gendered hierarchy of labor that emerged in the barricades. This chapter focuses in particular on the "everyday" as it was theorized and experienced in the late 1960s student movement. Sources produced by student activists, particularly those created by female student activists, describe how activists in the late 1960s built barricades at university campuses as part of their challenge to the everyday of the state and capital, which also opened up the time and space for young people to experience daily life outside of mainstream society and imagine potential political and personal alternative ways of living. State-led efforts to reorganize higher education in the service of the growing economy formed the larger context for a proliferation of campus-based protests and occupations and led many students to question the value system that bolstered an expanding middle-class lifestyle. Students felt that violence in nearby Southeast Asia contributed to the affluence they enjoyed in daily life, and they sought to disrupt the organization of the state and industry interests that contributed to war. However, the persistence of gendered definitions of labor in the student movement, as reflected in the daily practices in the barricades, led many female student activists to question the real-life limits of the New Left and to become aware of how sexual difference set limits on their political involvement.

Chapter 4 focuses on late 1968 and 1969, when the student movement faced not only rising state oppression but also increasing marginalization by the mass media. This chapter considers how New Left ideals of gendered action responded to a perceived crisis of masculinity in the postwar period and how those understandings linked with larger frames about political vulnerability and violence. The construction of a masculine identity became important to a New Left that wanted to project an image of invulnerability and strength; in doing so, it cultivated a culture that disdained expressions of vulnerability and understood femininity as such a vulnerability. This emphasis on a masculine vision of the revolutionary hero focused on a kind of personal liberation, rather than political or economic liberation. Masculinist ideas about the proper political subject resonated with similar concerns on the far right, and ostensibly liberatory practices like sexual liberation or confrontations with authority actually created new forms of gendered exclusion. While the mass media emphasized New Left spectacles of violence, the police turned toward community outreach, cultivating a new image of the friendly police officer.

Japanese students referred to their violent actions as *Gewalt—gebaruto*—to distinguish their "counterviolence" from the violence employed by the state. However, the mass media soon picked up on the term to frame the student movement as a dangerous threat to social order and to disparage the students' actions. In this late 1960s moment, activist women, once considered particularly vulnerable to violence, became deeply associated with active incitement to violence. Chapter 5 explores how the mass media coded female student activism in particular as both terrifying and titillating through its imaginary construction of the "Gewalt Rosa" (Violent Rosa). The social meaning created by the relationship between female students and violence, as disseminated through the mass media, critically influenced public reception of student activism. When, in 1972, the mass media revealed a leftist group's bloody internal purge, it marked a moment many saw as the death of the New Left. The female leader of the group, Nagata Hiroko, stepped all too conveniently into existing media formulations of the Gewalt Rosa, leading to both disavowals of the student movement among feminists in the 1970s and also to mass media narratives that attacked feminism as a potentially violent movement.

I conclude by considering the gendered nuances of the New Left legacy in Japan and what it means to understand the history of a radical movement and its reception through the figure of the female activist, particularly in a society in which so much desire and fear is projected onto young women but their voices are so rarely heard. We need a nuanced accounting of the New Left's legacy now more than ever to understand the necessity of a feminist Left.

1 Naive Politics

A Maiden Sacrifice for Postwar Democracy

Beaten by the acacia rains
That is how I want to die
The night will end, the sun will rise
In the morning's light
He'll find my cold body
That certain someone
And I wonder if he'll shed tears for me
"When the Acacia Rains Stop," sung by Nishida Sawako

For many people in Japan who lived the events of the 1960s, Nishida Sawa-ko's hit ballad "When the Acacia Rains Stop" evokes the mass protests of 1959 and 1960. The lyrics describe a beautiful failure and the death of a young woman: "Beaten by the acacia rains / that is how I want to die / the night will end, the sun will rise / in the morning's light / he'll find my cold body." For many, this song, released just before the rainy season—the "plum rains" (*tsuyu*)—of June 1960, provided the soundtrack not only for the dramatic street confrontations of that month but also for the aftermath of mourning for a young woman who had indeed died, tragically, in clashes with police after forcing entry into the Diet compound with a contingent of New Left student activists on the evening of June 15, 1960. Kanba

Michiko's "cold body" was found by the entire nation in the early morning hours of June 16, 1960.

Here I position the twenty-two-year-old student activist Kanba Michiko within the larger, gendered context of postwar politics to understand how, in death, she became available to a wide variety of political actors as a figure around which to rally. The results of her autopsies offered conflicting narratives of the cause of death, and opinions remained divided about whether she was strangled by the police or trampled by fellow protesters. Yet the dominant narrative that framed the death of the University of Tokyo senior Kanba was that she became a maiden sacrifice for postwar democracy in Japan.

Kanba's gender was incidental to her death, but her death as a young female protester created meaning because it fit into a narrative about postwar democracy and the role of female political participation therein. Preexisting discussions about the political participation of young, middle-class female students in postwar protest often linked ideas about a particularly female vulnerability with Japan's nascent postwar democracy. It was into these narratives that Kanba stepped, tragically and inadvertently, with her June 15, 1960, death at a mass protest, becoming a symbol of the fragility of postwar democracy.

Yet Kanba's writings underscore a discrepancy between her public significance and her personal relationship to radical politics. In a January 1959 letter to a friend, Kanba expressed her desire in blocking the renewal of the U.S.-Japan Security Treaty and ousting Prime Minister Kishi Nobusuke (and the entire Liberal Democratic Party) in this way: "I want to scream 'Why don't we seriously tackle the struggle to overthrow the capitalist class!'"[1] Kanba's own radical politics were undermined by various attempts to speak on her behalf and fit her into gendered frames of popular empathy. How did a student interested in Marxist theories of class conflict become a symbol of postwar liberal democracy?

I understand the political context of the mass protests of 1960 in which Kanba died as one in which "naive politics" framed popular understandings about acceptable political behavior. What I refer to here as a postwar narrative of naive politics describes the tension that emerged between what was considered the wartime politics of male experts and what was suggested as a possible counter to the "masculine" militarist excesses of the war. Specifically, I use *naive politics* to indicate a politico-emotive ideal in the postwar period, in which democratic participation and political authenticity became linked with ideas about intuition and feeling in such a way that those presumed to be least politically experienced—"ordinary" women—could formulate powerful political appeals based on assumptions about women's political naivete.[2]

In many ways, new social movements spearheaded by women in the 1940s and 1950s in Japan introduced a radical political subjectivity newly available to women. However, many such movements often employed strategies that linked women to the household and to family care to legitimize political interventions by "ordinary" women. They framed their activism as that of political outsiders defending the average household from the political plots of male establishment politicians and business elites. This kind of politico-emotive ideal of nonideological naive politics legitimized women's political interventions, but it also harbored a risk: the subjects expected to represent such politics—or political affects and emotions—can be cut off from other kinds of politics. This became true for Kanba Michiko, who in death became cast as a political naïf; she was a woman of twenty-two who became interpreted as an innocent maiden to make a political appeal for postwar liberal democracy that spoke to a broad swath of the Japanese population. Her own voice was supplanted by a symbol of her forged by others.

PREEXISTING NARRATIVES: WOMEN AND NAIVE POLITICS

The Allied Occupation of Japan (1945–1952) inaugurated a gendered political culture that construed female participation in an essentializing way, specifically understanding women as nonviolent. Efforts to imagine the ideal postwar political citizen embraced defeat as a moment of rupture and instated a political culture in which participation by women also symbolized a break with the past.

The U.S. occupying authorities, primarily Douglas MacArthur, demanded women's suffrage as a pillar of postwar democracy; MacArthur based his opinion on ideas popular in the United States about women as a moderating political force. This idea about Japanese women had been popularized in the U.S. mass media specifically as the war wound down, which, as Lisa Yoneyama argues, set up Japanese women as "subject-objects of American liberation and recipients of Cold War liberal tutelage."[3] On the Japanese side, Prime Minister Shidehara Kijūrō agreed and argued to skeptical Japanese lawmakers that women were nonideological and politically moderate and had a simplicity that could benefit that nation.[4] The

December 1945 revisions to the election law that gave women in Japan the right to vote strengthened a narrative of how moderate female political participation could bolster a postwar politics that sought to avoid radical excesses in Japan's nascent democracy; this narrative was important to both the supreme commander of the Allied forces and the postwar Japanese cabinet. Japan's wartime experience and the particular ways in which women were imagined to figure in its resolution offered women a privileged place from which to speak as new citizens, although U.S. ideals of domestic womanhood also shaped what form such citizenship could take.[5]

In this new postwar formulation, women's suffrage was a bulwark against state violence, after women had endured repression and political exclusion in the dark valley of wartime. This narrative elided women's wartime political participation. In the period of total war, women had entered public spaces in unprecedented numbers. They had participated in government-led campaigns via such organizations as the Patriotic Women's Association (Aikoku fujinkai) and the Greater Japan National Defense Women's Association (Dai Nippon kokubo fujinkai), including engaging in certain forms of street activism.[6] There had been an indigenous movement for women's suffrage as well, and although one of its leaders, Ichikawa Fusae, became a celebrated champion for democracy and gender equality in the postwar period, she had cooperated with the wartime state's colonial and militarist projects.[7] Further, standard postwar accounts ignored the history of prewar proletarian women's alliances, which had also demanded "full suffrage" (that is, access to the vote for all adult men and women).[8]

Indeed, within a dominant narrative that defined women's suffrage as key to ensuring the success of postwar liberal democracy and pacifism, there was little space for radical women. The cases of women active in the late Meiji and interwar periods, such as Kanno Suga (1881–1911), Itō Noe (1895–1923), and Kaneko Fumiko (1906–1926), sat uneasily alongside the triumphant history of women's suffrage as a force for liberalism and peace. All three had become infamous in their time for embracing radical thought, ranging from anarchism to nihilism, as well as for defying moral codes for women. The Japanese mass media had reacted to these women with fear and scorn; all three died in confrontations with the state.[9] Postwar discussions about women as new political actors elided strong links forged in the prewar and wartime periods between women and state violence, as well as between women and radical violence.

A longer political formulation in Japan linked women with a nonideological politics of purity, often grounded in an understanding of women's work in the home. The imagined association between women and a politics free from ideological (oftentimes meaning "leftist radical") influence and affiliation was not new in the postwar period. Before the war, women's groups had campaigned against prostitution or partisan politics based on such an understanding. In some cases, conservative male bureaucrats in the prewar period had supported giving women the vote, assuming that women would act as a stabilizing force and counter the potential influence of radical male candidates.[10]

In the postwar period, ideas about the militaristic excesses of a kind of male politics created a new context and meaning for female political participation based on ideas of women's political naivete and vulnerability. In the context of the Allied Occupation immediately after the war, this also followed a Western colonial discursive pattern, in which U.S. reformers in Japan understood Japanese women as helpless victims of feudal Japanese male chauvinism.[11] Sharing an understanding of women as potentially most vulnerable to state violence also formed activist strategies in the postwar period. By the late 1950s, the image of the teary woman linked to the postwar peace movement was an established cliché.[12]

But, as Wesley Sasaki-Uemura has observed, this also meant that discussions of the relationship between politics and domesticity—and women's proper social roles therein—actually formed the basis for a new, rather radical political subjectivity available to women in the postwar period.[13] In the late 1940s and throughout the 1950s, women marshaled ideas about characteristics identified as feminine—nurturing, care, and an inherent connection to everyday life—to mobilize key postwar activist movements associated with consumer rights and the peace movement. Demonstrations immediately after the war often featured female speakers with infants strapped to their backs.[14] Groups like the Women's Democratic Club (Fujin minshu kurabu), formed in 1947, and the Federation of Housewives (Shufuren), formed in 1948, prided themselves on defending daily household needs against government officials and expert elites. The official journal of the Federation of Housewives published a December 5, 1948, article that declared, "The greatest success of the Federated Housewives' movement to date has been the establishment of a pipeline into government officialdom so that the voice of female consumers can be heard in quarters that have heretofore been reserved for business elites only."[15] In making demands, women often organized around the figure of the housewife and thus tapped into a political strategy of female naivete about formal politics. They participated in politics as ostensibly apolitical actors.

So while postwar women's activism obscured the history of women's wartime mobilization in support of Japan's imperial and militaristic project by framing women as inherently victims of male authority during the war, it also set up a powerful postwar political strategy for women as defenders of the naive daily-life issues faced by the ordinary citizen against the machinations of a corrupt and authoritarian political elite. This postwar context of female victimization and naive politics also informed understandings of female student participation in the postwar student movement.

FEMALE STUDENT AS POLITICAL ACTIVIST

Portrayals of female student activism often depicted young women as challengers of outmoded social customs. One sympathetic fictionalized account of an angry protest by female students against the rigid, feudal administration of their school appears in Kinoshita Keisuke's 1954 film *Garden of Women (Onna no en)*. The film, about a group of students at a women's college battling to form a student council at their restrictive school, portrayed the young heroines as victims of feudal rules. The institution's unyielding and outdated regulations, enforced for their own sake, crush one young woman in particular, played by cinema idol Takamine Hideko. Her suicide prompts school administrators to blame leftist "Red elements." The film indicts the unyieldingly hierarchical and strict system of the women's college for trapping not only the female students but also their teachers and parents. Ultimately, however, the young women remained most vulnerable, and their angered reactions come across as just and earnest. In this film the young women's affirmation of their democratic agency against the restrictive rules of their college dramatizes impassioned political pleas by female students; although the conflict remains restricted to a women's school, all segments of society—class differences, gender inequalities, and family expectations—are implicated in a corrupt and cruel situation that results in the death of a female student and provokes all the young women to come together in denouncing their school.

Kinoshita's film was a mainstream depiction of female student activism, but fictional representations of the student Left at newly coeducational higher education institutions that came out of "student literature" also featured female students. Short stories by Ōe Kenzaburō and Kurahashi Yumiko, young student writers breaking onto the literary scene in the late 1950s, narrated critiques of and disillusionment with the "old" establishment Left from the perspective of female student activists who acted out of an intuitive sense of justice.[16] Although expressing different political hopes and appealing to different audiences, these fictional representations of young women as agents of political rebellion and change demonstrated how young activist women became loaded with meaning as new subjects within postwar democracy and, for those who were interested in radical interpretations of postwar democracy, within radical politics.

A further example of the symbolic significance of the young female in postwar Japanese politics is a 1959 painting by the politically engaged artist Nakamura Hiroshi. The piece depicts a slightly monstrous figure in a schoolgirl uniform, her wide eyes gazing out of a fantastic train meshed with an enormous feudal castle in a chaotic and gray landscape. The title of the piece urges *Rise Up, Girl!* (*Hōki seyo, shōjo*). The uniformed schoolgirl would become a frequent personal symbol in Nakamura's art and has also become a key figure in the contemporary Japanese erotic imaginary. However, in response to later questions about the erotics of girls in his work, Nakamura clarified that in 1959 he saw the erotic dimension of the schoolgirl as less about sex and more about revolutionary thought.[17] That is, Nakamura saw the young girl not as an object of desire but as a subject of political agency. In a postcard to a friend written in 1959, Nakamura urged his (also male) friend to become a *shōjo*, a young girl, noting that "our antiestablishment consciousness alone qualifies us as shōjo."[18] Nakamura's painting and his interpretation of the painting at the time illustrate a narrative that associated young females with new forms of specifically antiestablishment postwar political action. In Nakamura's case, he also linked the figure of the maiden with the New Left, noting to a friend that his subtitle for *Rise Up, Girl!* was *Offering to the Zengakuren*. Zengakuren (short for Zen Nihon gakusei jichikai sōrengō, or All-Japan General Alliance of Student Self-Governing Associations) was the nationwide student alliance that by 1959 had organized as a radical alternative to the establishment Left.

After the end of the war in 1945, high school and university students were among the first in Japan to apply the new democratic ideals of access and voice to the institutions that governed them. The first student strike of the postwar period took place at a women's high school, Ueno Gakuen High School, when 150 female students initiated a strike on October 8, 1945. They protested the misappropriation of rations at their school and demanded the firing of faculty who had supported the war effort and the hiring of new teachers who advocated democracy.[19] A series of isolated student protests at various schools—including women's colleges and high schools—culminated in the formation of student self-governance associations, or *jichikai*, beginning at the University of Tokyo in January 1947. As students from various campuses began to unite to fight fee hikes and the government's educational policy, the call for a general student association led to the September 1948 founding of Zengakuren. The resolutions adopted by 250 student representatives from 145 campuses invoked the language of democracy, freedom of study, and student political engagement and identified their collective enemy, in the very first resolution, as "the fascist-colonialistic reorganization of education."[20] Although the context in which students would act shifted over the next two decades, how education was organized and how it related to state power would remain a central concern for campus-based activists.

TOWARD A NEW LEFT

The influence of the wartime history of authoritarianism and militarism also shaped the leftist character of postwar student activism in Japan. Although Zengakuren was ostensibly nonpartisan, students affiliated with the postwar Japanese Communist Party (JCP) had been deeply involved in the group's formation and quickly took control of Zengakuren leadership. Aside from the general appeal of Marxism among students, which had an antecedent in the prewar period, the history of Communist resistance to Japanese militarism attracted many; the party consisted of men and women who had suffered imprisonment or exile for their opposition to the wartime state.[21] For those seeking models of strong-willed individuals who had resisted imperialism and militarism, these Communists offered living examples.

However, the postwar JCP did not escape the factionalism of the prewar Marxist movement in Japan, and by the late 1950s, tensions brewing between the JCP leadership and Zengakuren activists came to a head. At the Sixth Party Congress (Rokuzenkyō) in 1955, the JCP withdrew its support for armed struggle in Japan, which disenchanted a generation of earnest would-be guerrillas who had left the universities to foment revolution in the countryside.[22] The JCP's decision to cultivate a larger presence in elections rather than focusing on direct agitation contrasted starkly with ongoing conflicts in Japan, such as antibase struggles and strikes, that brought politics into the streets.

In 1956 chaotic events in international Communism—Nikita Khrush-chev's de-Stalinization speech, the brutal Soviet suppression of a people's movement in Budapest, and the Soviet Union's complicity with U.S. policy over the Suez Canal crisis—led many left-leaning students to feel that the institutional Left at home and abroad was more interested in maintaining the contemporary power balance than in achieving a just social order.

Students who might otherwise have sympathized with a left-leaning cri-tique of contemporary issues were also wary of the paranoia and inflexible dogmatism that had become associated with the student movement under JCP leadership. In the context of a postwar ideal of active political sub-jectivity willing to speak truth to power, the JCP-led student movements seemed to harden in the 1950s into a system that suppressed individual voices. In 1957 some dissident JCP members, including student activists, es-tablished Japan's first New Left groups. The Japan Trotskyist League (Ni-hon Torotsukisuto renmei, or Toro-ren for short) formed first, and soon thereafter the Revolutionary Communist League (Nihon kakumeiteki kyōsanshugisha dōmei, or Kakukyōdō) grew out of the Japan Trotskyist League. In December 1958 a group of fifty students formed another anties-tablishment Left group, the Communist League (Kyōsanshugisha dōmei). To indicate their attempt to return to the roots of Marxism, they named their group after Karl Marx's first organization and went by the German name Bund (Bunto) for short. Kanba Michiko was a founding member of Bund, working in their makeshift office until the organization got more traction at university campuses.[23]

In the late 1950s, leading up to the movement opposing the U.S.-Japan Security Treaty, these New Left groups came to control the mainstream of Zengakuren, ending the JCP's control of the organization. New Left coali-tions could be fragile, but the New Left–led Zengakuren unified as an alter-native to the JCP's institutionalized ideology in the late 1950s, and the pro-JCP Zengakuren, known as the Yoyogi Faction because their headquarters were located in Yoyogi in western Tokyo, became a minority movement.

The New Left did not emphasize only class conflict; issues of demo-cratic access resonated widely in student activism of the late 1950s, influ-encing demands for Japan's autonomy from U.S. Cold War policy as well as for campus policies that ensured student access to self-governance.[24] Key issues for the student movement in Japan at this time included protests against the expansion of Tachikawa Air Base—a U.S. military bastion—and struggles against state policies that could be used to encroach on edu-cational and political freedoms, such as the reinstitution of moral education and a rating system for teacher efficiency, as well as the 1958 Police Duties Bill (Keishoku hō). Above all, however, the most iconic mass mobilization in the period was that against the 1960 renewal of the U.S.-Japan Security Treaty, known colloquially as Anpo.[25]

ANPO: STATE VIOLENCE AND VULNERABLE DEMOCRACY

What came to be known as the "Anpo struggle" (*Anpo tōsō*) against the renewal of the Treaty of Mutual Cooperation and Security between the United States and Japan (Nichibei anzen hoshō jōyaku, shortened to Anpo) began as a conflict over Japan's position within U.S. Cold War policy but rapidly became understood as a battle to preserve Japan's nascent postwar democracy against the arrogance of Prime Minister Kishi and his Liberal Democratic Party (LDP) administration. As such, demonstrations against the treaty's renewal drew not just left-leaning students but also a wide swath of the Japanese population; estimates put the number of participants in protest activities between the spring of 1959 and the fall of 1960 at 16 million.[26] The New Left–led Zengakuren became a key group in the prolonged series of protests opposing the treaty.

Although U.S. observers typically interpreted the anti-Anpo protests of 1959 and 1960 as anti-American rioting, internal conflict over the treaty's renewal reflected a strong antiwar sensibility rather than just anti-Americanism. The treaty had originated in the negotiations between Japan and the United States that ended the Allied Occupation in 1952 and incorporated Japan into the larger framework of U.S. postwar military strategies in East Asia.[27] Under the terms of the treaty, U.S. troops waged the Korean War (1950–1953)—the first hot war of the Cold War—from bases in Japan, and Okinawa remained occupied by the U.S. military. Although the Korean War had jumpstarted manufacturing in postwar Japan, for a war-weary population, the threat of being dragged into another conflict because of an alliance with the United States felt very real. One major newspaper's public opinion poll in the summer of 1959 showed that almost half of those polled feared that the new treaty would increase the chances that Japan would become involved in war.[28] Many on the Left desired closer relations with the Soviet Union and China.

However, as the heavy-handed tactics of Prime Minister Kishi increasingly worried political observers and citizens, the issue at stake in the revised treaty's ratification became less the content of the treaty than the way politics functioned. Kishi's authoritarian maneuvering became understood as a threat to Japan's democracy. Leading up to the treaty revisions, in October 1958 Kishi sought expanded policing powers with a revision of the Police Duties Bill. He employed aggressive tactics—blindsiding the opposition with controversial proposals at the very end of Diet sessions— and the protests became cast more and more as a battle against the rise of pre-1945-style Japanese militarism.[29] Many of the political actors, such as Kishi and the house speaker at the time, Kiyose Ichirō, had been involved in Japan's wartime imperial project. A return to militarism did not feel too far-fetched to many observers.

The bad behavior of these elected politicians increased popular sympathy for anti-Anpo protests, which in many ways transformed into an "anti-Kishi movement."[30] As opposition mounted in the streets, quarrels broke out within the Diet itself on May 19, 1960. Physical scuffles between the Socialist-led opposition and the ruling LDP concluded with the admission of five hundred police officers to remove the Socialists, who had attempted a sit-in to block the LDP. Amid the confusion, the vote to approve the new treaty was deferred, resulting in a situation where, instead of requiring an affirmative vote, the revision would automatically gain Diet approval on June 19, 1960, if the House of Councillors took no action against it. The press reported this as the unilateral approval of the treaty by the LDP. Many observers of the chaos in the Diet defined the LDP as a threat to Japan's nascent democracy.

Zengakuren activists engaged in direct-action tactics that took this battle into the streets: they broke into the Diet grounds during a large protest on November 27, 1969, and they organized an occupation at Haneda Airport on January 15, 1960, to block Kishi from traveling to the United States. Zengakuren's willingness to take risks at demonstrations, framed within a common interpretation that ordinary people's inaction during wartime had allowed a militarist government to wage war, drew the admiration of several influential intellectuals in Japan and of large swaths of the general population as well. George Packard, a U.S. intelligence officer hardly sympathetic to the strategies and the politics of Zengakuren, nevertheless noted that "the student activists threw themselves into causes with raw energy and naïve idealism, and were tolerated, if not openly admired, by much of the rest of society."[31] Their appeal depended, however, on their apparent vulnerability when pitted against state power. Within this context female participants became understood as particularly vulnerable to state violence, based on a powerful gendered postwar narrative of naive politics.

News articles, participant accounts, and even Diet debates about the mass demonstrations against Anpo often employed the presence of young women to emphasize the approachability, vulnerability, and moral authority of the New Left. Even for those Japanese who were not particularly invested in leftist ideology, young women's interest in political participation on the street held tremendous persuasive power; the presence of female students at protests emphasized how nonthreatening the student movement could be. In many personal narratives of citizen activism during the Anpo protests, young women figured as key actors encouraging people to participate: a business owner notes that it was his teenage daughter who urged him to march; a middle-aged housewife describes the friendly young female activist who encouraged her to join a street demonstration.[32] These stories fit a shared narrative of postwar politics in which young women's outrage, based on nonideological naive politics, provided legitimate justification for public protest.

Observers reported feeling excitement at seeing young women in street demonstrations, even if they personally opposed the Zengakuren's confrontational strategies. Tanaka Sumie, a female screenplay writer for Kinoshita Keisuke, among others, wrote a piece to try to dissuade students from engaging in violent tactics "as an elder, as a mother." But she also noted that the "four hundred female students" who participated in the Zengakuren actions made her question her own more apolitical poststudent life.[33] Tanaka thrilled to the sight of young women in street demonstrations.

Parents and schools still restricted female students' activities in particular, but many young women were able to join the street protests focused on the Diet building in Tokyo because they had been allowed to leave home to pursue their education. Families and schools attempted to restrict women's full integration into coed schools and demonstrations. Many parents persuaded their daughters to attend short-term and women's colleges to protect them from the perceived dangers of full coeducation.[34] But even women's schools like Joshibi University of Art and Design and Ochanomizu University gained radical reputations. Women's dormitories often attempted to curtail their residents' activism with strict curfews, but institutional rules meant little without proper enforcement. Minagawa Kanae, who had protested Anpo while an undergraduate at Japan Women's University, recalled that her dorm matron had sympathized with her political engagement and offered encouragement: making rice balls for her to take

to demonstrations and quietly opening the door for her if she returned after curfew.[35] Parents' reactions to their daughters' activism also varied,
ranging from letters and phone calls forbidding any form of political participation, to the tacit support of progressive parents, to—in the case of at
least one family with mixed politics—a loud debate with one parent and a
quietly encouraging "be careful" from the other.[36]

The idea of a female student activist as an inherently good citizen, rather
than a dangerous radical, influenced interpretations of the young women
who acted as leaders in the student movement. As part of a February 1960
House of Councillors hearing on the correct application of the Subversive
Activities Prevention Law (Hakai katsudō bōshi hō) of 1952, the peace activist Takada Nahoko argued against police abuse of the law, citing the
detainment of female students—including "Kanbajima [sic] Michiko and
Shimoinoue Yoshiko" from the University of Tokyo—at the Zengakuren
sit-in at Haneda Airport in January 1960. Takada criticized what she saw
as undue police prosecution of student leaders and emphasized that these
young women came from good families, were passionate about their studies, and should not be the targets of the Subversive Activities Prevention
Law.[37] Takada brought up female students as particularly sympathetic examples of democratic dissent. Policing of protest came across as most insidious when it targeted young women.

Just as the presence of young female bodies at protests legitimated the
political activism of the student movement, police violence against female
bodies provoked the deepest critiques of state power. Police aggression toward female student activists prompted sympathetic media reports about
"angry" young women and student demonstrations. The tabloid Shūkan
shinchō focused its coverage of the April 26, 1960, demonstrations, the first
held at the Diet since November 1959, on what it dubbed the "angry maidens of April 26."[38] As in the demonstrations of November 1959, students
clashed with police.[39] However, a series of full-page photographs printed
in the periodical rendered female students chiefly as victims, exposing
through images the physical force that police had used against them (figures 1.1 and 1.2).

Although the journal describes the young women as "angry maidens,"
the female protesters are shown cringing, roughly jostled by policemen.
The photographs in Shūkan shinchō's double-page spread emphasize the
male hands of authority that grab at female bodies. The young women's
hands are empty, raised to protect their heads or, in one case, defiantly
wrestling a comrade from a detective's grip. By contrast, police hands seize

警官と怒れる娘たち

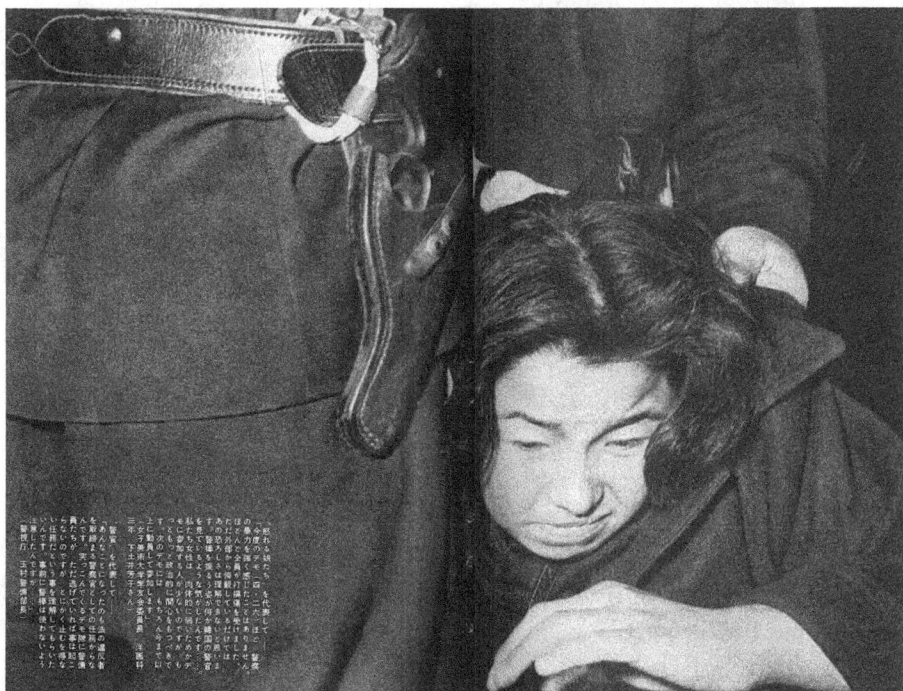

FIGURE 1.1 (*opposite*) An image of a policeman wrestling a female student activist from the "Police and the angry maidens" photo essay in *Shūkan shinchō*, May 16, 1960.

FIGURE 1.2 (*above*) Police force down the head of young female activist. *Shūkan shinchō*, May 16, 1960.

young women by their necks. One image captures the young face of a female activist as the hands of authority force her head down. All that can be seen of the policemen manipulating her are a holster and hands gripping the collar of her coat. The photograph evokes an almost sexual violence, showing a young woman's troubled face forced down to groin height, her face level with the butt of a police gun. Such images suggested that while the young women may be "angry," the police employed undue force and rough treatment.

Superimposed on the photograph is a quote from a student at the prestigious Women's College of Fine Arts decrying the force employed by the police against the weaker bodies of women. She also noted that the police she faced behaved like Korean police, referring to the force used by South Korean soldiers in concurrent protests by laborers and students across the Tsushima Strait and suggesting that it was the actions of the police, not the protesters, that threatened Japan's democracy.[40] For many observers of student protests, the state's willingness to confront women's bodies with violence represented an excess of state force.

KANBA MICHIKO AS FEMALE VICTIM

Although Takada misstated the name of the female student activist Kanba Michiko in her House of Councillors testimony, after June 15, 1960, no one in Japan could make such a mistake. The death of Kanba, a student at the University of Tokyo and a New Left activist, at the South Gate of the Diet compound in clashes between students and police became the most famous of the postwar student Left. That Kanba was female meant she could also fit into a narrative already in motion that equated female students with vulnerability and an ideal form of nonideological naive politics. Kanba's death gave that narrative real-life confirmation. Kanba did not necessarily die because she was female, but her death became legible within preexisting ideas about female vulnerability and state violence. She was not the first to die in postwar protests; two activists died in the Bloody May Day of 1952, when police fired their handguns into a crowd of demonstrators. However, Kanba, as a middle-class female student at an elite university, fit into ideas about the ideal citizen of the postwar liberal state. Kanba's "sacrifice" tapped into public sympathy for the activism of female students and prompted intellectuals and citizens to criticize the state, which contributed to Prime Minister Kishi's decision to resign a month later. But images of Kanba's feminine purity also eclipsed her articulations of a radical political stance.

In the political confusion following the June 15, 1960, demonstration in which Kanba died, the only "truth" all parties could agree on was the identity of Kanba as the victim. The identity of the victimizer, meanwhile, became a matter of ideological conviction. Major newspapers issued a general statement condemning violence, while student activists and their supporters countered with charges of undue "violence by authorities."[41] Kanba had been taken by ambulance to the police hospital, where an autopsy declared that she had been crushed to death. Her family demanded another autopsy, which concluded that she was likely strangled. A group of lawyers and activists who sought to document the events of June 15, 1960, noted that other protesters—including a journalist and a professor—recalled police beating them back with one hand and grabbing at their throats with the other. This and other protesters' testimony, along with the results of one of the autopsies, convinced them that Kanba had been asphyxiated by the police.[42]

Many were injured in the dramatic confrontations among demonstrators, authorities, and right-wing groups on June 15, 1960 (figure 1.3), but it was Kanba's death that represented for most Japanese the ultimate sacrifice. Some publications, ranging from the mass-audience *Asahi jaanaru* to the campus newspaper of the University of Tokyo, even ran photographs of her lifeless body laid out in the police hospital.[43] Such media treatment represented Kanba as a passive subject and vulnerable victim. Newspaper coverage often separated Kanba out from the protesting students altogether; for example, the front page of the June 16, 1960, morning edition of the *Mainichi shimbun* declared that a "female University of Tokyo student" had died while student activists and police clashed. The distinction suggested that Kanba had been an unfortunate caught between the two, whereas she had in fact been a vocal leader of the anti-Anpo New Left.

Kanba was more legible as an "ordinary girl" rather than an activist; she was a more powerful symbol of the hopes for Japan's future and a more sympathetic figure as a political innocent crushed between student radicals and state authority. As Hirakawa Hiroko has written, many accounts emphasized Kanba's death as a foreclosing of a middle-class maternal future in forging a mythology of her sacrifice for "New Japan."[44] At her funeral, this twenty-two-year-old young adult was portrayed as a "maiden" (shōjo).[45] Her parents reinforced the idea that she was ordinary, even though, with her upper-middle-class upbringing in an intellectual and cos-

FIGURE 1.3 Activists injured in the June 15, 1960, clashes with police during anti-Anpo protests. Although it is impossible to verify the identity of the bloodied figure in white on the left, lifted by police, the *Kyodo tsūshin* caption reads, "Kanba Michiko once again in the spotlight."

mopolitan family (her father was a professor, and her mother a Christian active in community groups), Kanba was rather unusual. Her level of political commitment was also not simply ordinary, nor girlish.

KANBA MICHIKO AS POLITICAL ACTIVIST

The posthumous framing of Kanba Michiko as a female sacrifice and an ordinary daughter of postwar Japan leapfrogged over Kanba's own attempts to articulate her political stance, which focused on a critique of postwar liberal democracy. With her death, Kanba increasingly represented the vulnerability of the individual citizen—in particular, the individual female citizen—in political conflict, but Kanba herself had opposed the postwar democratic ideal of a liberal individual citizen and challenged an emphasis on peace without an understanding of the dynamics of conflict, or an emphasis on democracy without an understanding of history and conflict.

This discrepancy between Kanba's popular image as a maiden sacrifice and her actual radicalism remained even when her own writings became available—and popular—after her death. Her mother, Kanba Mitsuko, assembled and published a collection of Kanba Michiko's writings within months of her daughter's death. Although the volume—titled *The Smile Nobody Knows* based on a poem she had written—included the political essays she had penned for university publications, it was Kanba's private writings that generated the greatest impact. Few accounts of the collection's influence—for example, those given by the later 1960s generation of activists—included comments on the political essays. Indeed, many described the book as deeply affecting *in spite of* their disagreements with Kanba's political convictions. Yamamoto Chie, a high school student at the time of Kanba's death, reflected that while she did not care for Kanba's politics, she nevertheless devoured Kanba's writings. Even years later, she felt that the experience of reading Kanba's words forged a deep connection; it made "[Kanba's] death feel like a part of my life."[46] As the title suggests, the collection of intimate materials, from journal entries to personal letters, appealed to those who wished to encounter the "real" Kanba Michiko; the writings promised to reveal "the smile nobody knows."

The posthumous collection included writings stretching back to Kanba's childhood and offered the reader a sense of familiarity and a comprehensive view into her life. Kanba's writings as an elementary school student reveal a postwar upper-middle-class upbringing, defined by the consumer lifestyle available to an increasingly wider segment of Japanese society. She filled her girlhood journals—most likely kept as part of school assignments over summer and winter vacations—with references to the cinema, shopping, and ice cream. Such activities mark Kanba's upbringing as defined by increased access to the high-growth-era consumer culture of Japan's urban spaces. Other activities of Kanba's were familiar to many suburban and also rural families: she joined her father and brother in weeding the family's vegetable garden in the summer, and she sewed while she and her family followed the national high school baseball championships on the radio.

Kanba conducted her first investigation of leftist ideology in middle school, during the early 1950s, for a school report she wrote, titled "On Socialism." In her attempt to get to the bottom of the issue, the young Kanba consulted newspapers and "adult magazines" such as *Kaizō* and *Ushio*. The publications she found lying about her house revealed her politically progressive and intellectual home environment. Some of the articles they contained—for example, one on the conditions facing African Americans in the United States, the "so-called representative of democracy"— shocked her.[47] Although Kanba concludes her essay unsure of which "ideology," that of the Communist Eastern Bloc or that of the West, will become hers, her discussion reflects many of the issues, such as lingering racial inequality, that made student activists throughout the 1960s skeptical of the American model of liberal democracy.

A college essay by Kanba critiquing postwar educational guidelines for teaching the social sciences offers an idea of how she framed her ideological stance vis-à-vis postwar democracy. Reflecting on the relationship between pedagogy and citizenship, Kanba rejected the postwar democratic ideal of a liberal individual citizen. She argued that Occupation-era educational reforms, drawn up to create democratic citizens, fell short because they emphasized democracy but slighted history.[48] The problem with a stress on democracy, Kanba argued, lay in the liberal definition of democratic citizens as individuals. Kanba noted that in describing how individual citizens relate to other individuals, to nature, and to society, the 1947 social studies guidelines erased the role of collective units, such as class.

Kanba argued that emphasizing the individual citizen in contemporary society also effaced larger, structural causes for historical change. For example, Kanba identified in the postwar social studies curriculum a failure to address the roots of war in explaining international wars and conflict. The lesson for students was that atomized individual citizens should assume the responsibility to avoid war and embrace peace: "In this interpretation, the actual causes for war are not sought, and blame is shifted to some sense that war can be avoided through each individual's efforts." She also pointed out that while the guidelines mentioned helping students understand the constitutional role of the emperor, they did not mention Article 9, which forbade war.[49] Kanba felt that social studies pedagogy in postwar Japan was thus stripped of historical analysis and conflated "simple growth and progress," which only confirmed the current social order.[50]

Kanba's analysis in her college essay displays a left-leaning concern for the historical category of class and its role in producing social contradictions. Kanba argued that an emphasis on individual responsibility for democracy and peace actually failed to cultivate an "active attitude" toward history. For Kanba, creating an "active attitude" demanded understanding conflict and resistance.[51] She concluded that recent educational guidelines "put to sleep an active attitude." Instead of cultivating an active citizen subjectivity, Kanba found that contemporary social science pedagogy "erases the people from contemporary society. Organized groups also disappear, leaving only scattered individuals who are supposed to cooperate."[52] The popular interpretation of Kanba's individual death as a demand for democracy and peace became an ironic counterpoint to her own preferred mode of historical analysis, which defined her participation in the self-consciously Marxist student New Left that formed in the late 1950s in Japan.

If Kanba Michiko showed some precocious interest in global politics, she also became interested early on in participating in the new democratic form of campus politics available to young people at school. In high school, Kanba was class president in a class with many more boys than girls. According to a school friend, however, this may have had less to do with Kanba's personality than with the general mood; there was actually a vogue for having a female class president at the time.[53] In high school she gave a speech to support a female candidate for the student council, appealing to a sense of duty and dissatisfaction with the current order of things.[54] With some other friends, she organized an informal discussion group to address current social issues. This group's mission grew out of frustration with the gap between the abstract lessons offered by teachers and the world they saw around them. In a collectively penned document, they wrote, "We look with eyes of indignation and anxiety at our society. What ought to be done is not done. In particular, we notice too many problems with the way women in Japan live."[55] Kanba and her friends identified some of the problems facing women in Japan in their own experiences at high school, where they felt stymied in their academic and political pursuits. They felt "powerless" to bridge the gap between their reality and the imperative of "equal rights for men and women" enshrined in the postwar constitution. However, they hoped to better define the issues they faced together and proposed diverse topics for group discussion, from the personal (university studies, work, marriage, issues at home) to the political (student government, national government, religion, and education).[56] Kanba and her cohort were not unaware of women's issues, but they set those aside when they engaged in anti-Anpo New Left activism.

Through familiarity with the Kanba Michiko represented in the newspapers and weekly journals, many in the general public felt a sense of intimacy with the idea of Kanba. That feeling of intimacy, of knowing someone actually unknown to them, was often based on how well Kanba's image fit into ideas already circulating about young women and political activism. A variety of voices contributed to the formulation in which Kanba became defined by her vulnerability, as a young woman whose death was interpreted as a sacrifice for postwar democracy.

Up until Kanba Michiko's death, her father—Kanba Toshio, a professor at Chuo University—had opposed his daughter's participation in aggressive political actions, and it had been a source of a great deal of tension between them. In August 1960 he wrote an article, "The Daughter Who Disappeared in the Tempest at the Diet," in which he described his conflicts with Michiko, in particular after her arrest during the Zengakuren demonstrations at Haneda Airport in January 1960.[57] In March of that year he had even published an article headlined "Zengakuren Stole My Daughter."[58] Half a year later, however, after Michiko's death, Toshio shifted from chiding the student movement for "stealing" his daughter to indicting the larger political "tempest" that had made her disappear. Although Toshio described his daughter as confrontational, standing up to him on matters of politics, both of his articles frame Michiko as politically vulnerable. In both cases, although the aggressor changes, Michiko the daughter remains a victim.

Kanba Toshio elided his daughter's radicalism after her death and was quoted on June 16, 1960, as declaring Michiko "a sacrifice for the people [kokumin]."[59] He affirmed that her actions represented the political will of all citizens, that she participated in the protests at the Diet for the very same reasons as everyone else did. As a father, Toshio emphasized that Michiko, and by extension the movement she participated in, always desired what was right in the world. In a later commemoration, he also defended her choice to enter the Diet compound with the front line of student activists, even with "the body of a female student." He declared that what many called a "dangerous place" for women was the proper place for a student demonstration protesting the government's antidemocratic actions.[60]

Like many other ordinary citizens, Toshio had supported the anti-Anpo movement and was also protesting in the streets around the Diet on the evening of June 15, 1960. He even participated in the moment of silence demanded by a student standing atop an armored police vehicle at the South Gate to commemorate an unnamed "fallen female student." Only when Toshio stopped at an eatery on the way home did he hear, over the radio, the name of his daughter announced as the killed student.[61] As he mourned her death, he affirmed her political actions on behalf of "the people" and "democracy."

Michiko became representative of a simplified ideal of postwar democratic agency and thereby delinked from her radical activist politics. Echoing postwar debates about how to overcome what was interpreted as Japanese subjects' passive acceptance of wartime militarism via an "active" democratic subjectivity, Michiko's father defined her death as a failure of democracy: although the postwar constitution promised a new democratic order, without action that democracy remained only a promise. Toshio hoped that Michiko's death would mobilize "citizens awakened to democracy," for if peace and democracy prevailed, he would not regret the death of his only daughter.[62] Michiko, through the accident of her gender and her death in a demonstration interpreted as an expression of democratic citizens, confirmed the impression of antidemocratic violence as a masculine force that victimized women in particular.

With Kanba Michiko's death, her parents, as the chief mourners, became guardians and interpreters of the meaning of their daughter's death. They insisted on her representation as an ordinary daughter and framed her not as a radical student activist but as a symbol of the fragility of postwar democracy. Kanba Toshio already enjoyed access to mass media sources by virtue of his social position as a university professor. But Kanba Mitsuko, her mother, also became launched into the public sphere in the aftermath of June 15, 1960. It was Mitsuko who took the initiative in publishing an influential collection of Michiko's poems, stories, letters, and essays. She also published her own essays on Michiko in various news outlets and journals.[63] Mitsuko would retain close links to later generations of student activists as well.[64] However, she continually insisted on her daughter's ordinariness and described her as "truly a sweet child."[65] Mitsuko's declaration that "Michiko was an ordinary daughter" affirmed the intimacy that others felt toward her in spite of not knowing her personally.[66] Calling Michiko "Japan's best daughter" caught on among commentators as well.[67] Embedding Michiko within her family, and portraying her family as an ordinary Japanese family, made her death feel more immediate to many people, who projected their ideas and feelings about the young women and daughters close to them onto the maiden sacrifice.

Although Zengakuren's aggressive tactics leading up to June 15, 1960, frequently divided generations in their opinions about the proper mode of active politics, Kanba Michiko's death united public sentiment around the idea of her sacrifice. In the wake of Kanba's death, a young woman attending college in Tokyo sent her parents in Nagoya a letter in which she declared that the general mood among students had shifted to one in which self-sacrifice seemed necessary and that if she were to die in a demonstration, her parents ought not to "say something embarrassing like 'Zengakuren took my child.'" The mother reacted to this stand with pride; she submitted her daughter's letter to the regional edition of the daily *Asahi shimbun*.[68] By sending her daughter's private letter to a public source, the mother legitimated her daughter's desire to sacrifice herself publicly for the cause of postwar democracy, based on the general sympathy for Kanba's death.

Public intellectuals also responded to Kanba's death in an intimate way. Tsurumi Kazuko, a female intellectual and cofounder of the left-leaning periodical *Shisō no kagaku*, reported her first reaction to the news of the tragedy in July 1960 as the thought, "If I was young, that girl could have been me."[69] Although Tsurumi did not know Kanba, nor her motivations, she identified completely with Kanba's actions and her death, based in part on both being female. Tsurumi's article also related several telephone conversations she had with other powerful intellectual women as the news of a young woman's death flew among them; the women often expressed their anger as mothers and wives. "From a mother's position I can't stay silent. I'm calling Mrs. Kishi [wife of Prime Minister Kishi] in protest," one woman declared. Another remarked, "How about calling the wife of the Chief Cabinet Secretary?"[70] These women framed their critiques of state authority around the moral prerogative accorded to wives and mothers and felt an imperative to speak, not directly to power, but to the women married to power. As women, they felt they understood how Kanba felt; as mothers, they felt it was their duty to appeal to other women and protect other young people from violence by making appeals to male political authority.

FROM POLITICAL CRITIQUE TO MORALITY TALE

Equating Kanba Michiko with an ideal of postwar democracy painted contemporary political struggles in broad moral strokes. This not only was the tenor of articles in mainstream newspapers and journals but also colored personal interpretations, as can be seen in a collection of mostly amateur poets reacting to Kanba's death, published by a group of Kyoto University students. The poetry of the three groups represented in the volume—workers, students, and "ordinary people"—celebrated Kanba's particularly feminine virtues. The collection, titled *Unending Footsteps*, emphasized the emotional power of a young woman's death for many people who had never met her. The authors affirmed a collective mourning for the maiden sacrifice. Many poems refer to Kanba's death as "pure," and to Kanba as a "maiden" and a "white-throated female student."[71] Many poems also likened Kanba to a flower. By contrast, the cause of Kanba's death is described variously as a bestial evil—"this goblin known as government"—or even as "Satan."[72] A poem written by "a worker," addressed "to Kanba-san's spirit," describes the death of her "white flesh" and the spilling of her blood as a purification ritual for the government.[73] Such poetic interpretations cast the complicated political struggles over Anpo as a morality tale in which evil crushed a pure, budding maiden, and in which her death also purified postwar politics.

Kanba as a sacrifice became conflated with a more general indictment of the violence of the ostensibly peaceful postwar state and of its male representatives. Criticisms of the police, and also of the police's links to organized crime, could employ Kanba as a kind of shorthand for the vulnerability of democratic protest. Her body featured in a political cartoon critical of the intimacy between the police and the yakuza, which portrayed a gangster lighting a cigarette for a policeman who bears a resemblance to Kishi as they stand over Kanba's corpse while both holding blunt instruments in front of the blood-spattered Diet building.[74] Her body made the violence of the postwar state, and its links to violent organizations, visible in such an illustration.

Writing about Kanba after her death, poet Ono Tōsaburō noted that the "bright voices" of his women's junior college students as they played tennis after class evoked Kanba for him, although he had never met her. Conflating their cheerful voices and healthy bodies with the idea of Kanba as the pure victim of the failures of postwar democracy, Ono urged his readers to "stand with the spirit of the young female student who confronted her enemy."[75] Ono invoked the purity of the young female student: her enemy ought to be "our" enemy, although the enemy is ambiguously defined.

Outpourings of sympathetic gestures by "the people" reflected the sympathy many people felt for Kanba as a vulnerable symbol of the excesses of the postwar state. Altars built "by the people's hands" at the Diet's South

FIGURE 1.4 Chūkaku activists carry Kanba Michiko's memorial portrait on their way to a June 14, 1970, anti-Anpo demonstration in front of the National Diet Building, where Kanba died almost a decade earlier. Credit: *Kyodo tsūshin.*

Gate demonstrated how Kanba as a maiden sacrifice resonated with popular opinion. Kanba's father noted an unexpected impact among "ordinary citizens," evidenced also by the "tens of thousands" of people, "old, young, men, women," who came out for her memorial demonstration on June 18, 1960.[76] A widely circulated portrait of Kanba, used at her June 18, 1960, University of Tokyo memorial service, and at the memorial services that mobilized her memory in subsequent years, offers viewers an image of a round-faced young woman with tidy, modestly coiffed hair and a face free of makeup (figure 1.4). This photograph conveyed an image of middle-class femininity.

In the creation of Kanba the maiden sacrifice after her death, memorializations overlooked her analytic words in preference for her poetic words. One of Kanba's own poems, frequently published after her death, was titled "Brumaire," a reference to the second month in the French Republican calendar established by the French Revolution and part of the title of Marx's critique of the dictatorial rise of Louis-Napoléon Bonaparte in 1851. Marx's *The Eighteenth Brumaire of Louis Bonaparte*, originally published in 1852, includes one of his most famous aphorisms, modifying Georg Wilhelm Friedrich Hegel, that history repeats itself "the first time as tragedy, the second as farce."[77] After Kanba's death, the "purity" she invoked in her poem was often ascribed to her, yet the poem demonstrated in a simple way her belief that radical change was qualitative change, demanding violence and "ugliness":

> There is ugliness
> Like there was in the American Revolution
> Like there was in the French Revolution
> There is human ugliness
> There is tragedy
> But
> There is unsurpassed, earnest purity
> There is a spirit that seeks freedom beyond freedom
> These are also there
> I think of it this way[78]

Her parents offered this and other poems by Kanba to bolster her image as a sacrifice. Kanba's father, while rejecting the idea of "glorifying Michiko's death," recommended in his introduction to Kanba's collected writings that readers should peruse her words and "calmly reflect on why this person had to die."[79] His comment intimated inevitability, suggesting that the political battles of 1960 had required the death of someone pure. Although Kanba's father described himself as reluctant to glorify his daughter's death, Kanba's mother, in her afterword to the same volume, quoted from a letter written by one of Kanba's close female college friends: "Kanba's purity could surprise you. She was too pure. I've known since our early days at college that Kanba was braver than any of the male students, even those who said radical things."[80] Although contributing to the popular appraisal of Kanba as pure with this statement, Kanba's friend also pointed out that purity did not necessarily equal a soft purity. In her description, Kanba's purity is one of willpower and bravery.

CONCLUSION

Another dynamic emerged regarding popular reception of radical female activists in the late 1960s. Although Kanba's death confirmed existing ideas about how young women participated politically as particularly vulnerable actors, those close to Kanba recalled the potentially terrifying character of her political commitment. As one of her male professors noted in an article dedicated to Kanba's memory for the University of Tokyo newspaper,

Kanba's devotion to radical activities was impressive but also a bit frightening. In particular, after her arrest at Haneda Airport in January 1960, Kanba declared to her professor that her father and older brother had abandoned her, forcing her to "get over the petit-bourgeois nature that was inside of me." The professor noted that in the face of Kanba's radical change, "timid male students" feared her.[81] In subsequent chapters I introduce several cases in which female student activists in the late 1960s failed to galvanize sympathy because they did not fit narratives of young female activists as vulnerable and instead fell into other narratives that share more with this figure of the dangerous (or ridiculous) female activist than with that of a sympathetic female sacrifice.

Using the case of Kanba, I considered here how a gendered ideal of naive politics legitimized the activism of young women, which both made space for new forms of political participation but also ultimately reinforced gendered norms and emotional standards. There was something particularly radical about the way female student activists became involved in campus activism and the New Left in the postwar period, protesting at the time of Anpo. However, their actions and their voices were often subsumed into larger, gendered discourses of political participation. This can be seen most prominently in the mass media's portrayal of Kanba. Kanba was posthumously evacuated of her analytic voice by appeals to gendered politico-emotive ideas about young women as particularly vulnerable to political violence, and her transformation into a maiden sacrifice for postwar democracy elided her relationship to radical politics and her critiques of the postwar liberal democratic order in Japan.

2 "My Love and Rebellion"

The Politics of Nurturing, the Logic of Capital, and the Rationalization of Coeducation

With only philosophy, without feeling
Humanity is lost
More than knowledge, kindness is critical
Without kindness only violence remains
Tokoro Mitsuko, November 1967

This chapter explores the ostensibly postpolitical moment after the mass demonstrations against Anpo through the figure of Tokoro Mitsuko and her writings, particularly as they responded to the rise of a national discourse that shifted the focus from political debate to economic prosperity. Tokoro had participated in the 1960 Anpo protests as an undergraduate student and continued to write on political themes as a graduate student until her death on January 27, 1968, from a connective tissue disease (figure 2.1). Like Kanba Michiko's posthumously publishing writings, the volume that came out after Tokoro's death, *My Love and Rebellion*, included not only her intellectual work but also intimate diary entries and letters. Tokoro argued passionately against the economic and scientific rationalism that facilitated modern war and the post-Anpo emphasis on economic prosperity. Tokoro herself was a scientist, working toward her doctorate

FIGURE 2.1 Tokoro Mitsuko, date unknown. Credit: *Asahi shimbun*.

in biology. But she became well known in activist circles for her work insisting on a compassionate Left, a compassion she imagined could be fostered by applying a kind of "women's logic" of care for the most vulnerable members of society. Tokoro insisted that without nurturing, "only violence remains."[1]

Here I trace how Tokoro articulated her ideas about nonhierarchical New Left activism through the frame of feminine nurturing as a challenge to the violence of scientific and economic rationalism, particularly in the context of geopolitical violence. Tokoro's history demonstrates how the 1960 Anpo generation of student activists continued to organize and influenced the late 1960s wave of campus activism. Tokoro's analyses, based on her experiences as a female student activist, also attempted to integrate women and values traditionally associated with femininity into political discourse.

While Tokoro's ideas about "women's logic" were based on a manufactured historical amnesia at the time about women's wartime role and replicated essentialist discourses about women's inherent urge to protect the vulnerable and refrain from violence, she wrote in the context of raging debates about the potential threat posed by female students and coeducation. In the mid-1960s, male experts warned that "coeds ruin the nation" and reaffirmed a gendered division of labor that removed women from a male public sphere. These discussions framed the coed as a social threat and set the ground for the public reception of young women as they participated in the radical student movement of the late 1960s.

WOMEN'S LOGIC AND THE LEFT

Tokoro Mitsuko's works have been cited as an influence on the late 1960s New Left, demonstrating how a female student activist shaped the postwar student movement. Her ideas, particularly about the importance of a women's logic of protecting the vulnerable, countered the emphasis on economic rationalization in the 1960s. Fighting the rationalization of higher education as it undergirded economic growth also became a major focus for the New Left in the same period. Japan's economic rationalization contained a gendered dimension, as political forces called for reconsolidating women's role in the domestic sphere. Tokoro experienced this personally as a female researcher, and she identified how the "objectivity" of rationalization affected different people differently, and in some cases violently. Tokoro imagined nurturing as a site for critique of postwar Japanese capitalism. She called on an understanding of women's logic as a counter to what she saw as the masculine logic of capitalist accumulation and rationalization, since she located nurturing as inherent to women's capacity to become mothers, although Tokoro imagined that men could also adopt nurturing roles. However, the link between women and nurturing also became critical to arguments in policy circles and mass media debates that emphasized the importance of female care in the home.

Tokoro's theoretical pieces on how to create a horizontal style of organizing in a political movement, written in reaction to the strongly hierarchical system of the establishment Left of the Japanese Communist Party (JCP) and the Japanese Socialist Party, drew on her personal experiences in leftist activism, including the experience of the post-Anpo disintegration of the Bund New Left. Her writings on women's logic as a potential source of opposition to the rationalist logic of economic efficiency and war influenced post–New Left feminists. It was absurd, Tokoro argued, to employ the logic of capitalist rationalization to facilitate a movement against capitalism:

While, ideally, we aim to respect the subjectivity [*shutaisei*] of every member, when we get close to realizing our aims in the middle of a struggle, participants' various actions come to resemble a thermodynamic process in which hierarchical communication overwhelms horizontal communication. So far, since this is the only way our organizations have been realized in concrete form, we know that our organization, which aims to reject capitalism, has not avoided the logic of capitalism: ranking humans by their production value.[2]

Her criticisms of the establishment Left echo the dilemma Carl Boggs Jr. identified among many Marxist revolutionary movements: the tension between the instrumental politics necessary to capture power and the prefigurative politics that are the ostensible goal: How could one ultimately create a society that no longer subjected its members to the older forms of political and economic authority if one employed older forms of political organizing?[3] Tokoro was not persuaded by the JCP's instrumentalist argument that its members needed to wait for the revolution it would organize before they could pursue human liberation.

Much like Kanba Michiko's, Tokoro's writings were also published posthumously, in some ways transforming her into another maiden sacrifice of the New Left, although Tokoro died of disease and not in a street protest. Similarly, this meant that some aspects of Tokoro's ideas were heard, and others were not. Although the protest movement at the University of Tokyo strove to employ Tokoro's ideas of horizontality and "endless debate," it dropped the link she made between the need for nurturing values in leftist activism and concerns about the role of women in society, demonstrating how women's issues were often erased in the late 1960s student movement.

Tokoro's ideas about women's logic are also problematic, often based on essentialist discourses about women as basically vulnerable and nurturing, an understanding that is not inherently radical or opposed to structures of power. And although Tokoro attempted to understand how a gendered subjectivity created meaning in society, and how one could listen to those voices excluded from hierarchies of power, her writings also reflected a gender-coded contradiction at the heart of the postwar political imaginary: male political power and violence versus female care in everyday life and vulnerability. This echoed the discourses of "naive politics," which I described in the previous chapter as a powerful postwar sentiment that women operated as emotional outsiders to male political power.

In spite of these problems, in many cases replicated in subsequent feminist discourses in the 1970s and 1980s, Tokoro's writings illuminate one critical aspect of the context in which campus-based protests arose in Japan in the 1960s: the battle over the rationalization of universities in the service of the national economy. This rationalization depended on not only tracking students by trade and thus class but also reinforcing gendered spheres of labor. Although Tokoro and other female students rejected such a rationalization of labor, and particularly women's labor, the divide between the public sphere of politics and the private sphere of the home was in many ways based on the same understanding of a gendered relationship with nurturing that Tokoro outlined. As postwar education turned toward educating Japanese citizens to serve the national economy, understandings about women as nurturers facilitated women taking on the care work in the home that undergirded the postwar economy.

THE END OF THE POLITICAL SEASON?

In the wake of Kanba Michiko's death on June 15, 1960, Prime Minister Kishi Nobusuke resigned. However, the vast numbers of citizens protesting in the streets failed to prevent the renewal of the unpopular U.S.-Japan Security Treaty, and the party of the disgraced Kishi, the Liberal Democratic Party, carried the elections of July 1960. The Bund-led Zengakuren (short for Zen Nihon gakusei jichikai sōrengō, or All-Japan General Alliance of Student Self-Governing Associations) dissolved, diminishing the student movement. Furthermore, the end of a yearlong strike by coal miners at the Mitsui Miike Coal Mine in Kyushu signaled to many the end of open confrontation between labor and capital. When Ikeda Hayato replaced Kishi as prime minister, he sidestepped ideological debates about postwar democracy and made the economy his top priority. His "double-income plan" expanded public-sector spending and lowered taxes, and he drew attention away from Japan's political position vis-à-vis U.S. power and Cold War influence and focused instead on national economic growth. Many observers have discussed this shift in policy as the end of the "political season" of Anpo. Ikeda's adoption of a "low-posture" strategy shifted away from his predecessor's highly political and forceful tactics, at home and abroad, and stabilized conservative rule while also strengthening the diplomatic and trade partnership with the United States.[4]

But political activism didn't disappear in Japan. There was still a New Left, although after the arrests of many activists and the disbanding of the Bund, it had lost a great deal of momentum. Campus-based activism would erupt with great force in the late 1960s, however, and many of the participants were graduate students with 1960 Anpo-era experience, along with a younger generation who had watched the 1960 Anpo protests with great interest as children and, often feeling deep empathy with Kanba Michiko, understood activism as an integral part of being a university student.[5]

Tokoro Mitsuko's personal history illustrates the continuation of activist commitments after Anpo in 1960. She participated in demonstrations against what activists decried as the "neocolonial" treaty Japan signed with South Korea in 1965 and also engaged in antibase and antiwar protests. She collapsed in 1968 from exhaustion as she rushed from activist engagements at the U.S. base at Sunagawa to a protest at Haneda Airport. Her daily work included corresponding with various activist and student groups, passing on news from Tokyo to those in regional schools, organizing students to participate in various actions, and speaking at events organized by student activists.

In the massive campus-based uprisings of 1968–1969, graduate students affiliated with the University of Tokyo News Research Center, of which Tokoro was a member, became key organizers and leaders. Through that group Tokoro became close with Yamamoto Yoshitaka, who would become the most high-profile student movement leader at the University of Tokyo during the campus occupations in the late 1960s. Although in many ways less visible than at the height of the anti-Anpo protests, the student New Left continued to organize on campuses throughout the nation.

TOKORO MITSUKO AND A POST-ANPO NEW LEFT

Not only had Tokoro Mitsuko participated in the student activism of the early 1960s in Japan, but her writings also influenced the forms that leftist activism took on campuses in the late 1960s. In particular, the Zenkyōtō (short for Zengaku kyōtō kaigi, or All-Campus Joint Struggle Committees) that formed on campuses in the late 1960s sought to employ her ideas about how to avoid rigid hierarchies and dogmatic politics through nonsectarian horizontality and "endless debate." In contrast, the sectarian New Left factions (ha), although sometimes distinguished by minor doctrinal differences, generally demanded a great deal from their members in terms of commitment, discipline, and loyalty and were often structured in a strictly hierarchical fashion.

Tokoro first came to activism as a third-year undergraduate at the all-women Ochanomizu University, mobilizing to counter the U.S.-Japan Security Treaty, and she continued to join demonstrations as a graduate student in biology at Osaka University and Ochanomizu University. Her experiences as an activist, and as a female activist in particular, shaped her analyses of the direction of leftist politics in Japan, which she published in various publications, ranging from progressive journals to student movement magazines to publications targeting the science community. Similar to Kanba's published works, Tokoro's posthumously published collection, *My Love and Rebellion*, encouraged the reader not just to sympathize with Tokoro as a thinker but also to see Tokoro as a vulnerable and specifically female person. Tokoro's collected writings, also published after an untimely death, drew a parallel with Kanba's premature death, echoing the role of the maiden sacrifice.

Tokoro's ideas helped shape post-Anpo activism at university campuses across the nation in the late 1960s, and her understandings of what had happened in 1960 and what needed to happen from the mid-1960s onward reflect the emergent understanding of what constituted the New Left not only in Japan but worldwide. In 1967 the left-leaning magazine *Asahi jaanaru* invited Tokoro to represent the concerns of the Japanese New Left in dialogue with Barbara Garson, a veteran of the University of California, Berkeley, Free Speech Movement and the author of the play *MacBird!* The journal had published the script of *MacBird!* because they liked its anti–Vietnam War message and felt it offered a good introduction to the not yet widely known "New Left movement" (*nyū refuto undō*). Also, considering the play's tremendous popularity in the United States at the time, it seemed the sort of thing that would sell magazines.[6]

When the theater group that had staged the play invited Garson to Japan, editors at *Asahi jaanaru* thought it would be a great opportunity to introduce the Japanese intelligentsia (their desired readership) to the American New Left and decided that Tokoro, as a kind of "Japanese Barbara," would make an appropriate interviewer.[7] The relatively unknown Tokoro appealed to the editors, although they had considered several prominent progressive and antiwar male intellectuals: Tsurumi Shunsuke, Oda Makoto, and Iida Momo. They found Tokoro through Yamamoto Yoshitaka, a graduate student at the University of Tokyo who would become a central figure in the movement there, and felt her background in the 1960 Anpo protests matched Garson's. They decided to organize a discussion between the two young female activists as an introduction to the concept of the New Left as it existed outside Japan.

At Tokoro's first meeting with an *Asahi jaanaru* editor, she struck him as a bit ignorant about U.S. politics but intrigued him with the questions she had prepared to discuss with Garson. She topped the list with a question comparing the two "New Lefts": the one in Japan that had escaped from the classical interpretations of Marxism dominated by the JCP and the one in the United States that had emerged from personal desires in a country ostensibly without a Communist party. Tokoro also wanted to ask about what she saw as the most pressing issues facing the New Left now: how to respond to the new challenges of the computer age, the age of growing administration, the age of human alienation. The editor's overall impression was that Tokoro was a "rather boisterous young lady." She talked about Simone Weil, spoke almost like an anarchist, and sang a parody song about the JCP for him as they sat in the Art Coffee café.[8]

In spite of (and, the editor noted, partly because of) her eccentricities, one of Japan's leading progressive magazines introduced the concept of the New Left (*nyū refuto*)—distinct from the sectarian shinsayoku—to Japanese readers through the transcribed dialogue between the two young women: Tokoro Mitsuko and Barbara Garson. Although, in one editor's opinion, Tokoro overwhelmed Garson, the conversation ran in the July 1967 issue of *Asahi jaanaru*. Their discussion offers a working definition of a transnational New Left and highlights many of the issues that remained important to the movement in Japan after 1960 Anpo. It also pointed to issues that would come to figure prominently in the late 1960s student movement. Although Tokoro and Garson came to their definitions of the New Left through their own specific experiences, their discussion demonstrated a shared, transnational working definition of the New Left as a movement that often formed on university campuses, was dedicated to direct action, and was defined through its opposition to established liberal and leftist organizations.

The key themes on which Tokoro and Garson spoke were the role of action versus theory in politics, what they felt liberals and the established Left lacked, and the challenges of the information age. Both of them had come to political action through participation in movements as university students: Garson was involved in the Free Speech Movement at the University of California, Berkeley, and Tokoro was involved in the anti-Anpo demonstrations in 1960. They both lamented how they had witnessed such dramatic mobilizations of people that had yielded such negligible political changes. Tokoro noted, "In the case of Japan, after Anpo we fell into a state of despondency. There were suicides, people who disappeared. Also, most students just returned to an outwardly normal life but became like spiritual vagabonds who carried the convictions and feelings we had in the struggle, and the memories of those dead and debilitated." She noted, "I'm no longer a person promoting a movement. I just show up for the demonstration." Garson expressed her frustration that even as demonstrations continued in the United States, nothing changed: "The bigger the demonstration, the bigger the sense of defeat. Because the actual point isn't just to gather a large group of people."[9]

One of the political realities that confronted them as they participated in activism was the reluctance of many progressives and the established Left to support radical change. Garson recounted her surprise at how quickly liberal politicians and university officials crushed the Free Speech Movement.[10] Tokoro decried how "during Anpo, many people had the illusion that then–prime minister Kishi was the root of all the bad, and if we could just get him to quit we'd get along somehow. But Ikeda, the cool-headed bureaucrat who came afterward, has managed things [workplace rationalization, expanding policing powers, militarization] Kishi couldn't do."[11] She also railed against the strictly hierarchical organization of the JCP, particularly as it dissuaded lower-ranking members from participating in directing political initiatives.[12] Both of them defined the New Left not only as a movement against the policies of the United States in the world but also as a reaction to the Communist Parties and the actions of the Soviet Union in the world. They both noted that their experiences as activists and organizers taught them more about these political realities in their societies than any study of political theory could have done.

TOKORO'S LOVE AND THE ZENKYŌTŌ'S REBELLION

Tokoro Mitsuko died on January 27, 1968, the very day that the University of Tokyo medical students voted 229 to 28 to embark on a strike. In her short life, Tokoro had participated in all the key battles of the student New Left: she had been at the Diet on June 15, 1960, when Kanba Michiko was killed. She had been at protests against the Korea-Japan Security Pact in 1965 and in demonstrations against the Vietnam War. She had also been at antibase protests at Sunagawa and at those opposing the docking of the

USS *Enterprise* at Sasebo in January 1968.[13] Yamamoto Yoshitaka, as chairman of the nationally influential Zenkyōtō at the University of Tokyo, memorialized Tokoro's death as a kind of sacrifice marking the beginning of the Zenkyōtō, adopting a flower metaphor and expressing a sentiment not dissimilar to the outpourings prompted by Kanba's 1960 death: "The Zenkyōtō movement began on the day of Tokoro Mitsuko's funeral. The Zenkyōtō movement inherited her approach to life, and it was in the movement that it blossomed."[14]

The "Zenkyōtō movement" to which Yamamoto referred began at the University of Tokyo but quickly spread to other campuses throughout the nation. Zenkyōtō, although only one of the names under which students organized campus-based activism in the late 1960s, also became a byword for the student movement in the late 1960s in general. The term originated in the University of Tokyo struggle in early July 1968, when a Zenkyōtō (All-Campus Joint Struggle Committee) was formed at a meeting attended by occupying student activists, including both members of factions and also nonaligned students.[15]

A loosely structured group of like-minded students appealed to many students because it contrasted with the traditional structure of leftist organizations in Japan, which tended toward a hierarchical style and made demands of their members, requiring them to follow the party line and participate in various actions. The dogmatism of the established leftist parties was at the root of young activists' critiques of the JCP in the late 1950s and prompted the splintering of the Zengakuren just before the anti-Anpo demonstrations of 1959–1960. While the Bund headed the mainstream of the Zengakuren during the protest season of Anpo, the JCP-organized youth group (Minsei) also organized students and formed an antimainstream faction of the Zengakuren. Bund splintered after Anpo, in July 1960. Such splintering into various factions would continue throughout the 1960s.

Brief alliances and coordinated "struggles" (*tōsō*) or protests would unite factions in action. Much of the campus-based activism of the late 1960s took place under a three-sect coalition known as Sanpa (Three Factions), which took control of the Zengakuren in 1964. In the Sanpa coalition, Chūkaku (the National Committee of the Revolutionary Communist League, Nucleus Faction), Shagakudō (Shakai shugi gakusei dōmei, the Socialist Students League) , and Shaseidō Kaihō (the Liberation Group of the Socialist Youth League) could set aside some of their different positions regarding Stalin, party structure, China's Cultural Revolution, and nuclear testing.

However, sectarian competition for control of student self-governance associations (*jichikai*) also channeled a great deal of activists' energies into intersectarian fighting. Intersectarian fighting would emerge as a particularly violent legacy of the university-based student movement in the 1960s and into the 1970s, as I discuss in chapter 4. But already in the 1950s and early 1960s, factions' demands for total loyalty and commitment from their members made many left-leaning students wary. The student movement of the late 1960s mobilized mainly to oppose the rationalization of higher education and the Vietnam War, and the ideal of loosely organized Zenkyōtō defined this generation of student activists' associative aspirations.

In discussing the late 1960s student movement under the widely employed term *Zenkyōtō*, it is important to note that a rich heterogeneity of Zenkyōtō experiences became lumped together under one tent, obscuring variations by region, class, and age of participants. All shared a politicized ideal of the student and a myth of spontaneity: that open, nonhierarchical, nonsectarian movements blossomed on hundreds of campuses nationwide in 1968–1969. However, in very few cases were the ostensibly nonsectarian Zenkyōtō actually free from sectarian power plays, and the two emblematic Zenkyōtō that in many ways were—those of the University of Tokyo and Nihon University—were ultimately short-lived, although influential, as I discuss in chapter 3.

When Tokoro's ideas are linked to the development of campus-based Zenkyōtō, many point to the essay "Toward the Coming Organization," written under Tokoro's pen name, Tomano Mimie.[16] In this essay Tokoro addressed the issues that prompted many student activists to leave the JCP in the late 1950s. Tokoro was concerned with how an organization could respect the individuality of its members, and her essay articulated the guiding principles for the nonsectarian New Left Zenkyōtō that arose in the late 1960s on college campuses. Tokoro decried an organization that demanded that its members subsume their desires to the group's goals. However, she also rejected an individualist solution, retaining hope for collective action. In her judgment, this would require ongoing debate—"endless debate"—and noncoercive and nonhierarchical structures. Zenkyōtō groups attempted to employ these strategies through, for example, inviting all members to participate in debates and not requiring that all members participate in the group's actions.

The movement at the University of Tokyo strove to employ her ideas about horizontality and debate but dropped Tokoro's insistence that a less coercive organizational style demonstrated a nurturing "women's logic."[17]

The Zenkyōtō movement ultimately did not address issues of gendered subjectivity, calling for a universalist ideal of revolutionary subjectivity. Many women who broke off from the New Left to form a women-only movement in the early 1970s criticized the New Left formulation of universal human liberation as assuming a masculine subjectivity.[18] Tokoro's ideas about women and feminine politics also influenced many 1970s women's liberation activists after they splintered off from the New Left.[19] Tokoro's writing had highlighted a potential problem in the New Left: that it would replicate larger social structures of power, which privileged men and masculinity.

Tokoro's own experience as an activist inspired her theories of a different future organization, one that made space for individual autonomy and eschewed hierarchy. She also responded enthusiastically to thinkers such as Takamure Itsue and Simone Weil, finding in the writings of both these female intellectuals a broader theory of "women's logic." She posited women's logic as a contrast to the utilitarian, rationalist scientific thinking of the wartime state in Japan and of postwar global capitalism.

Tokoro articulated her theories on women's logic more clearly in a later essay that made it into the pages of a special February 1967 issue of *Shisō no kagaku* dedicated to the question "What Is the Nation to Us?"[20] Again writing under her pen name, she explored the theme of women's logic in "How Do Women Want to Be?"

Tokoro defined "women's logic" as that which determines existence itself to be enough and sees value in everything, from the "head of a salted salmon" to the "tail of a radish."[21] This supposedly derived from women's urge to nurture even the "useless" bodies of weak or disabled children and was a worldview that Tokoro imagined as a challenge to utilitarian logic or the logic of U.S. military scientists, who were busily computing how to most effectively kill people in the Vietnam War. It is the logic of women, Tokoro argued, to exhaust all resources to nurture life without calculating the value of that life, whereas what she saw as the male logic of science and capital exerted itself to assess the most effective means of eliminating lives considered valueless, regardless of the villages, villagers, jungles, and rice fields that might also be destroyed.[22]

Tokoro tried to illustrate the potentially gendered subjective experiences of historical events by opening her essay with a brief mention of what many noted as a key rupture in Japanese history, quoting the science fiction writer Komatsu Sakyō, who was a fourteen-year-old boy when he listened to the emperor's voice read the Imperial Rescript on the Termination of the War. In formal Japanese, the previously unheard voice of the Shōwa emperor, Hirohito, announced the end of the war on August 15, 1945, via a prerecorded radio broadcast. During wartime Hirohito had been a distant and divine figure. In this moment his voice entered the public spaces of cities, towns, and villages for the first time. Komatsu noted that this "hard to hear" voice on the radio had suddenly transformed the "battleground" into "ruins." He recalled this as a moment of absolute internal temporal rupture: "A clock inside of me broke at that moment."[23]

Komatsu was a male adolescent at the time, and Tokoro wonders about how the situation must have been experienced by the many women gathered around radios all over the nation listening to the same broadcast, struggling to decipher the stilted classical speech of their emperor. Tokoro wonders if "for women who had been forbidden to mourn husbands lost in battle or sons deployed to the front, this 'moment' in which all became 'ruins' also existed."[24] Tokoro is interested in how this key moment—which many described as a vertiginous shift in reality—operated in the space of the home front, a space from which adult men had disappeared, where only women remained alongside the fragile lives they had to nurture: those of the elderly and children. Perhaps, Tokoro ventures, women did not experience this moment in which men's dreams of the Greater East Asian Co-Prosperity Sphere crumbled as a rupture: "Men were dumbfounded when struck by the moment [toki] at which the dream of the Greater East Asian Co-Prosperity Sphere collapsed. Women, in spite of having lost their sons, even their beloved husbands, stolen from them by men's dream, uttered no grudge and diligently offered tribute to those shelled-out people who lost their livelihoods and their pride. I don't think it's an exaggeration to say that for these women, 'ruins' reflected nothing more than a battleground where they fought starvation."[25]

Women occupied a battleground in which the enemy was hunger, not other humans. Their battles were not fought with guns and swords in strategic missions but were organized around mealtimes. It was not the war of violent spectacles but that of everyday needs. While Tokoro's interpretation is based only on her imagination of women's experiences, she encourages a kind of mental exercise by which we can imagine how the moments that standard national histories mark as breaks might actually be experienced as continuities, or how daily concerns might override eventfulness as defined by national history.

But the basic problem with Tokoro's articulation of women's logic is that it is ahistorical and essentialist, based on the assumption that a feminine urge toward nurturing inherently undermines power hierarchies and systems of oppression. She assumes that such a naive politics would save the space of daily life from the taint of the greater, rationalist structures of male political violence. To counter the demands of national interest over the innate value of each life, Tokoro argues for women's logic and refers to the historical example of women on the home front in wartime Japan to illustrate how ideas about furthering the national interest can perform violence and actually victimize the nation's people.

However, Tokoro's account of wartime women elides the role women played in Japan's empire and militant mobilization; in describing Japanese women as the victims of war who stoically "uttered no grudge" even as they lost beloved sons and husbands to "men's dream" of war, she echoes the arguments of postwar democracy advocates who insisted that incorporating women into the political process would prevent a resurgence of militarism. In advocating for a political organization that responded to women's logic, she perpetuated an essentialist philosophy of women's political purity and pacifism.

This association between women and peace reflects the context in which Tokoro wrote and participated in political activism: a time in which there was a strong assumption that women were inherently pacifist and nurturing. That idea—what Lisa Yoneyama has dubbed "feminized memory"—was critical to discussions about how integrating women into formerly all-male social institutions (education and politics in particular) would rehabilitate Japan's militarist past (imagined as male).[26]

The limits of an essentialist vision of the oppositional power of feminine nurturing were already apparent in the writing of Takamure Itsue, whose ideas about women's history and women's logic deeply attracted Tokoro. Takamure's writing spanned genres (poetry, political commentary, history) and ideologies (anarchism, nationalistic emperor worship) over her career, which traversed the prewar and postwar decades. Her legacy as an influence on contemporary Japanese feminism is mixed. As Sonia Ryang has pointed out, Takamure "made powerful connections between past history and present politics with a potential to fundamentally subvert conventional understandings of gender relations in Japan" in her postwar work on women's history, but she also praised, in 1944, the role played by Japanese women and their intrinsic maternal love in waging "sacred war."[27] Takamure's concern with individual freedoms reflected her attraction to anarchism as a more total way to oppose all forms of power, including patriarchal power. This put her in opposition to socialist feminists in the prewar period, who insisted on the primacy of challenging oppression created by the class system.[28] But Takamure's understanding of women's love, which she posits as an alternative to the "artificial" social institutions men constructed to dominate the weak and powerless, is, in the words of Ryang, "not historically envisioned and remains in the realm of the abstract."[29] Furthermore, in the prewar period, Takamure conflated the authenticity of feminine, maternal love with the authenticity of Japanese agrarian communities and the emperor system, a configuration that combined maternalist feminism and fascism.[30]

While Tokoro attempted to reformulate women's logic as something that would challenge the nationalist imperial project of wartime Japan, the historical reality is that Takamure's essentialist understanding of the nurturing power of women had actually undergirded her arguments in support of Japanese imperialism in the prewar period. An ahistorical ideal of women as the repository of sentimental politics is not only a fiction that subsumes distinctions of class, ethnicity, and nationality but also a myth that can be mobilized to support larger projects of oppression as easily as it can be used to chip away at those projects.

Tokoro likely did not know about Takamure's support of the imperial project, however. The postwar swell of women's histories, beginning with Inoue Kiyoshi's 1948 book *Japanese Women's History* and Takamure's four-volume *Women's History* (1954–1958), drew on leftist theories of class struggle but generally contributed to a historical amnesia about how women were emotionally mobilized during the war. Not until the late 1970s, when feminist academics and activists began investigating and documenting Japanese women's complicity with the state's imperialist and militarist projects, did a critique develop against the strong pacifist and maternalist narratives associated with women in postwar Japan.[31] As I discussed in the previous chapter, this historical narrative supported women's inclusion in citizenship after the war, based on ideas about women as an inherently good force for politics. Such claims were based on understanding women as a collectively oppressed group and led to many scholarly efforts to trace the historical roots of that oppression. Tokoro's interpretations of women as instinctively respectful and loving toward all things living drew from Takamure's *Women's History*, in which Takamure traced an arc from an idyllic premodern time in which women were central to the rise of an increasingly oppressive patriarchal system in which "women's culture" was abhorred and shunned.

In the postwar period, Takamure's work in support of the empire—and her prewar anarchist writings—were left out of her collected writings (the ten-volume *Complete works of Takamure Itsue*, 1966–1967).[32] In her postwar women's history, which included theories of motherly and female culture, Takamure also does not mention her support for the mother ideology of the national imperial project. Instead, Takamure reframed her insights about women's history to fit the new discourse about inherently pacifist women. Tokoro's writing in the 1960s, inspired by Takamure's work that was published in the 1950s and 1960s, reflected the larger gendered discourse in the postwar period: that the ultranationalism of the 1930s and 1940s had been a male project, of which women were the victims. Women who had experienced the wartime as mothers were just beginning to publish their own accounts, in which they often described feeling torn between the state's ideal of the patriotic mother and "the role they actually performed of an intensely loving mother."[33]

The specific inspiration for Tokoro's investigation into the historical voices of Japanese women seems to have actually been her own mother's personal story, which she heard secondhand. According to a diary entry she penned on January 3, 1967, she wanted to build an argument about the danger of half the world's population—women—being made voiceless, hidden in the shade cast by "the intellectual history of MAN."[34] Tokoro's own mother's history seemed an example of how many women lived outside of intellectual history. Her mother was drawn to socialist thought as a young woman and married for love, a rejection of traditional marriage in Japan. But she also soon began having children, giving birth to her first child at twenty and several more thereafter. Tokoro wrote, "How a woman who read *Capital* in her teens and lived that [radical] life became an ordinary woman. That's what I want to understand." She longed to hear her mother talk about her life raising five children, often scraping by during the war and immediately afterward while her father was involved in the labor movement.[35] Tokoro's father was also busy with work and labor activism, yet he had time to write a fictionalized account of his youth. In contrast, Tokoro witnessed how care work constantly demanded her mother's attention. This work of caring for the vulnerable and needy in the family exhausted Tokoro's mother and erased her historical voice. How the burden of care work threatened women's intellectual production was something Tokoro and her friends discussed. Quoting something another friend said, Tokoro noted, "Let's see [Simone de] Beauvoir do her work while raising children."[36]

So while Tokoro framed her piece around the male war and the everyday struggles on the female home front of care, casting women's logic as a foil for the violent and supposedly masculine logic of imperial aggression,

Tokoro's concerns were very much rooted in how the domestic labor demands placed on women had historically erased their voices not only in the militant national project but also among labor unions and the Left. In her ideas about an ideal future organization for political action, Tokoro proposed bringing nonviolent and nurturing values, which she imagined as feminine, to politics in general. It seems that she imagined a more general sharing of nurturing that would liberate women from their individual households. In her essay "Toward the Coming Organization," she called for "a society of many mothers, all nurturing their shared human children, rather than a society in which each child is raised by one mother as one household's private project."[37]

In her article "How Do Women Want to Be?" Tokoro demonstrates an ambivalence toward the segregation that forces women to live a life of (maternal) care. Although Tokoro affirms a nurturing women's logic against the destructive logic of capital and the nation, she also describes the experience of women on the home front as being trapped in a "mother-child space-time": "Women have a solemn existence in an uninterrupted, unseverable mother-child space-time. They can't escape it, can't fulfill any other dreams. Their compassion for children sinks other enlivened spirits. They are faced with a history-less existence."[38] Although, Tokoro argues, nurturing creates a logic antithetical to rationalism and violence, she notes that the home front—and perhaps by extension the household—was also a space that confined.

CAPITALIST LOGIC AND EDUCATION IN THE 1960S

Tokoro's writing in the mid-1960s demonstrated how she struggled to understand the role of science in a capitalist society, in particular when scientific and economic rationales could promote violent strategies over the sea in Southeast Asia or undermine individual laborers' livelihoods at home. She saw how scientific discourses were deployed to streamline the workplace, guaranteeing that workers would lose their jobs.[39] Science in the modern era, she wrote, helped to extract even more value from labor and thus dehumanized workers.[40]

In a letter to a friend from May 1966, she noted that she was uncomfortable with scientific rationalism critiquing war as irrational. Rather than allow rationalism to determine whether humans would kill each other or not, she preferred Takamure's "logic of love."[41] How love for a group of people could guide political action and not lapse into a fascistic overidentification with the group would remain an unresolved issue in the Japanese New Left.[42] As one professor, Kōuchi Saburō, who knew Tokoro through a study group at the University of Tokyo interpreted it, Tokoro struggled to understand how to transform potentially problematic ideas about fascistic unity in community (kyōdōtai) into a more radical ideal of "commune."[43]

From Kōuchi's perspective, Tokoro wrote to explore the issues that came up for her in her experiences of activism: the process of negating oneself in a movement and the way that also undermined the movement of the 1950s, when an elite group of intellectual activists imagined that they represented the proletariat.[44] The nagging questions for her were about whether humans could really consider themselves as having progressed, in light of the continued carnage all through the modern era (at the time most forcefully illustrated in Southeast Asia). This led Tokoro to question the role of scientific research and the university in contemporary Japan, and she imagined, influenced by Takamure, that women's experiences offered potential alternatives.

The JCP didn't offer a viable alternative, Tokoro believed, because of their actions during the 1959–1960 demonstrations against the U.S.-Japan Security Treaty. Not only did the JCP not support more radical protest strategies, but they also distanced themselves from any potential class conflict. Instead, she reflected in 1965, the labor movement got lost in the citizens' movement, and Anpo became framed as a classless "war of nationalist unity" while Japanese laborers were crushed by Japanese capital, as symbolized by the denouement of the yearlong dispute at the Mitsui Miike Coal Mine in Kyushu.[45] She urged her fellow scientists to be independent from capital and political authorities and free from the JCP as well.[46]

Tokoro wrote this at a time of increasing contestation over what kind of relationship research and higher education institutions should ideally have with industry and the national economy. From the 1950s, business interests in Japan had lobbied for a national educational system organized around industry's labor needs rather than around the initial postwar focus of molding democratic citizens.[47] A mission statement by the Japan–United States Productivity Conference (Nichibei seisansei kyōgikai)—which formed in February 1955 with the encouragement of Japan's key industry representatives: the Nikkeiren (Japan Federation of Employers' Associations), Keidanren (Japan Business Federation), Nisshō (the Japan Chamber of Commerce and Industry), and Keizai dōyūkai (Japan Association of Corporate Executives), along with the U.S. Foreign Operations Administration—called for using the nation's resources and workforce "effectively" and "scientifically."[48] In 1953 Nikkeiren urged the nation (*kokumin*) to pull together the nation's resources and "rationalize" industry to make Japan globally competitive.[49] Tokoro, like many other progressives in postwar Japan, identified in these pronouncements the rhetoric of capitalist profit seeking alongside the strategies of the prewar Japanese state, which had urged the population to make personal sacrifices to benefit the nation, its economy, and its geopolitical standing.

Government policy makers and industry leaders anticipated that the nation's education would be organized to facilitate their economic growth goals. After the contentious "political season" of Anpo under Kishi Nobusuke's leadership, Prime Minister Ikeda Hayato's policies focused on economic development and favored investment in technological fields for export. Expanding prioritized industries required more students of science and technology and more graduates from technical high schools. Throughout the 1960s, business interests hounded the Ministry of Education to address "the serious problem of technical manpower shortage."[50]

Industry leaders felt that higher education not only owed the nation the kind of graduates that would contribute to expanding the national economy but also owed industry a voice in guiding educational policies because of its role in creating jobs for graduates. As one senior businessman declared in 1969, "the business-industrial community absorbing more than 70% of annual college graduates has not only the right but also the obligation to speak out on educational policy."[51]

The problem with these demands was that, in their insistence that education contribute to national economic goals, they ignored other issues that had been essential during postwar educational reforms: namely, that education foster critical thinking and shape the citizen participants of a democratic system. Instead, business groups attacked the "undue emphasis" many higher education institutions placed on nonscience majors.[52] Nikkeiren demanded measures to curb what it perceived as excesses in postwar education reform as soon as the Occupation ended in 1952. Rather than the new single-track system, designed to open up higher education to a greater swath of the population, Nikkeiren argued for a system to "diversify" education, ostensibly to meet individual students' needs and competences. Such a system closely mirrored the prewar system in which students had been tracked and groomed early on to fill specific roles in the national economy.[53]

The kind of diversification of educational tracks that industry desired in Japanese higher education also perpetuated socioeconomic inequalities. As had been the case under the prewar education system, the prestigious national universities would continue to cultivate the elite bureaucrats and politicians who would manage national resources, while a range of private and technical schools would deliver midlevel managerial staff and factory labor.

Student activism in the 1960s began to engage with this philosophical battle over the meaning of education. While demonstrations against Japan's cozy relationship with the United States had prompted most left-leaning student mobilizations in the late 1950s and in 1960, student protest in the mid-1960s often targeted universities themselves. As private universities rushed to meet the higher education demands of the postwar baby boom generation, campus-based activism often reacted to the tuition hikes implemented by private universities to bankroll their expansion. Between 1960 and 1966, the number of students entering universities and junior colleges doubled.[54] Many private institutions ran on shoestring budgets, resulting in inadequate facilities and personnel. At the same time, the tuition disparity between private and national universities meant that private university students often paid about seven times the national university tuition rate.[55]

Even in the late 1960s, when a broad swath of university students sympathized and identified with a generally left-leaning critique of global capitalism and militarism in the context of the Vietnam War and various postcolonial national liberation struggles, many campus-based movements mobilized largely around campus-based complaints. Of the thirty-one major university disputes one mainstream newspaper identified in 1968, eleven centered around issues related to university finances (tuition hikes, lack of adequate teaching staff or campus facilities), while nine centered on issues of democratic process and university autonomy. Students at Kagoshima University rallied in opposition to "industrial-academic cooperation."[56]

Particularly sensitive to the recent history of wartime mass mobilization, which had organized education to facilitate the national projects of imperialism and militarism, students in the 1960s mounted challenges to what seemed like a reformulation of this ethos in the name of the postwar national economy. One specific example is the 1966–1967 strikes and barricades at International Christian University in Tokyo, which were mobilized to oppose the university's plan to use an aptitude exam (*nōken*) similar to the U.S. College Entrance Examination Board's test. Students attacked the exam, ostensibly a more uniform way to measure prospective students, as a way to undermine a humanitarian approach to education.[57] They argued that reducing students to a numerical score served the interests of industrial rationalization rather than the needs of the students.

THE GENDERED WORK OF RATIONALIZING NATIONAL RESOURCES

Rationalizing national resources, including human resources, was also an inherently gendered task. In an effort to abolish the prewar educational hierarchy, postwar higher education had been organized into two-year junior colleges and four-year universities.[58] This new system was supposed to make higher education more democratic than in the multitracked prewar system. What emerged, however, was a different hierarchy of higher education, one that ultimately tracked students by gender. In 1950 not quite 40 percent of junior college students were female (38.9 percent), but by the mid-1950s, they made up half of the student body.[59] This trend continued, and in the 1960s junior colleges definitively became female spaces of education.[60] By 1975, 86.2 percent of the students at junior colleges were young women.[61] The number of female students at universities remained much more modest, however; the largest increase was between 1950 and 1955.[62] Throughout the 1960s, female students at four-year universities remained under a fifth of the total university population.[63] In the late 1950s, ten years after the legal imperative toward coeducation, inequality persisted in practice.

Differing views on coeducation's purpose remained at the root of lagging efforts toward full integration of women into universities. As outlined in chapter 1, in the postwar drive toward radical democratization of key social institutions, female participation held the promise of purifying spaces associated with masculine wartime militarism. But how much participation was necessary? According to many experts, it was enough to allow young women to attend dances with male students or to form hiking groups. These kinds of social activities would allow young people to explore what was assumed to be their heterosexual attraction. College became an opportunity not for intellectual exchange but for romantic love. One male author of several advice manuals for women disagreed with students at women's colleges who desired more opportunities for coeducational scholarship. After all, he declared, "there's no need [for male and female students] to debate philosophy."[64] In the context of an expanding higher education system driven less by concern about cultivating a political subjectivity and more by interest in how graduates contributed to the growing Japanese economy, what need was there for anyone to debate philosophy?

In the 1950s Kanba Michiko had already written about how she viewed gendered equality as impossible in a capitalist system precisely because of the capitalist urge toward rationalization. While many other progressive observers in postwar Japan blamed lingering "feudal elements" for obstructing women's access to full equality in the workplace, Kanba had written, "Even if feudalism remains in their hearts, the heads of industrialists surely have a modern structure—the tireless pursuit of personal profit."[65] In this modern capitalist system, Kanba noted, labor productivity defined the worth of a human life, and this necessarily put women at a disadvantage because of their potential to bear children and need to withdraw from production when they do the work of reproduction. Kanba declared that without social services such as childcare and communal eating facilities, without "liberation from the odd jobs of the household [*katei*]" real equality between men and women—as workers—was not possible.[66] However, Kanba also questioned whether real parity could occur within the structure of a capitalist economy. She closed her article by noting, "If competing enterprises also employ women, along with equality becoming a reality, I think that [the fact] that unemployed males would increase would invite a basic drawback for all capitalists—a crisis of existence."[67]

The postwar Japanese economy in the 1960s relied increasingly on a gendered division of labor that tapped female labor in the home as support for male "breadwinning" wages and also as a source of cheap and flexible domestic labor. Tokoro noticed this as a female researcher. When the professor under whom Tokoro worked had boasted about obtaining funds with which he intended to hire "girls" to conduct research, Tokoro noted that she understood that the male professor's discussion of "girls" was a way of discussing low-wage workers by another name, which bothered her. But it bothered her even more when she asked about what those female researchers would do when the money ran out. The professor responded that they could just get married if they could not find other work.[68] This professor's comments exposed to her the underlying rationale for precarious and low-paid female labor: when women were no longer needed in paid positions, they should find employment as housewives. This assumption fit with an understanding of the national economy as structured around family economies in which male wages supported female dependents. Even highly educated women labored in a milieu in which they were expected, at any moment, to exit the workforce and enter the household. This supposedly offered women an economic safety net as economic dependents on men's salaries, but these expectations also became tied to discourses about the potential violence done to the family when women's labor was diverted from household care work.

THE VULNERABILITY OF THE POSTWAR FAMILY

In the mid-1960s, in debates waged in the mass media and the state bureaucracy, several mostly male "experts," ranging from professors to politicians, also reasserted the link between female education and the household. In the post-1945 milieu, the government could not invoke the language of "Good Wife, Wise Mother," which had associations with the wartime ethics curriculum. That powerful ideal of women's role in society did not immediately disappear, however.[69] And those who voiced concerns about the degraded state of the postwar family often pointed to a postwar emphasis on women's role in public, arguing that it came at the expense of their important roles at home.

Attempts by government commissions in the 1960s to forge a homogeneous national ideal of a Japanese family drew on prewar models, which required both female labor in the home and a link between the family and the nation. Policy makers' reports and documents from the early 1960s expressed concern for the health of the family at a time of rapid postwar social change and suggested enforcing gendered labor in the home as a solution. A rise in youth crime in the late 1950s and early 1960s drew attention to how the household ought to function. Not until 1960 did a Central Child Welfare Commission document actually link this juvenile violence— usually petty theft—with the health of the family. In the late 1950s, the main culprit was seen as mass culture: movies and late-night coffeehouses. However, the 1960 report made it clear that the experts at the commission saw a "healthy family" with "husband and wife and children at the heart" as a necessary basis for a democratic society and identified the postwar "collapse of the family system" as a threat to democracy.[70] In 1963 a government white paper on child welfare pointed to "a deficiency in the level of nurturing" that put postwar children at risk; this "decline in child welfare" came "in the wake of women's increased penetration of the workforce."[71]

Basically, society became particularly vulnerable when female attention turned away from nurturing duties in the home.

In the meantime, the so-called Housewife Debates brought issues surrounding female labor in the home into the pages of popular magazines. Sparked by a 1955 article by Ishigaki Ayako, a female journalist critical of the "secondary occupation" of housewife, in the women's magazine *Fujin kōron*, the back-and-forth spanned two decades in at least thirty-three articles and many more letters from readers.[72] The debate demonstrated the dynamic chorus of voices that negotiated the value of female domestic labor in a period of high economic growth and rapid social change in Japan. But, as Hiroko Takeda has pointed out, one of the assumptions underlying the debates about the social and economic role of the housewife remained a sexual division of labor that made the work of maintaining "'happiness' at home and 'the quality' of children"—that is, nurturing care work—women's work.[73]

The discourse about the vulnerability of the postwar home and the debates about the role of the housewife existed alongside state labor policies in the mid-1960s that sought to mobilize female labor to manage a shortage in workers. This mobilization was understood as a way to tap female labor as supplementary to men's and thus as a flexible workforce. As the Economic Deliberative Council's 1963 report emphasized, the ideal form of work for married women remained "reentry employment" and "part-time" work. This allowed women to fulfill their expected roles as domestic laborers, while married women also functioned as a flexible workforce that supplemented the full-time employment of unmarried women and unmarried and married men.[74] This was a fine balance to strike: the growing economy needed women to work but not to work too much.

In the mid-1960s, the Ministry of Education emphasized that women's education needed to address women's role not only in society but also in the family. The ministry included "the necessity of improving women's qualities as citizens and their important role as educator at home" in its objectives for women's education, thereby particularizing domestic labor as female and including education as an essential part of that work.[75] This Ministry of Education statement, although employing the democratic language of citizenship, nevertheless emphasized the gendered future of a young woman's labor in the home. Much like late Meiji definitions about the particularly female duties of women subjects, government policy in the early and mid-1960s emphasized the specifically domestic duties assigned to women, while they also employed the postwar rhetoric of equal citizenship and democracy.

COEDS RUIN THE NATION

At the same time as the government and industry strove to bolster postwar economic growth in high-tech sectors through educational reforms, professors of the humanities who witnessed the diminishing powers of their departments blamed the rising admissions of young women. Coeds were visible markers of social change and became scapegoats for all kinds of shifts in the hierarchies associated with higher education.[76] As presented in the periodical press, intellectuals often framed their concerns about the democratization of higher education, and the diminished position of the humanities in a technology-driven economy, through attacks on female students.[77] In 1962, for example, the violence done to universities through admitting young women became a sensational theme in the tabloid press. Waseda University professor Teruoka Yasutaka sparked an infamous debate with an article in the March 1962 issue of the journal *Fujin kōron*, in which he outlined his view of coeducation at the university level under the hyperbolic title "Coeds Ruin the Nation Theory" ("Joshigakusei bōkokuron").[78] Teruoka based his "theory" on the assumption that a humanities education was wasted on young women, who would retreat into the domestic sphere upon graduation. Teruoka went so far as to declare that young men were sacrificed in the drive to educate these young women who wasted knowledge, and he recommended quotas limiting the number of women admitted to humanities departments: "For the sake of Japanese culture, I'd like to limit it to 2,500 [female students] if possible and admit more men instead."[79] Not only were the male workforce and the postwar family threatened by female labor, but female education also endangered the quality of male education.

For Teruoka, a professor of the humanities, his academic field lost its social value if his students did not enter the workforce, and he assumed that his female students would not. Even if the political ideals of Japan's postwar constitutional order included integrating women into the public sphere, Teruoka played on an assumption that women—and women's education—belonged to the domestic sphere. Furthermore, at a time when the humanities were increasingly de-emphasized in favor of the industry-supporting sciences, Teruoka chose to define the threat to Japanese culture not as an economic preference for training that had industrial applications but instead as the admission of too many women to literature departments. Teruoka's attacks on female students for "ruining" the humanities seem especially misguided in light of one conservative politician's 1960 suggestion that the government abolish humanities and social science departments altogether.[80] Anxieties about rationalized mass education in the service of the economy, however, targeted the figure of the coed rather than the authorities directing educational policy.

Tokoro had mused on the gendered dimension of the differentiation between elites and "the masses" in postwar Japanese education. Tokoro described the "Coeds Ruin the Nation Theory" as a product of a process of specialization that demanded that women perform domestic labor after graduation.[81] As such, she found it a backward kind of theory, judging women's capabilities based on social expectations of women's labor rather than women's actual intellectual merit. Tokoro believed that coeducation was needed to subvert that tracking of male and female talents. Although she had attended a women's university for her undergraduate education—a university whose female alumni had fought hard to keep it women-only after the war—Tokoro interpreted the existence of women-only institutions as a way to preserve elite tracks for men: "Women's universities—of course these exist to protect boys."[82] She traced the process by which Japanese education contributed to perpetuating social hierarchies, including those of gendered labor, and groomed a national elite through determining what students were "able" to do and what was beyond their capacity as early as junior high school and then creating distinctions in higher education based on what students could afford.[83] Gender played into it when educators and mentors continually emphasized marriage as a primary goal for female students. According to Tokoro, this resulted in young women terrified that they might fail to marry, at which point "men's purposes are mostly completed. From that fear women will then narrow their own radius of what they do, or what they feel, on their own."[84]

While Tokoro's critique of a failure to fully integrate women turned toward an analysis of women's logic, other young women who entered universities eager to participate in intellectual life in the late 1950s and early 1960s in Japan found that the way male professors tended to steer them into analyzing "women's issues" (*josei mondai*) made them feel excluded from real scholarship or politics, and thus they rejected studying problems specific to women. Some recalled that they felt marginalized when male teachers and colleagues encouraged them to research women's history, for example. Katō Katsuko, who became involved in Anpo activism as an undergraduate at the University of Tokyo, recalled later how she felt hostile when a professor proposed such a subject of study: "I just hated being told to do the woman thing because I'm a woman."[85] Yamamoto Chie, a high school student in Tokyo at the time of the 1960 Anpo, described a similar experience as a student in the early 1960s: "At that time, I wanted to live proactively as a person and thought that stopping at 'women's history' was a retreat. It felt like yielding to being a woman."[86] Young women who insisted on participating in academic and political ventures often refused to claim "woman" as their primary identification, since they saw that as a barrier to full engagement in serious study or political activism. The early 1970s feminist critique of the 1960s student movement—that it lacked consciousness of issues facing women—sometimes obscures how an earlier generation saw focusing on women's issues as an isolated and marginalized field of study or mode of political participation.

As the mid-1960s student protests and university crises eclipsed the "Coeds Ruin the Nation Theory," female students could imagine that youth revolt would sweep away demands confining women to the home. However, as Maruyama Kunio noted in a 1966 article in the progressive journal *Shisō no kagaku*, female students underestimated conservative opposition at their own risk. Maruyama, the younger and more radical brother of prominent liberal intellectual Maruyama Masao, reflected on the "Coeds Ruin the Nation" debate and described a higher education atmosphere in which university administrators and professors continued to blame young women for ruining university departments.[87]

Addressing the ahistoricity with which the popular discourse often discussed the importance of the household and the training of an expert in home economics, he ironically proposed instead the establishment of "household studies" as an academic department. Instead of assuming that the family ought to play a certain role in society, Maruyama described a real course of household studies as one that "would have to include raising questions, from those about the processes that formed the household to those about what the household is at this point in time." He went on to describe how he would organize his hypothetical "household studies department," including which public intellectuals he would hire and insisting that it—like other higher education departments—would be coeducational. "Since men and women would study together, it would be sure to be seething with controversies between students. Among them probably some 'new Noras' [Henrik Ibsen's dramatic protagonist in *The Dollhouse*] would arise who reject modern home life, reject the one-husband one-wife system, and leave the home on their own."[88]

Although Maruyama's proposal was tongue-in-cheek, he urged young women to articulate a serious counterattack to the "Coeds Ruin the Nation Theory." He reported several conversations he had shared with female students who dismissed the argument as simply outdated sexism or who even welcomed the kind of "ruination" coeducation would bring. One young woman told him, "If this is a country that will be ruined by women occupying the universities, then it doesn't matter if it is ruined."[89] Although young educated young women tended to dismiss such debates as too silly to merit an organized counterargument, Maruyama believed that young women needed to assert themselves, or else they would "half affirm their critics."[90]

Of course, many women were aware of the violent potential of such public debates and responded in force to the more threatening pronouncements of gendered politics. For example, women of all ages reacted with organized resistance to the statements of Prime Minister Satō Eisaku, made shortly after his 1964 election, that Japanese women ought to bear more children. Satō's declaration raised the specter of the state's wartime pronatalist policies, and the sensitivity of women's groups to such rhetoric illustrated what Sandra Buckley has called "the multiplicity of feminisms" that emerged in Japan not only in the 1970s but also in the 1960s.[91]

However, state policies interpreting women's work and education as essentially bound to domestic responsibilities triumphed in the 1960s. While young women scoffed at tabloid debates that derided women's place in coeducation, the Ministry of Education issued a directive in 1969 that required high school girls to take homemaking courses.[92] What made the gendered divisions of labor in the coed revolution of the late 1960s, which I consider next, so insidious was the way in which an ostensibly radical movement designed to challenge the received wisdom and hierarchies of postwar Japanese society also replicated the sexist division and rationalization of labor that was rolling back any gender equality promised by democratic postwar reforms.

CONCLUSION

Tokoro Mitsuko's writings, which influenced the campus-based student movement of the late 1960s, demonstrate both that women were critical in formulating issues for the New Left in Japan and also that their theories about activism drew from their experience of a coed revolution. Although Tokoro's assessment of women's logic bears many of the marks of an essentialist and romantic analysis of womanhood, her writings also reflect an attempt to understand how a society or social movement can organize around a recognition of varying positions of power and vulnerability through the examples offered by women's experiences. Although her ideas about horizontal decision-making based on "endless debate" inspired the organizational ideas of the late 1960s student movement, the practices of student activists in the barricades replicated the marginalization of the labor of everyday care that was gendered female.

Whether or not embracing an intuitive women's logic offered a solution to the logics of science, capital, and nation, the late 1960s student movement certainly valorized a kind of masculinist logic that ultimately betrayed the experiences of many of its participants. Although the movement attempted to employ horizontal structures to increase access to the movement and to disrupt the hierarchical structures of science, capital, and nation, the iconic battleground of the late 1960s student movement remained confrontational spectacles. The work of meeting the everyday needs of the movement—through rice balls, mimeographed pamphlets, jail support for those arrested—remained invisible, trapping female activists relegated to these activities again in a space-time in which they tended a home front, although many came to activism attracted to its expansive calls to undermine the logic of everyday life of the state and capital in postwar Japan. I examine the potential and pitfalls surrounding the New Left attempts to create a nonhierarchical movement in the next chapter.

3   Is the Personal Political?

Everyday Life as a Site of Struggle in the
Campus New Left

Isn't a "return to the everyday" actually a defeat? Doesn't "another strike"
actually open up the prospect of victory? Let's overcome the sectarian
battles with an all-campus wave of energy!
Nonpolitical Antiwar Group at the University of Tokyo

Student activists in the late 1960s began to occupy university spaces as a
strategy of disrupting the business of the university and, they imagined,
the business of Japanese business. Students built barricades (*barikeedo*)
from desks and chairs to occupy university buildings and create spaces
in which they organized, debated, ate, and slept. They saw these places as
challenges to the everyday life that sustained the Japanese state and capital and thus the violent geopolitical order on which the state and industry
relied. As a flier distributed by one antiwar group at the University of Tokyo announced, to allow the institution to "return to the everyday" would
mean defeat; they defined victory for their *nonpori* (nonpolitical) political
activism as the successful disruption of the everyday operations of their
school.[1]

Here I introduce the rise of the Zenkyōtō movement and its insistence
on the primacy of everyday life as a site of political struggle and then con-

sider how the everyday operated in the barricaded spaces of the Zenkyōtō (short for Zengaku kyōtō kaigi, or All-Campus Joint Struggle Committees), particularly in the experiences of female student activists in the late 1960s New Left. In many cases the barricades offered student activists a degree of autonomy and liberation from received ideas about proper social roles, including gendered social expectations. However, the gendered expectations that came to define the work in the barricades exposed a major gap between the theories and the practices of the coed student movement. Within the campus spaces activists occupied, where they organized their disruptions of the everyday of state and capital, female student participants in particular experienced contradictions embedded in the everyday of the New Left.

As students organized in autonomous spaces behind the barricades of campus occupations, they felt the potential to create a new kind of everyday. This was the lived daily life in which people defined and redefined their intimate relationships and explored the multiple ways in which they could challenge a hegemonic ideal of how they ought to structure those relations. Through barricading university buildings, the New Left attempted a rupture with the prevailing common sense that prioritized national economic growth. But the gendered division of labor in the barricades showed how the organization of the New Left also employed received common sense ideas about gendered social roles.

Many of the sources used in this chapter that were written by female student activists were produced after the campus occupations. There is a reason for this temporal lag: many female student activists did not write about what were seen as "women's issues" (*josei mondai*) while in the barricades. Their experience of sexism within the barricades of the coed revolution led them to retrospectively declare that the late 1960s student movement had operated according to a sexist logic that marginalized women. The persistence of a gendered hierarchy that perpetuated the gendered everyday values of mainstream Japanese society within the lived daily life of the radical New Left led many female participants to question the structures that continually privileged masculine modes of activism. Young women participated in campus-based activism in late 1960s Japan, but their contributions remained undervalued and their voices unheard; what was understood as feminine care work in the campus-based movement became invisible and supplementary. This kind of invisible activism was the actual lived experience of most female activists in the New Left, and recovering that labor is part of writing women back into the New Left.

Many participants in campus-based activism in the late 1960s in Japan employed the term *the everyday (nichijō)* or *everyday life (nichijō seikatsu)* to indicate the broad set of institutions and practices they challenged, based on links connecting those institutions and practices to war, capitalism, and global inequality. Student activists sought to disrupt this everyday perpetuation of systems of power in affluent postwar Japanese society through strikes, campus occupations, and street battles.

The New Left use of the concept of the everyday in many cases drew from what students described as their experiences of an increasingly disciplined daily life at universities. However, their use of the term *the everyday* was also influenced, if often indirectly, by the works of an earlier generation of thinkers. Intellectuals such as Henri Lefebvre in France and Tosaka Jun in Japan analyzed the links between capitalism and everyday life in their respective societies in the 1930s, while the influential and popular postwar journal *Shisō no kagaku* built on earlier examinations of popular culture to encourage readers to examine the complexity and significance of their everyday lives as part of its mission to democratize philosophy.[2] Radical cultural experiments that had linked intellectuals with workers in the 1950s and critical art practices in the 1960s in Japan also targeted everyday life.[3] New Left ideas about the politics of everyday life in many ways reflected these intellectual and cultural debates, while young student activists also focused on everyday life as a political space and time because of their experiences of education and its relationship with postwar affluence.[4]

Student activism in Japan in the late 1960s mobilized around two key themes: the violence of war in Southeast Asia and the rationalization of Japanese society. Participants linked these two issues based on their critiques of capitalism and U.S. militarism, arguing that the peace and prosperity enjoyed in Japan in the 1960s was based on the exploitation of other nations. Indeed, as Japan entered a period of high economic growth from the mid-1950s, it became clear that Japan had resumed certain exploitative economic relationships with its Asian neighbors. New Left activists had decried the forging of a security pact between Japan and the Republic of Korea in 1965 as the start of a neocolonial relationship with South Korea. Japanese manufacturers sought markets for their goods in Southeast Asia as well, including South Vietnam.[5] These new relationships, although protected under U.S. Cold War policies, seemed to echo the older relations forged under the Japanese Empire; furthermore, many leaders in postwar

Japan had also been powerful in wartime Japan.[6] Although Japan was not a combatant in the Vietnam War, the United States waged its military campaigns in Southeast Asia from bases in Japan. Postwar Japan was ostensibly a peaceful state, but there was no question that its policies perpetuated war.

The death of a student activist at an anti–Vietnam War demonstration in the fall of 1967 in many ways prompted a rise in student activism in the late 1960s.[7] Yamazaki Hiroaki, a student at Kyoto University, died on October 8, 1967, while protesting Prime Minister Satō Eisaku's visit to South Vietnam at Haneda Airport. Yamazaki's death called to mind earlier struggles at Haneda Airport during the 1960 anti-Anpo demonstrations and evoked also the 1960 death of female student activist Kanba Michiko. These past events framed students' interpretations of Yamazaki's death. The controversies over how Yamazaki died also echoed those over Kanba's death. Similarly to Kanba's case, many witnesses and photographs attested to police brutality in the clash between activists and police in which Yamazaki died. While the police report declared that Yamazaki had died as a result of being run over by a police truck commandeered by a fellow activist, the original death certificate declared a blow to the head as the direct cause of death. Activists present at the demonstration suspected that a note about "suspicions of injuries to the chest and stomach" (such as would result from being run over) was added under police pressure.[8]

In refuting mass media claims that a student who had hijacked a police bus had killed Yamazaki, an activist group at the time sought sympathy for this most recent sacrifice in a struggle against state authority by evoking the generally sympathetic figure of Kanba.[9] In a flier distributed at the University of Tokyo in October 1967, they drew clear parallels between Kanba's death in 1960 and Yamazaki's death in 1967.

Although the actions of university administrations and the Japanese government had distressed students even before Yamazaki's death, his death provoked many students who had watched the protests from the outside to become involved in activism. Even if their politics were vague, a sense of the necessity of immediate political action gripped many students at the news that a fellow student had died. One female student related conversations she had with otherwise apolitical students who felt unclear about leftist jargon about overthrowing imperialism or promoting Marxism but nevertheless felt they needed to do something in the wake of Yamazaki's death.[10] Kashiwazaki Chieko, a University of Tokyo graduate student who became a leader in the Maoist Marxist Leninist League (ML dōmei), reflected that she had been immersed in research instead of the struggle and reproached herself upon hearing of Yamazaki's death: "It was not state power that killed Yamazaki. I was the one who killed this person who gave his life in solidarity with the Vietnamese people."[11] She interpreted his death as something that could have been avoided had she been actively participating in protest.

That Yamazaki's death catalyzed the late 1960s student New Left also illustrates another common characteristic among several campus-based movements of the time: the rapidity with which students linked conflicts with university administrations to the larger geopolitical struggles of neo-imperialism, represented most vividly through the war in Vietnam.[12] In part, students linked the Vietnam War with the rising power of Japan's consumer economy. As one female student activist wrote, she felt the new fetish for private homeownership in Japan was built on the dead bodies of Vietnamese people.[13] Another female student invoked Che Guevara's demand for "two, three, many Vietnams" when she explained how Yamazaki's death had spurred her to political action; she wanted to bring the war home and disrupt the peace of postwar Japanese affluence.[14]

Student activists also linked postwar Japanese prosperity with the university's role in bolstering the national economy. Oda Makoto, a prominent anti–Vietnam War peace activist, remarked that it often bewildered outside observers that student activists in Japan so directly linked their campus-based struggles against rising tuitions and other university policies with assisting the people of Vietnam.[15] But students argued for links between the university, the everyday of Japanese capital, and the institutions that supported military intervention in Vietnam. In the late 1960s, student strikes and occupations became strategies to disrupt the edu-industrial-military complex. As discussed in the previous chapter, many students acted through Zenkyōtō that were less rigidly organized than New Left sects and Zenkyōtō created flexible coalitions of activists from various factions as well as nonaligned, nonpori participants.

In an article on the "philosophy of the barricades" during a protracted campus occupation in the fall of 1968, University of Tokyo Zenkyōtō chairman Yamamoto Yoshitaka attacked the institution for facilitating research that undergirded the existing order in which the United States buttressed Japanese capitalism while waging war in Vietnam and continuing a military occupation of Okinawa.[16] Yamamoto echoed Tokoro in noting that "the ideology of capitalist society is recognized as rationalism" and outlined the philosophy of the barricades as an attempt to disrupt the rationalist logic of capital and authority as manifested in the university.[17] Yamamoto declared that one of the main goals of the barricades was to "confront the malicious and everyday-supporting ideology on campus."[18]

The University of Tokyo Zenkyōtō's idea of the barricades, as articulated by Yamamoto, mobilized an understanding of the everyday as the rationalized time that obscured contestations between labor and management, between the oppressed and the oppressing elites. Yamamoto identified the barricades and unlimited strikes of the mid- to late 1968 campus movements as a key tactic to interrupt the process by which universities acted as factories that produced workers to serve capital.[19] The barricades of which Yamamoto wrote—and in which he wrote—in November 1968 were those of the highly publicized student occupation of the University of Tokyo, which lasted from early July 1968 through January 1969, when the university administration finally called in the riot police to besiege and dislodge students.

RISE OF THE ZENKYŌTŌ

The first Zenkyōtō formed out of protests at the University of Tokyo in early July 1968. In a call for a radically democratic, nonsectarian organizational structure and the autonomy of campus space, occupying students in solidarity with "ordinary students" formed what they called an All-Campus Joint Struggle Committee (Zenkyōtō).[20] The Zenkyōtō united students across the university in a movement that had begun as a limited campus dispute on the part of medical students, who had protested an internship system that forced them to work without pay. The medical students' strike, which involved a little over two hundred students and began in January 1968, sparked the much larger debates about the role of the university and its students in Japanese society that became associated with the Zenkyōtō movement. After repeated failed negotiations between the administration and the expanding student movement, students at the University of Tokyo organized a Zenkyōtō on July 2, 1968, and all departments at the University of Tokyo went on strike in September 1968. By the time President Ōkōchi Kazuo resigned and Katō Ichirō, dean of the Law Department, became the emergency acting president, the slogans of the movement expressed how expansive student demands had become. One declared: "Destroy the University of Tokyo!"[21] Photographs of Zenkyōtō rallies show the scale of participation (figure 3.1).

FIGURE 3.1 The January 15, 1969, All Zenkyōtō Rally held outside the student-occupied Yasuda Tower on the University of Tokyo's Hongo campus. Credit: *Kyodo tsūshin*.

The prominence of the University of Tokyo Zenkyōtō in both the mass media and also the general social imagination meant that the experience of the barricades at that institution was often generalized to describe the Zenkyōtō experience as a whole, although a diversity of experiences made up what is often thought of now as the "Zenkyōtō generation."[22] While students represented a significant political demographic at the time of the 1960 U.S.-Japan Security Treaty protests and the birth of the Japanese New Left, they also remained an elite group at that time. This had changed with mass higher education in the 1960s. In 1963 Japan was already third in the world in the number of higher education institutions, behind only the United States and the Soviet Union.[23] By the late 1960s, not only had the postwar baby boom generation come of age, but they were also attending higher education institutions at an unprecedented rate.[24]

It is hard to summarize the events of the late 1960s campus-based student movement. Some statistics give a sense of the scope of disruption at universities and the scale of the police response to the campus-based New Left in the late 1960s: riot police entered campuses to break up barricades and quell student disturbances 969 times in 1968 and 1969, and police made a total of 16,175 arrests related to the student movement.[25] One contemporary source estimated that 40 percent of all university students in Japan were unable to attend classes in June 1969 alone because of "campus disorders."[26] At the peak of campus disputes in the late 1960s, about 80 percent of the nation's campuses—165 schools—were involved in some kind of struggle.[27] At seventy of these, students built barricades.[28] Particularly in the late 1960s, campus-organized protests and occupations became a significant part of the educational experience for a wide swath of young people in Japan and facilitated student activist participation in a variety of protests across the nation (figure 3.2). Many of these campus disruptions took place under the banner of loosely affiliated Zenkyōtō.

Mass higher education guaranteed a tremendous impact from student protests, while the rationalization of education at rapidly expanding universities also fueled student discontent and sparked campus-based protests. This was particularly the case at such mammoth private universities as Nihon University. Although Nihon University's president had boasted about the lack of student activism there when other schools became embroiled in disputes in the mid-1960s, the Nihon University Zenkyōtō came to rival the University of Tokyo Zenkyōtō in terms of national prominence in late spring of 1968 when free-floating student frustrations with Nihon University management exploded into mass demonstrations, strikes, and

FIGURE 3.2 Young woman being cared for in the first-aid station in a corner of the municipal grounds in Narita, Chiba, at the March 10, 1968, meeting to organize a call to action to counter the building of a new airport. The image also appeared in a March 25, 1968, article in *Josei jishin* about female student activists with a more romantic caption, "Aah, I'm worn out. Is this also a kind of youthful satisfaction?" Credit: *Kyodo tsūshin*.

occupations upon newspaper revelations that university funds had gone missing.[29]

Even as Zenkyōtō formed at several campuses nationwide, each with its own history and specific set of concerns, the nation's attention fixed on two schools—the University of Tokyo and Nihon University—based in central Tokyo. Both universities' student movements were supposed to be examples of truly nonsectarian Zenkyōtō, even as the schools occupied very different positions in the national hierarchy of universities.[30] Nihon University was a sprawling institution: at ninety thousand, its student body was the largest in Japan.[31] The physical space of the university was diffuse, and it lacked any kind of geographic symbol that could play the same role as the University of Tokyo's Hongo campus clock tower. Also, the University of Tokyo celebrated a long history of activism and protest, which stretched from the prewar period to the death of undergraduate Kanba Michiko in 1960. Nihon University, in contrast, was considered a school for apolitical students, lacking the New Left factions that had established some kind of presence at most Japanese universities. Students at Nihon University were apparently known for responding to their diminishing freedoms at the school "like docile sheep."[32]

When activism finally erupted at Nihon University campuses and a Zenkyōtō formed, the popular image of how that activism compared to that at the University of Tokyo was conveyed by the saying: "The University of Tokyo struggle is a revolt of the intellect; the Nihon University struggle is a peasant riot."[33] This saying was dismissive of Nihon University students inasmuch as it classified their movement as lacking theoretical rigor, but it was also embraced by Nihon University Zenkyōtō activists, who were eager to link themselves to a longer Japanese history of spontaneous rebellion, the peasant rebellions known as *ikki*.[34]

In addition, Nihon University's position as an enormous institution designed to churn out midlevel workers and its lack of an activist history contributed to the sense that its Zenkyōtō best embodied the ideals of that movement: its emergence was spontaneous and nonsectarian, and its demands for radical democratic access swelled up from a student body that represented the ordinary masses. When Nihon University students first began to hold demonstrations, so few of them were familiar with New Left activist culture that they sang the school song instead of "The Internationale" as was standard in leftist circles.[35] Akita Akehiro, the representative of Nihon University's Zenkyōtō, stated in a roundtable with University of Tokyo Zenkyōtō chairman Yamamoto Yoshitaka that Nihon

FIGURE 3.3 Riot police attacking the student-constructed barricades at the main entrance to the Nihon University Faculty of Arts in Nerima, Tokyo, on November 12, 1968. Credit: *Kyodo tsūshin*.

University's struggle didn't share the University of Tokyo's focus on such abstract questions as the "autonomy of the university" or "freedom of research." The Nihon University struggle, he insisted, was based on more general human hopes and desires and therefore couldn't help but be an absolute struggle (figure 3.3).[36] Akita also evaluated Nihon University's lack of a tradition of activism as something that made them "free from any ghosts and phantoms. Therefore, Nihon University students' struggle didn't know past failures and was astonishingly liberated."[37] That an activist movement—or rather, considering the particularly loose nature of the Nihon University Zenkyōtō, an activist moment—could emerge at a formerly apolitical mass institution suggested that the student activism of the late 1960s was no longer an elite avant-garde. If it was an absolute struggle for humanity, there should be no limits on its demands or on access to its practices.

Nevertheless, the University of Tokyo's position as the nation's premier university placed its barricades at the center of the national story of the late 1960s New Left. Many school administrations called in the riot police to break up these occupations; the entrance of the riot police into the University of Tokyo campus in particular, however, prompted debates in the National Diet about state intervention into academic freedom. Of the total money allocated to state universities by the Japanese government, 10 percent went to the University of Tokyo, and many of the nation's elite—politicians and bureaucrats—were alumni of that school. Indeed, the University of Tokyo, as several student slogans reminded the public, had originally been Tokyo Imperial University, an institution founded to meet the needs of the imperial state. Even with the collapse of the empire, the state and the university retained a deep intimacy. The final siege of Yasuda Tower in which riot police ejected the occupying students on January 18–19, 1969, induced six of seven Tokyo television stations to drop their planned programming and offer audiences all-day live coverage.[38]

In a demonstration of the relative position of Nihon University and the diversity of Zenkyōtō experiences, from the beginning Nihon University students did not share the same protection from state force that University of Tokyo students enjoyed. The Nihon University administration was particularly quick to squash any signs of a movement. Not only were the riot police called for several demonstrations, but right-wing students and student athletic clubs also meted out vigilante justice to demonstrators, to which university officials turned a blind eye.[39] The "peasants" of Nihon University did not share the protected status of University of Tokyo students; many people in places of power considered the University of Tokyo campus an inviolable space, beyond the reach of the state and the police.

Intervention by force at Nihon University only increased the numbers that turned out for demonstrations, however. After right-wing students broke up the first demonstration of a few hundred students on May 23, 1968, five thousand students assembled to protest on May 25 in Kanda Misakichō in central Tokyo. Soon the number of protesters doubled, and the administration canceled lectures and locked students out. On May 27 a Nihon University Zenkyōtō formed when students from the economics, literature, sciences, law, art, commercial science, and dentistry departments met and decided on a set of demands that ranged from requesting transparency in university accounting to allowing students freedom of assembly. On June 11 right-wing students and members of the student affairs office attacked another activist gathering at the economics department. Over two thousand students were injured in that clash. Rather than quelling student activism, the violence intensified it, and Nihon University students called a strike and occupied university buildings with barricades.[40]

The student self-governing associations of several departments at the University of Tokyo had also declared unlimited strikes—strikes with no definite end—to protest the admittance of police onto the campus. This meant student activists at the nation's largest university and at the nation's premier university had effectively shut down the nation's educational system by early summer 1968.

THE EVERYDAY LIFE OF THE STUDENT MOVEMENT

Many students participated in strikes and occupied campus spaces to disrupt the everyday operations of the universities. As the flier circulated on the University of Tokyo campus that was quoted at the opening of this chapter noted, students viewed a "return to the everyday" as a kind of defeat.[41] The student group that wrote that flier declared themselves nonpori and addressed other nonpori students, which emphasized how they saw themselves as free from the political dogmas and dramas of New Left factions.

Being nonpori still meant being politicized, however, and nonpori students participated not only in strikes but also in campus occupations. As William Marotti has noted, *nonpori* as a political classification confirmed how politics had become synonymous with a narrow range of activities on the part of government actors, political parties, and also ideological protesters. The term *nonpori* expanded the range of potential political actors and indicated a kind of not-yet position that "came increasingly to designate individuals who were likely to self-mobilize spontaneously."[42] That many Japanese students used the term *nonpori* to describe themselves in the 1960s points to the larger context in which many activists sought to emphasize their activism as nonideological.

The potential spontaneity with which people could erupt in protest became an important part of the self-understanding of the Zenkyōtō movement in particular as authentic. In this sense, nonpori politics operated similarly to the "naive politics" I outlined in chapter 1, which many people, particularly women, had embraced in the late 1950s and early 1960s to oppose the political experts responsible for the militarist past and the authoritarian ratification of the U.S.-Japan Security Treaty.

Although the symbolic focus of the University of Tokyo's New Left was the occupation of the central clock tower, a nonpori group of students erected a "tent village" in front of Yasuda Tower two days after activist students reoccupied the building in July 1968. The encampment in front of Yasuda Tower attracted many nonsectarian nonpori students, for whom it was a middle ground between occupation and apathy. This in-between space—not quite a barricaded building but still an occupied area—indicates the varying levels of commitment possible within and at the peripheries of the Zenkyōtō. The activities of students in the tent village included campus demonstrations, lectures, and debates. Students rotated sleeping there and held their own courses.[43] Students would begin most days with a persuasion picket march at eight in the morning and close the day with a recap discussion (sōkatsu) in the evening. They assigned themselves readings and wrote reports.[44] In a flier issued by the students creating the tent village, they declared their support for the students who retook the tower—many of them members of New Left factions—and noted that they could not be disinterested in the development: "Why is that? Because this issue involves us as well, and it's something we have to actively grapple with. Also because one of the reasons for this occupation, a decisive step that should have been avoided but was unavoidable, is the powerlessness of our current movement."[45] The nonpori students of the tent village characterized the barricading of campus space as rather extreme but justified in reaction to the actions of the administration. They encouraged other nonaligned students—those who shared concerns about the unfair punishments for medical students and about the riot police on campus—to gather at the tent village to show support and discuss the issues.

Students occupied campus spaces to claim them from the everyday processes of the university, and they also attempted to renegotiate the content and form of university study. While students boycotted classes, those occupying Yasuda Tower hosted "autonomous seminars" to address issues not usually discussed in formal seminars. For example, one discussed the Kin Kirō (Kwon Hyi-ro) incident of February 1968 and the issue of resident (zainichi) Koreans in Japan in general. Kin, an ethnic Korean born and raised in Japan, had come to national attention when he was chased down by police for killing a gang leader and held hostages in a hotel when besieged by officers. His demands for apologies from the police for discriminatory comments linked his plight with that of all resident Koreans in Japan. In the flier the students noted that such violence toward ethnic minorities was hidden by "the 'everyday life' of the 'good people' in Japan," emphasizing how the affluent postwar lifestyle enjoyed by so many people in Japanese society was built on the oppression and invisibility of minorities.[46] The spaces of barricaded campus buildings promised an autono-

FIGURE 3.4 Photograph taken inside the University of Tokyo Komaba campus barricades by Watanabe Hitomi, one of the few photographers allowed to enter. She captured rare images of the daily life of student activists inside their occupied spaces. This was probably taken during preparations to celebrate the New Year, in late December 1968. Credit: Watanabe Hitomi.

mous area within which students could reflect on the everyday life outside the barricades and criticize the inequalities and struggles hidden therein (figure 3.4).

Students linked the plight of resident Koreans in Japan with that of African Americans in the United States, influenced by what they could learn of the civil rights movement and black power. Students were also interested in the links between social movements and cultural movements, and a July 26, 1968, "extracurricular lecture" on black power included a "record concert" of the music of John Coltrane, Ornette Coleman, and others.[47] In the occupied spaces, students tried to expand the definition of what constituted knowledge worthy of study to include contemporary social issues, cultural products, and radical theory.

Unlike one-off demonstrations or protests, the barricades on campuses promised a continuous disruption of the everyday cycle of study and work that many students felt caged in by. One student who had some experience with demonstrations noted her disappointment when a protest would end and she would return to her "everyday cycle," saturated with paradoxes.[48] In contrast, the barricades and strikes of the student movement offered an exciting disruption of the everyday cycle of work and common sense and opened up spaces in which students could relate to each other and society in new ways.

THE GENDERED EVERYDAY OF THE CAMPUS BARRICADES

As campus-based activism intensified at coeducational universities nationwide, students negotiated activism in a context in which the demands included deep and radical challenges to social norms. The desire to escape everyday life in the barricades came up against the requirements of everyday life in the barricades. The promises of a greater liberation—from boring lectures, from a rationalized society, from social expectations—attracted many otherwise apolitical students to Zenkyōtō. Young women who were drawn to this expansive call for liberation found new freedoms and also encountered familiar constraints. While the ideal of nonhierarchical participation offered the potential for mutual nurturing, many female student activists found that the tasks of providing actual nourishment fell to them.

The movement's gesture toward openness made it possible for many young women to participate in Zenkyōtō, yet their experience of a gendered division of labor within the movement led many to question the structures that privileged masculine modes of activism. The persistence of a gendered hierarchy of labor in the movement's barricades reflected a failure of the radical student movement in Japan, which—dramatic and combative as it was—ultimately failed to disrupt the greater social structures against which it battled.

Ōhara Kimiko, in a memoir written in the spring of 1969, when the dust of the final siege of Yasuda Tower had not yet truly settled, described her personal path from reluctance to join sectarian activism to participation in the University of Tokyo Zenkyōtō, along with the promises and disappointments she found therein. It wasn't until the fall of 1968, Ōhara noted, when the Zenkyōtō had driven the student members of the Minsei faction (affiliated with the Japanese Communist Party) from the student council of the science department, that she felt engaged at a meeting of science students. At the late September meeting of about 250 students, she recalled that rather than engaging in the usual sectarian dogmatism, participants asked more fundamental questions about the radical democratic goals of the movement and the role of the University of Tokyo in servicing the Japanese state and capital more generally.[49] Through the social bonds created by chatting late into the night over a postmeeting plate of spaghetti, Ōhara felt she was able to see her individual worries as something shared with others.[50] Casual socializing united the students affectively, even as opening up a larger, more ambitious framework for thinking about issues at the university gave them a sense of a great mission and of overcoming the narrow sectarian debates that often dominated student politics.

In general, Zenkyōtō attracted many students like Ōhara who were otherwise intimidated or alienated by factions and conflict. As one former activist at Nihon University noted, it was difficult to draw attendees if one advertised protests under the name of Sanpa Zengakuren, the "Three-Faction Zengakuren" (short for Zen Nihon gakusei jichikai sōrengō, or All-Japan General Alliance of Student Self-Governing Associations) coalition composed of Chūkaku-ha (National Committee of the Revolutionary Communist League, Nucleus Faction), Shagukō (short for Shakai shugi gakusei dōmei, the Socialist Students League), and Shaseidō Kaihō-ha (the Liberation Group of the Socialist Youth League), which had spearheaded radical Zengakuren actions such as the Haneda protests of 1967. The term Zenkyōtō implied a more open and democratic structure.[51] Activism on the ground often meant cooperation across sects and nonsectarian groups rather than a complete experiment in radical participatory democracy. But in the late 1960s student movement, the appeal of a participatory democratic structure contributed to its broad base of support among many students who might not otherwise define themselves as political, and this probably encouraged many of them to participate in confrontational tactics such as street protests, strikes, and campus barricades, since organizing around consensus gave a wider range of participants a sense of ownership over actions.[52]

Many former student activists recalled feelings similar to Ōhara's: there was a moment in which campus politics shifted from entrenched sectarian debates to an earnest attempt at communication, and this is the moment they point to as defining the nonpori New Left of the late 1960s. For a female student at Waseda University, Tokuyama Haruko, this moment came in 1966, when negotiations with the school administration over rising tuition costs broke down and student barricades prevented classes from being held. Although the two major competing sects at Waseda University at the time were the New-Left sect Kakumaru (short for Nihon kakumei-teki kyōsanshugisha dōmei kakumeiteki marukusu shugi-ha, Japanese Revolutionary Communist League Revolutionary Marxist Faction), which controlled the official university student council, and Minsei, which had set up their own unofficial student council, she recalled that the small meeting of thirty-five students in her class on how to react to the barricades was the first nonsectarian political meeting in which people expressed their individual opinions instead of entrenched political stances. She recalled it as feeling very fresh and novel, an attempt at real communication. After a month of continuous debate, the class of thirty-five students decided they were against the tuition hikes and also agreed to go on strike. She felt that, unlike the street demonstrations she had participated in before, which required a commitment to extreme action, this was a kind of "everyday activism."[53]

Tokuyama's use of the term *everyday* drew on a definition of the everyday as a potential site of resistance to the everyday of nation and capital. Her use of *the everyday* demonstrates the double meaning contained in this term: how student activists of the 1960s in Japan understood everyday life as both the daily reproductions of the conditions for capital and the state and also as a terrain in which they could organize against those authorities. In this case, Tokuyama pointed out that a protracted strike, rather than a one-off demonstration, was both a less spectacular action and also a more sustainable disruption. Although the activism she described was not organized as a Zenkyōtō, this campus-focused form of activism protesting tuition hikes at Waseda reflects the more expansive definition of the New Left that I apply to the campus-based activism of the late 1960s, which incorporated many students beyond those affiliated with what are known literally in Japan as the "New Left" (shinsayoku) of factions.

Many young women who participated in the campus-based New Left recalled the barricades as spaces that offered a new degree of freedom. Shigenobu Fusako, later prominent for her involvement with the Japan Red Army's international actions, attended night school at Meiji University while working for Kikkoman, a major soy sauce manufacturer, in the mid-1960s. She stumbled on the student movement just before the entrance ceremony in the spring of 1965 and was impressed by the students sitting in protest of rising fees, since it seemed that they were acting not on their own behalf but for the next generation of students. She described the Meiji University barricades as a place where young people were able to come together and discuss their lives. It wasn't just Meiji University students either: "At some point students from nearby Bunka Gakuin, some high school students and girls who'd run away from home, joined our group. It became a kind of counseling service."[54]

Although these barricades predated the more famous Zenkyōtō occupations of the late 1960s, the social functions of a student-run space were similar. They were peer groups in which, removed from everyday social hierarchies and constraints, students felt they were able to articulate concerns they could not otherwise discuss. Yonezu Tomoko, who would become a well-known women's liberation activist, recalled that she was first able to talk about the physical disabilities that had long convinced her that she'd never live the life of a normal woman in the "extraordinarily liberated space" of the student barricades.[55] She felt freed in a space apart from the everyday logic that defined normalcy.

Another young woman, Katō Mitsuko, reflecting on the University of Tokyo Komaba campus barricades in 1970 recalled: "When in the 'exitless' space of Building 8, I was released from my social positions (as a female, as somebody's child, as a University of Tokyo student, etc.). I lived only in a 'now' that floated away from its position in connecting the past and the future."[56] For this female student activist, the barricades acted as a spatial rupture that also prompted a temporal rupture, demonstrating how occupying the spaces in which society operated—in this case the university— also felt like a disruption of the time of society and released students from the social expectations they usually felt. It seemed to facilitate new forms of engagement with others.

Katō may have felt hungry and cold in the dark occupied buildings at the University of Tokyo's Komaba campus in January 1969, but she also felt free. "In the barricades," she noted, "we began to have our own lifestyle."[57] It was exciting to feel that one could change the way one lived in the world by controlling and changing one's physical surroundings. As Kuwabara Yōko, a student at Sophia University noted, "When a classroom was transformed into a bedroom, a dining hall, a study, my world was born." She remembered the cigarettes smoked there as more delicious.[58] Very soon after the barricades fell, many female students wrote of nostalgia for those spaces. One noted that she felt like a discarded kitten and was given to repeating, "I want to go home to the barricades."[59]

Because students felt that they were forging something new and redefining the received common sense of society at large, young women could also understand their nurturing of their comrades as distinct from the nurturing expected of women in society. For example, as conflicted as she came to feel about her role as a woman within an often masculinist movement, Katō Mitsuko also defended her role as a cook in the barricades. She found her work rewarding and explained that the rules she experienced in the "commune" of the Komaba barricades were different from those "in the world": she took on those tasks freely, without feeling she was forced to do so because she was subordinate to a man.[60]

Many female students noted, however, the incongruity between the liberated space of the movement's barricades and the quotidian sexism that assigned them tasks because of their gender while increasingly privileging the masculine roles associated with more and more aggressive strategies of protest. The understanding that women would do the cooking and cleaning was often unarticulated. As one male activist remarked to me retrospectively, "No one *asked* the women to cook. No one *told* them they had to clean up."[61] But account after account of various student movements at various universities describe the expectations that women would manage the New Left's home front. A photo essay by Asakura Toshihiro about the Kyoto University barricades featured in the magazine *Asahi gurafu* captured young women performing secretarial duties and making rice balls (*onigiri*). Rice balls in particular became a synecdoche for the sexism of the student movement in Japan in women's narratives.[62] Women recalled making piles and piles and piles of rice balls (figure 3.5).[63]

The social mechanics that limited female leadership in the campus-based movement were complex. At times, it was not only male students' expectations of women's roles but also young women's own reluctance to lead that limited female presence in the more public roles of the movement. Ōhara felt that her female comrades shrank from roles like "agitation" (speech making), some of them fearing they would ruin their chances at marriage or upset their families. Mori Setsuko, a former student activist at Tama Arts University, noticed that the women in the barricades cleaned up after the men of their own volition. Her refusal to do this was challenged by a male student. A male student leader then came to her defense, noting that "even though" she was a woman, she also did "real" work: she wrote fliers and gave speeches.[64] Even when a woman could step into other roles, she often did so as an honorary exception. There were thus hierarchies of tasks—masculine leadership roles were more valuable than feminine support roles—and also hierarchies of women: women who performed intellectual work were more fully activists than women

FIGURE 3.5 A female student making rice balls in the Kyoto University barricades. Credit: Asakura Toshihiro.

who organized food preparation, the mimeographing of fliers, or jail support.

It was not only male students who privileged the more prominent work of writing and agitating; a former female activist looked back on her participation in the student movement and Marxism, wondering if she had joined up in order to become "male" and escape the weaker social position allotted to women.[65] Another young woman at the University of Tokyo noted that she had first approached the Zenkyōtō movement as a way to liberate herself from a feminine passivity.[66] The allure of activism for some young women was its promise of an alternative subjectivity, one not marked by gendered expectations of passive vulnerability.

In the gendered hierarchy that emerged in the New Left, however, militancy figured as a primarily masculine activity and was privileged as the most authentic expression of activist commitment. In the late 1960s in particular, student activists increasingly emphasized militant engagement, which they called *Gewalt* (*gebaruto*), employing a transliteration of the German word for "violence" or "force." German had a longer history of being associated with the elite, male world of university students in the prewar period and had strong associations with leftist theories in Japan as well.[67]

Like the barricades, student activists framed Gewalt—in particular the waging of spectacular street clashes—as a strategy to disrupt the everyday life of the nation and capital. Basically, provoking the police was seen as a way to make visible the violence that undergirded the ostensibly peaceful postwar Japanese society. Partly as a practical response to more violent confrontations on streets and campuses, partly as a matter of style, student activists in the late 1960s thus adopted a kind of Gewalt uniform: a helmet painted with one's sectarian affiliation (or nonpori status), a towel to protect one's face from tear gas (and police cameras and news cameras), and a "Gewalt stave" (gebabō) made of wood or bamboo to wield in battle (both against the police and also against rival factions).[68]

Katō Mitsuko noted that although "You're a girl, so you don't have to Gewalt" was never put into words, she felt that sentiment among male activists.[69] Ōhara Kimiko actually lamented, "I was frustrated that I didn't have a stout frame that could wield a sword like a boy."[70] Of course, some women did participate in Gewalt, as I discuss in chapter 5. However, within the New Left itself, the participation of some women in Gewalt did not necessarily trouble the gendered division of labor in the barricades. There remained two clear-cut and gendered roles within the movement: rice balls and Gewalt staves.

Many of the New Left's confrontational strategies prioritized the students' power to disrupt the everyday life cycles of capitalist Japanese society. However, as the students became an anti-institutional collective, they needed to reproduce themselves as a kind of counterinstitution. The labor that reproduced the daily needs of the movement—food, pamphlets and signs, jail support—was made invisible, thus rendering the mostly female labor that did this work invisible as well.

In contrast, female student activists at women's universities were shielded from some of the injustices of barricade sexism in the Zenkyōtō movement. One woman who had been an activist at all-women Ochanomizu University felt she couldn't really relate to the stories of Zenkyōtō sexism that other women told when she joined the women's liberation movement in the 1970s. She first discovered the gender gap when she left college and was looking for a job.[71] Until she entered the greater social structures in which she worked alongside men, she was not forced to address the social expectations that curtailed women's freedoms. However, a former student at Tokyo Women's University qualified the lack of sexism in the activism she participated in by noting that even in a women's college, she felt the long shadow cast by "men's governance."[72] Another woman who had been active at the same university referred to the liberation within their all-women movement as "freedom in a birdcage."[73]

Even a movement protected from the gendered expectations of male students was not immune to emerging hierarchies, however. One student activist who entered Tokyo Women's University and the Zenkyōtō a bit later, in 1969, felt busy all day with the movement's tasks: mimeographing pamphlets and drawing billboards, attending assemblies and debates, and distributing fliers occupied all her time. But she didn't feel a sense that she was expressing herself; she felt that she just did what the older women instructed her to do.[74] Other hierarchies developed in the ostensibly horizontal barricades. But in the cases in which men and women organized together, that hierarchy was primarily based on a gendered division of labor.

Coeducation played a significant role in allowing many young women to experience the contradiction between the theory of universal human liberation and the practices of differentiated labor and values attached to labor, sharpening their awareness of this gap as a social problem. Young women's participation in a coed activist movement that framed its demands in expansive and universal terms made female students conscious that they were somehow shut out from a universal subjectivity because of their gender. As Ōta Kyōko noted, the University of Tokyo struggle was supposed to be a total struggle in the name of humanity, but she felt that she was treated differently because she was a woman.[75]

What surprised female student activists was not sexism in general; it was how they came up against familiar gendered stereotypes in the supposedly radical student movement. The women involved in New Left activism were not ignorant of the many problems that faced women in bourgeois and capitalist society. There had been women's groups at universities before the rise of the Zenkyōtō movement, but many of the participants in these groups stopped attending those meetings while they devoted themselves to the collective project of campus struggles and barricades; sectarian affiliation felt more important than organizing as women during the campus occupations. However, when such women's groups began to reconvene after the breakup of the barricades, they became places where female students shared stories about their experiences of sexism within the coed New Left.[76] This compelled many of them to formulate women-only movements in the 1970s that worked to articulate how patriarchy intersected with capitalism to reproduce not just class-based exploitation but also sex-based exploitation.[77]

As discussed in the introduction, there was a longer history of a male chauvinist Left in Japan. Leftist female intellectuals such as Hayashi Fumiko and Hirabayashi Taiko had written about the limits of the radical imagination in prewar Japan as it regarded female participation and women's issues, and many female participants in the early postwar student Left had criticized the sexual politics of the movement before the campus barricades of the late 1960s. Imai Yasuko, a female member of the late 1950s student New Left, complained that the internal dynamics of their activist groups often held female participants to a different, feminine standard. Male student activists expected affection and emotional support from their female comrades, and she noted that the fight for "human liberation" was shaped by their "male romance," which included assumptions that women would conform to male expectations about feminine behavior and support. This extended to expectations that women would observe gendered linguistic conventions to soften and feminize their statements. Imai overheard male Bund leader Shima Shigeo's shocked reaction to a female activist's direct and forceful criticism of a male comrade: "This one's just like a child." Imai interpreted Shima's comment as reflecting a more general attitude toward women in Japan: that a grown woman ought to speak in a refined and feminine manner.[78] This was a kind of everyday gendered expectation that many prominent men in the movement did not question, although it could limit women's participation in political debates.

In a pattern established by many politically radical men in modern Japan, Shima Shigeo also organized his political and intellectual work around the economic support of his wife, Hiroko. Indeed, Hiroko recalled how Shigeo praised the politicians' wives of the Meiji era (1868–1912), those selfless creatures who offered up instant hospitality to the guests their husbands brought home with them. Knowing that was what Shigeo would admire in a wife, she aspired to meet the needs of the hundreds of people who passed through her house (Shigeo had moved in with Hiroko and her mother when they married) every year from 1960 until Shigeo's death in 2010. After his death, Hiroko noted her disappointment that Shigeo had not acknowledged her contributions to his political activism, from making rice balls to raising funds to support both his campaigns and his livelihood. However, she also dismissed herself as having no head for such big thoughts, even noting that she preferred that he didn't waste his time explaining things to her.[79] In other words, Hiroko affirmed the separation of the somehow more real politics of intellectual exchange from the practical matters of everyday life.

This division between the recognized labor of the New Left (its intellectual production and direct-action confrontation) and the invisible labor of the New Left (generally care work and support) remained gendered. The care work of the student New Left in Japan was gendered feminine, and the low regard for such work mirrored the low status accorded to it in mainstream society, even as the movement depended on such everyday care work. The late 1960s student movement politicized the concept of the everyday, however, which opened up new spaces to question received ideas about gendered social roles. In many ways, the expansive definition of politics in the late 1960s New Left made it possible to think of personal and intimate issues like care work as political.

CONCLUSION

That the gendered expectations that came to define the work in the barricades exposed a major gap between the theories and the practices of the student movement also informed subsequent feminist evaluations of the late 1960s student New Left as a male movement. Former activists' recorded narratives of the late 1960s New Left in Japan are often divided along gendered lines: male former student activists publish celebratory memoirs of the campus occupations, while female former student activists have tended to publish accounts that consider how campus activism led them to feminist activism.[80] For many young women in the late 1960s, the barricades were exciting, but the sense of betrayal by male activists and the significance of subsequent women-only activism remain the most salient legacies for them.[81] However, when the campus-based activism of 1968 in Japan is characterized as only male, this erases women's experiences and obscures a key tension that developed within the coed New Left.

Tokoro Mitsuko had hoped that the "women's logic" of nurturing would influence leftist movements in Japan after the 1960 Anpo. Although her ideas about a less hierarchical and more open organization influenced the late 1960s campus-based student activism, certain tasks in the movement became gendered, retrapping young women in a kind of mothering role that affirmed for many of them the necessity of creating a women-only movement. Instead of embracing the influence of a logic of nurturing, the culture of the late 1960s New Left sought to affirm an aggressive and violent pose to counter the demands of liberal society and often self-consciously defined that as a masculinist ethos. Again predicated on a binary of female care and male violence, the New Left cultures of masculine bravado contributed to the hypervisibility of the movement's spectacles of violence and eclipsed the feminized care work of the New Left.

4 "When You Fuck a Vanguard Girl . . . "

The Spectacle of New Left Masculinity

"When you fuck a Vanguard girl, you better analyze the base."
New Left parody song

A book of songs "for the current student movement generation" compiled by the "Tokyo Metropolitan University Zenkyōtō Rubbernecker Corps" includes lyrics for a parody ditty it calls "Counting the Zengakuren." The song enumerates the various New Left groups active at campuses in the late 1960s with puns conflating tactical strategies and sexual acts performed on women aligned with various factions: "When you fuck a Liberation girl, you better penetrate at one point; when you fuck a Bund girl, you better do organized violence."[1] The song suggests both the richness and the intertextuality of campus-based New Left culture, which was constantly borrowing and adapting phrases and words from the mass media and activist *minikomi* (minicommunications), and it also demonstrates the heterosexual masculinist subjectivity that often defined the active subject of New Left activism.

This chapter focuses on the political meaning of masculinity in the New Left in the late 1960s, when the student New Left embraced a particularly masculinist interpretation, adopting an aggressive and violent pose to counter Japan's postwar liberal society. As discussed in the previous chapter, female student activists who participated in the Zenkyōtō (short for

Zengaku kyōtō kaigi, or All-Campus Joint Struggle Committees) experienced how a gendered dichotomy of leadership versus maintenance, and of violence versus nurturing, created a new hierarchy in the ostensibly nonhierarchical New Left of 1968–1969.[2] Katō Mitsuko, a female student activist at the University of Tokyo, identified a pervasive theoretical formulation that "MAN = universal human" in the campus-based New Left. She noted that this dynamic emerged in spite of the coed makeup of participants: "This wasn't because those who undertook the University of Tokyo struggle were overwhelmingly male. Rather, it came from the basic philosophical premises of the movement."[3]

Here I explore how some of the cultural aspects of the New Left conspired to define the New Left activist as a male figure in the late 1960s. Whereas the previous chapter teased out the gendered hierarchies of activist labor within the New Left, this chapter considers how New Left ideals of gendered action reacted to understandings about masculinity in the postwar liberal order and how those understandings linked with larger frames about political vulnerability and violence. The construction of a masculine identity became important to a New Left that wanted to project an image of invulnerability and strength; in doing so, it cultivated a culture that disdained expressions of vulnerability and understood femininity as weakness. This emphasis on affirming a masculine vision of the revolutionary hero ultimately focused on a kind of personal liberation rather than political or economic liberation. Ostensibly liberatory ideas about sexual liberation also most commonly defined "free sex" as unlimited heterosexual male access to female bodies, creating new forms of gendered exclusion in the name of freedom. The masculinist idealization of violence in the New Left resonated with similar ideas on the far right and also reduced the campus-based New Left's popular appeal—an appeal that had been based in part on appearing vulnerable to state violence—as the movement became defined by spectacular strategies of street fighting and infighting, which were often understood as masculine, while the police moved toward a more nurturing grassroots approach.

MASCULINITY AS AN ETHOS, FEMININITY AS AN INSULT

As related in the previous chapter, the gendered expectations associated with political action and behind-the-scenes support that were described by Bund activists during the 1960 Anpo persisted even as the late 1960s campus-based New Left of the Zenkyōtō sought to link politics and everyday practices. In the late 1960s, the activity most frequently associated with the masculine New Left subject also became Gewalt (gebaruto), the "counterviolence" with which student activists hoped to provoke and thus render visible the violent authority on which the ostensibly peaceful postwar liberal order rested. In this context, what was interpreted as particularly feminine nurturing and weakness also became an obstacle to revolutionary ambitions.

The cultural products of the Zenkyōtō often associated masculinity with action and courage, while femininity became a byword for passivity and cowardice. The graffiti scrawled on the walls of the barricades of the University of Tokyo often returned to the theme of the university affirming its masculinity through the Zenkyōtō movement. One line from the wall of an occupied building read, "With this, the University of Tokyo has also become a man."[4] Such scribblings on the walls of occupied buildings suggest that many students found masculine affirmation part of the allure of activism. Barricade graffiti often used the term *female* to indicate a passive contrast to male activism. In another scribble, a student denigrated Kakumaru (short for Nihon kakumeiteki kyōsanshugisha dōmei kakumeiteki marukusu shugi-ha, the Japanese Revolutionary Communist League Revolutionary Marxist Faction) using this gendered distinction: "Male University of Tokyo fought. Female Kakumaru does not fight."[5] An insult of "effeminate University of Tokyo" also framed the struggle as one that not only pitted male against female but also fought to eradicate any feminine affect among men.[6] Such graffiti appeared alongside other slogans, including those affirming "women's autonomy" and "women's liberation."[7] But statements associating femininity with cowardice indicate a streak of casual sexism that undermined attempts by anyone other than heterosexual men to participate fully in the New Left project. In a movement that valorized direct action, *female* became an insult.

In some ways, the New Left adopted more mainstream concerns about the social position of men in a postwar Japanese society that had granted women access to formerly all-male institutions. One former female student activist at Waseda University recalled reading a student movement billboard that declared, "Actresses can also enter, women can also enter, tuition also rises, the riot police also enter, there's no university student council, what a degraded thing is Waseda."[8] Student activists at Waseda University drew a parallel between the degradation of higher education and the admission of female students, aligning the logic of the New Left with the logic of more conservative observers who believed that the admission of women destroyed the quality of higher education, as discussed in chapter 2.

The cultural products that the campus-based New Left embraced also often linked authenticity, action, and a masculinist ethos. The emblematic poster for the student-organized University of Tokyo Komaba Festival of November 1968, a poster that celebrated the New Left disruptions at the institution, featured an image of a tattooed man evocative of the actor Takakura Ken, a popular actor famous for playing honorable yakuza. Referencing the famous gingko trees of the University of Tokyo, the text on the poster read, "Don't stop me, Mama. The gingko on my back are crying. Male Tokyo University is going somewhere."[9] In this rendering, not only is the activism at the university masculine (male Tokyo University), but it is also cast as a hypermasculine yakuza outlaw.[10] More than one observer has noted that Toei Studios' yakuza films were wildly popular with students in the late 1960s for their romantic portrayal of masculine codes of honor (*ninkyō*).[11] The image of manhood in yakuza films emphasized an ethos that contrasted sharply with the rationalized, domesticated masculinity of the postwar male white-collar worker. That worker, the "salaryman" (*sarariiman*), represented the new ideal of masculine responsibility in the high-economic-growth era of the late 1960s, based in a family structure that required men to earn enough to support women's work within the home. New Left slogans making claims about manliness set activist masculinity against what they saw as the subjugated nature of postwar liberal society and of the expanding managerial class within it.

The assumption of a male subjectivity for New Left revolutionary activism also framed debates around the idea of liberated sexuality in the coed movement. While the tabloid media constantly speculated about the rampant sexuality of the coed campus-based New Left, "free sex" became a buzzword among student activists only rather late in the Zenkyōtō movement. As I discuss in chapter 5, many activist groups actually attempted to constrain sexuality within campus barricades, particularly since rumors of debauchery threatened to undermine their political critiques. For some in the New Left, free sex, much like Gewalt, seemed to promise a liberation from and destruction of bourgeois social morality. However, personal liberation through free sex often turned out to mean free heterosexual male sexual access to female bodies.

As actually experienced by many female students, "free sex" became another way to express heterosexual male expectations about the sexual availability of female participants. Even those who did not oppose a more open attitude toward sexuality in principle criticized free sex as it was experimented with in the New Left. Female student activist Aoyama Michiko, writing in 1971, noted that she felt free sex liberated only part of her person, not the whole person.[12] Tanaka Mitsu, an activist and writer influential in the women's liberation movement, framed her ideas about how to liberate women as human beings around a critique of free-sex doctrines in the New Left. In her 1970 tract "Liberation from the Toilet," Tanaka wrote about how she felt men in contemporary Japan divided women into two distinct categories: "mothers" worthy of affection or "toilets" in which they could discharge their sexual desires. Tanaka pointed out how the former were considered fit partners for marriage, while the latter were partners for free sex. However, Tanaka noted, the designation of some women as "toilets" degraded not only women but also men as humans and sexual beings: "If women are 'toilets' to dispose of physical desire, that makes male sexuality 'shit.'"[13]

Free sex was a particularly loaded term when rape and sexual assault were realities for female activists involved in the New Left. Sexual assault took place between members of the same faction and also figured in the *uchigeba* (short for *uchi gebaruto*, "internal violence") between factions as they vied for control of various campuses. When Kakumaru attacked a female student member of rival sect Chūkaku (National Committee of the Revolutionary Communist League, Nucleus Faction) at Chiba University, the male assailants concluded their attack by raping her.[14] They hoped that the shame of a sexual assault would deter her from returning to the campus.[15] While intersectarian attacks were generally painful—and, over time, became deadly—affairs and involved not only battering but also torture, the use of sexual assault also incorporated the logic of gendered violence into political violence. "Using rape and sexual violence to punish women was an everyday thing," recalled one woman involved in the New Left.[16]

In light of these experiences, it also becomes difficult to overlook the cinematic depictions of rape so common in the cultural works linked to political radicalism in the late 1960s. In the late 1960s and early 1970s, erotic films that faced censorship for obscenity had many links to New Left critiques of the state and authority. Filmmaker Ōshima Nagisa expressed his hope that young people in the late 1960s were radically renegotiating gender relations through some kind of revolutionary sex in the campus barricades.[17] A member of an older generation of activists, Ōshima was a leading figure in Japan's New Wave of cinema and frequently explored themes in which erotics and politics overlapped. It is difficult to understand exactly what kind of sex would be truly revolutionary for Ōshima, who, like many other leftist male directors, often projected political violence and exploitation onto the bodies of women through depictions of sexual assault in his films.

Like many others involved in politically engaged films at the time, Ōshima was also an early champion of the "pink" soft-core pornographic film (pinku eiga) as a politically oppositional genre.[18] Pink films often faced legal challenges from censors, which the filmmakers and observers interpreted as evidence of their political radicalism and threat to the authorities. However, as feminist commentators noted in the early 1970s, these works often featured stereotypical gender roles that affirmed the patriarchal status quo. One columnist writing about such a film (Nishimura Shogorō's Osana tsuma no kokuhaku: shōgeki [Confessions of a Young Wife: Shock]) for a feminist publication, Onna eros, criticized the film's imaginative shortcomings in portraying a "pitiful woman" who succumbs to a rape and her sad fate: "In the end porno film is not able to set foot out of its dark little self-satisfied castle and fly the flag of progressivism."[19] While such films, like the student-built barricades, attempted to disrupt the everyday of the state and authority, the content created within this disruption was not necessarily radical. In both cases, a masculinist fantasy undermined the liberatory promises of the late 1960s New Left.

From 1970 onward, many female activists attempted to articulate this within the movement but found themselves and their critiques marginalized. This book opens with one such case, when the Thought Group S.E.X. female activists from Tama Arts University who attempted to intervene with feminist demands at an April 1970 New Left event felt chased off the stage.[20] Both Mori Setsuko and Yonezu Tomoko of Thought Group S.E.X. went on to participate in women's liberation at the Ribu Shinjuku Center, a major hub for the movement from 1972 to 1977, in a movement that both continued and also broke from their student activism.[21] One of the early women's liberation slogans in Japan was "What the hell is femininity?" In asking this, women's lib activists pointed to the heretofore-invisible order that regulated women's behavior in mainstream society and within the New Left.

Female student activists began to critique masculinist attitudes in the student movement at a moment when voices were beginning to challenge the ethnocentric limits of the New Left as well. At a national Zengakuren (short for Zen Nihon gakusei jichikai sōrengō, or All-Japan General Alliance of Student Self-Governing Associations) assembly held on July 15, 1971, one young woman cited recent critiques and protests by Chinese student activists in Japan about the Japanese chauvinism of the New Left to frame her larger denouncement of New Left men and the New Left women who supported them. She argued that a narrow focus on class struggle did not capture the ways in which the Japanese proletariat's advancement could oppress other people in Asia and women. Her speech attacked xenophobia and sexism, linking the privileging of a Japanese subject with the privileging of a masculine subject of the revolution. She closed by declaring, "Men, I don't want to enable you! Women, *don't hand over the initiative for your own liberation to men!* The ones to decide the future of Japan's class struggle are us women! [We should] describe ourselves with our own words! Make the revolution's intrinsic inevitability our own!"[22] She and many other female student activists argued that women needed to find the way forward on their own to liberate themselves from the sexist attitudes they had absorbed by growing up in a sexist society and participating in a sexist movement.

MAN TO MAN WITH THE FAR RIGHT

While the New Left did not foster conversations about the operations of femininity, its concerns about masculinity in the rationalized liberal postwar order paralleled the far right's anxieties about the state of Japanese masculinity. This became clear in a 1969 event staged by a group of University of Tokyo students that invited right-wing author Mishima Yukio, who would go on to kill himself in November 1970 while attempting to incite a coup with his small band of far-right youth. The mass media flocked to this event bringing together two ostensible enemies because the conversation between Mishima and students who declared themselves representatives of the University of Tokyo Zenkyōtō promised to present a clash between two extremes in the contemporary political and cultural milieu. Mishima represented his idiosyncratic extremist right-wing ideology, and the student group that took part under the banner of the Zenkyōtō claimed to represent the collectivist and leftist project of the student movement.

The underlying tone of the event reflected a shared assumption that political action emerged from a masculine subject. The resulting "debate" demonstrated a search for an ideal political subject, albeit one riddled

FIGURE 4.1 A photograph of the audience taken from behind the author Mishima Yukio at his debate with University of Tokyo Zenkyōtō students, held at the university's Komaba campus on May 13, 1969. Credit: *Kyodo tsūshin*.

with contradictions and half-baked ideas. What emerged clearly, however, was the all-male ensemble's shared hatred of the contemporary liberal Japanese state, a willingness—enthusiasm, even—to use violence, and a shared masculinist subjectivity.[23] For his part, Mishima was eager to align himself with the radical students' attacks on postwar liberalism, which both sides declared to be their shared enemy.[24]

In the encounter, Mishima earned their respect—one of them unthinkingly referred to him as *sensei* (an honorific reserved for figures of authority) in the debate—by performing what the students saw as the courageous act of coming into their midst alone (figure 4.1).[25] The campus-based New Left had by this time developed a reputation for violence, taking hostile faculty members hostage for "forced negotiations," sometimes for days on end.[26] Using this logic, the student who slipped up and called Mishima *sensei* defended his mistake by noting the courage it took to come into their midst alone, commenting that Mishima deserved the title more than many of their so-called teachers, many of whom feared them. Mishima's swagger protected him, while liberal University of Tokyo professors had been subjected to confrontations and "forced negotiations" with radical students. In the debate with Mishima, the student dubbed Zenkyōtō A offered a justification for such violence and a rebuttal to an accusation by Maruyama Masao, perhaps the most famous liberal intellectual in the postwar period, after student activists trashed his office that not even Nazis would have been so destructive: Yes, Zenkyōtō A declared, fascist Nazis would not have attacked the University of Tokyo, since the institution itself was in the service of fascism during the war.[27] Although the students and Mishima were all also products of the University of Tokyo (Mishima graduated from the Law Faculty in 1947) and in many ways owed their social prominence to their affiliation with that institution, they all framed themselves as enemies of the postwar liberal intellectualism for which the university stood.

It is unlikely that the student participants in the debate with Mishima understood exactly how strong the author's attraction to the politics of violence was. Mishima maintained a colorful, high-profile public image, and his oeuvre ranged from minor works with an avid housewife-reader audience to novels that drew the attention of the Nobel Prize committee. In conversation with the University of Tokyo Zenkyōtō, he described his political views as an "extremely radical conservative political philosophy" but delivered the line in such a manner that he prompted his audience to laugh.[28] It is hard to know where Mishima stood; he often adopted different tones and voices. In his debate with the student activists, he flattered them; in an article for the popular journal *Bungei shunjū*, however, he appealed to civil society against the student activists, calling on the public to "turn the University of Tokyo into a zoo" and isolate the barricaded students like animals in cages.[29]

Mishima adopted several different personas as a celebrity writer, and the ease with which he played these various roles made him seem ever playful and never sincere. He was, simultaneously, a militant, a dandy, queer, and a womanizer. Mishima's fascination with military culture and masculine violence led him to train with the Self-Defense Forces in 1967. And yet, while he was there, the readership of a popular weekly tabloid awarded him the number-one position in its "All-Japan Mr. Dandy" contest.[30] His 1951 serial novel *Forbidden Colors* (*Kinjiki*) introduced audiences to the underground world of gay bars in Tokyo, although Mishima also had love affairs with high-society women. Shōda Michiko, who married the crown prince in 1959, had even met with him for a formal marriage interview.[31] These roles were not necessarily contradictory: in many ways, both Mishima's dandyism and his militancy embraced varied iterations of masculinity.

For many of his contemporaries, Mishima's tone of aristocratic irony obscured just how invested he was in his militant rightist politics in the late 1960s. The student leftists' view of Mishima was also shaped by the author's foppish public image, and while they traded words with him in an often earnest effort to distinguish their own views from his romantic rightism, they likely did not realize the seriousness behind Mishima's frequent provocative flourishes.[32] In spite of whatever fears Mishima's associates may have had for his safety when entering the company of "violent" students, the mood of the May 1969 Mishima-versus-Zenkyōtō debate as recorded on film and in a transcription seems light: Mishima, dressed casually in a polo shirt, charms laughter out of his ostensibly antagonistic and thousand-person-strong student audience.[33]

Mishima's interest in political violence as a foil to the postwar liberal democratic order responded to a different set of geopolitical concerns than those of the Zenkyōtō he debated, although both sides ultimately privileged masculinist violence as a response. While the late 1960s student movement battled Japanese authorities to disrupt the everyday life of the state and capital that perpetuated violence in Vietnam, Mishima declared his support for U.S. military involvement in Vietnam when *Newsweek* consulted him in 1967. The Japanese weekly tabloid *Heibon panchi* contacted Mishima to clarify his statements in the American publication; Mishima replied, "You can take it as they put it," adding, "I'm still someone who affirms the Great East Asian War and I support America's Vietnam policy, too."[34] Mishima's support of the contemporary U.S. war in Southeast Asia, and also his unabashed admiration of Japan's wartime imperial project, made him an enemy of the Zenkyōtō. And yet Mishima's outreach to university youth addressed a concern common to both the right-wing men who joined his Shield Society and many who joined in militant left-wing activism.

Mishima's attraction to the Zenkyōtō and his fear of it arose from the possibility that the leftist student movement might offer young men an opportunity for a glorious death in a postwar society in which that option was supposed to have been foreclosed.[35] Confrontations between student occupiers and the police called in to dislodge them produced spectacular clashes in the late 1960s, and the students facing the police must have feared for their lives at many moments. Police also risked injury and death in skir-

mishes with New Left students; in a case that attracted a great deal of public sympathy, one officer died in 1968 when a piece of concrete thrown from
the Nihon University barricades struck his head. The siege through which
riot police ended the long-standing student occupation of the University
of Tokyo's Yasuda Tower on January 18, 1969, lasted seventy-two hours and
resulted in hundreds of casualties on both sides. Although there were no
fatalities, many injuries were serious. Of the 400 students arrested in that
single event, 270 were wounded. A list compiled by the students' defense
team gives a sense of the scope of the violence: tear gas canisters and police
batons broke teeth and split lips, tear gas burned skin and eyes, and water
cannons crushed bodies.[36] One student went blind.[37] After Mishima committed ritual suicide in the commandant's office at the Tokyo headquarters of the Eastern Command of the Self-Defense Forces on November 25,
1970, imagining that he might inspire a military coup, his mother speculated that witnessing New Left activists clash with the police prompted his
own turn to violence.[38] The symbolic power of the student movement, and
its ability to disrupt cities and capture the attention of the mass media and
the public captivated Mishima. By many accounts, he hoped to harness
these elements for his own political beliefs, which he framed as both defending against and exploiting the opportunities created by the New Left.

Several asides about sexual desire also revealed an underlying heterosexual male framing shared among the male participants of the Mishima-
versus-Zenkyōtō debate. Although Mishima was well known in the gay
underground of Tokyo, his debate with student activists remained within
the heterosexual logic of mainstream Japanese society, demonstrating a
limit in the student movement's ostensibly wide-ranging imagination. In
their discussions of free sex, in particular regarding the monogamy that
defined the modern imperial institution, it remained defined as male sexual access to women.[39] In a segment in which they considered the self and
the other, Mishima pointed out that it was not only violence that made
the distinction clear but also erotic desire. Mishima drew a parallel between violent and erotic confrontations in which the subjectivity of the
other presented an obstacle for the desiring self. Defining sexual desire in
heterosexual terms, Mishima declared that "one of the paradoxes of male-
female equality" remained the othering of the desired object.[40] Reflecting
the general erasure of gendered concerns within the New Left by 1969, the
students did not pursue the political implications of this line of thought
about imagined male active subjectivity in opposition to female passive
subjectivity. To this group of students, the emphasis on militancy pushed

out considerations of how affective interpersonal relations also formed political subjectivities.

An anxiety that postwar liberal democracy emasculated men informed both Mishima's and the students' formulations of the ideal political subject. For Mishima, this was linked to the postwar order in which, according to Article 9 of the postwar constitution, "the Japanese people forever renounce war as a sovereign right of the Nation."[41] In his 1967 "Temporary Proposal for JNG" (the "Japan National Guard" that Mishima outlined in this pamphlet, to be used for fundraising among corporations), Mishima—writing anonymously—declared, "The most important issue for Japan under present circumstances is the establishment of a national ideal and to make young men understand with their own bodies 'What is the Great Principle?'"[42] Notable in this statement is Mishima's desire to activate a physical knowledge in young men's "own bodies" and also to link it to "the Great Principle" (*taigi*), a term that echoed Japanese wartime militarism and ideology. Although militant New Left activists framed their protest against the Japanese state differently, they too sought a way to physically embody great principles.

However, unlike those on the homosocial far right, New Left activists had to negotiate their ideals of masculinity in a movement with both male and female participants. Within the New Left, then, an idealization of militant masculinity produced a dynamic tension among participants. Although the New Left also displayed a male chauvinist swagger that prompted comparisons with right-wing men, the campus-based New Left was a coed revolution and made claims about universal human liberation and democratic participation. The sexism of the New Left, as discussed in the previous chapter, created a productive dynamic in which young women began to articulate both the allure and the frustrations of the spaces of the student-erected barricades, based on their experiences of how a gendered dichotomy of leadership versus support created a new hierarchy in the ostensibly nonhierarchical Zenkyōtō of 1968–1969.

Far-right youth groups in Japan were more unabashedly sexist. Another "debate," this one published in the right-leaning magazine *Shokun!* in November 1969, pitted a "Zenkyōtō coed" against a "right-wing youth." Rather than a debate, the discussion reads like an interview of the right-wing male student by the leftist female student. Indeed, the framing question of the organizer, Yamada Masahiro, was why a young man who might otherwise be attracted to leftist politics joined a rightist group. At several points the right-wing youth, Suzuki Shin'ichi, and the leftist young woman, Fujita Mizue, discuss women. Although women could theoretically join his group, Suzuki also declares that he and his buddies hate what they see as women's inability to commit to political ideals. When Fujita sits in on a meeting of Suzuki's organization and presses the young men to elaborate on their philosophy and political strategies, they deflect her: "It's something a woman can't understand."[43] Their beliefs in the spiritual unification of the Japanese people through the figure of the emperor are also based on an image of women as lacking in both intuition and intellect.

Fujita's own leftist opinions are discussed little, perhaps because the guiding question of the article is why, in a political milieu of overwhelming youth participation in the New Left, a young person would be drawn to the far right. Undoubtedly, the fact that the guiding hand of the magazine was that of the conservative Ikejima Shinpei also limited any discussions of Fujita's New Left politics. Part of the mission of Shokun! was to amplify conservative voices in a period that Ikejima felt was too radically left-leaning. The organizer of the conversation noted that having a female interlocutor kept the tenor of the discussion civil, which focuses on Fujita's conformity to gendered social expectations rather than her political experiences. But Fujita's questions also cause Suzuki and his fellow right-wingers to appear a bit ridiculous at moments. Suzuki openly states that he views men as superior to women, but Fujita's questions lead the reader to understand this as the result of his "mother complex." Suzuki's mother is actually a leftist teacher, and Fujita presses him to elaborate on how his "mother complex" influenced his politics:

FUJITA: Are you saying your mother is too strong?

SUZUKI: Perhaps.

FUJITA: I want to hear more about that (laughs). Isn't your complex about men being superior to women?

SUZUKI: No.

FUJITA: Are you contradicting what you said earlier?

SUZUKI: Yeah. But if I have to come out and say it, I'd say I strongly believe that men are superior to women.[44]

Fujita manages to cast Suzuki's political convictions as a young man's attempt to overcome his overbearing mother through adopting a view of male superiority. This casual psychological analysis fit with popular conceptions of the dominant roles played by mothers in postwar society, an image influenced by the emphasis on the importance of women's new participation in politics as actors connected to daily life and domestic nurturing. While this forged a radical political subjectivity for ordinary women's naive politics, it also came to represent, for New Left activists, the dangerous complicity (and complacency) of domesticity and the state.

REVOLUTIONARY MEN OR CODDLED BOYS?

Mothers also figured in the imagination of the campus New Left, often as a stand-in for affective familial ties that might obstruct action or as symbols of the bourgeois family. The slogan of the aforementioned University of Tokyo Komaba campus festival poster—"Don't stop me, Mama!"—framed a masculine gangster's declarations against the possible objections of "Mama," advocating a rejection of maternal love that might hold him back from his manly tasks. A December 1968 article in the University of Tokyo Zenkyōtō's journal *Shingeki*, "Overcome Mama," equated mothers with "everydayness" in the sense of the hegemonic everyday of the state and capital. The author noted, "What is 'Mama' to us fighting this struggle? 'Mama' is a symbol of the household," and called for campus activists to "overcome Mama" as part of the movement's battle against all forms of social collectivity (*kyōdōtai*, a term that often evoked historical fascism in Japan) that undergirded the established social order. "'Mama' is the simplest form of calling for a return to the most powerful order of established kyōdōtai (= everydayness)."[45]

The idea that "Mama" posed an obstacle to university students' activism was not only metaphorical. The "Overcome Mama" article opens by describing the women, some from faraway regions, who flocked to the University of Tokyo and handed out candies, oranges, and cakes to students, urging them to "stop the struggle" and to "be careful not to catch a cold."[46] These women became known as "Caramel Mamas." Ōhara Kimiko of the University of Tokyo's Zenkyōtō criticized the intellectually vapid tenor of their objections as they "without trying to understand anything only talked about how you have to take care of your body."[47] These Caramel Mamas attempted to persuade young people through emphasizing the social role of the mother, offering sweet rewards to good children. To Ōhara and other student activists, however, mothers like this represented the bourgeois household that undergirded the Japanese state. Caramel Mamas presented a case in which mothers reprised an earlier role of feminine

FIGURE 4.2 A "Caramel Mama" passes out sweets at the University of Tokyo in front of Nakamura Hiroshi's Komaba campus festival poster in late November 1968. Credit: *Yomiuri shimbun*.

ideological suasion, with a difference. Whereas during the war mothers had often prepared care packages to encourage their sons' participation in the state's war, the Caramel Mama appealed to young people to avoid conflict and thus support the state's postwar order.

While many student activists attempted to reject the affective ties of the bourgeois household, as represented by the mother, the Caramel Mamas patrolling the borders of the student New Left also offered an image of emboldened women in postwar Japan. A full-page photograph published in December 1968 in the tabloid *Shūkan yomiuri* featured a kimono-clad Caramel Mama, armed with her box of sweets, outside the placards around the Komaba campus of the University of Tokyo (figure 4.2). The woman stands confidently between the viewer and the festival poster that demands, "Don't stop me, Mama!" In contrast with the poised figure of the mother, a uniformed guard behind the photo fidgets and gazes at the ground. This photograph pits the Caramel Mama against the tattooed illustration in the poster and situates the mother as the vigilant patroller of the campus's borders. The title of the photo series adopts the "Don't stop me, Mama!" slogan, while the photograph of the Caramel Mama suggests that Mama is a formidable force indeed, arresting the viewer with her competent gaze.

However, student activists also sought to "overcome Mama" because of a widespread belief that equated feminine gentleness and nurturing with weakness. Writing retrospectively, Ōsawa Toshirō noted that a "taboo" prevented activists in the campus barricades from discussing their families, particularly their mothers: "Within our day-to-day experiences, what was probably taboo was essentially our own spiritual vulnerability, kindness toward others."[48] The perception that affective bonds, and perhaps particularly one's affective bond with one's mother, were potential obstacles to political action informed the context in which Carmen Maki's hit single "Sometimes Like a Motherless Child" resonated with student activists in the campus occupations of 1969. One former student activist recalled listening to the popular song, with lyrics by Terayama Shūji, in the Waseda University barricades. The mournful song expressed a longing to cut oneself off from the key familial relationship with "Mama," and the activist found that it resonated with how he felt at the time.[49] Terayama's lyrics detailed a yearning to, "at times," live "like a motherless child." Terayama's words described a tension between, on one hand, the desire to break free of the mother-child affective bond and thereby experience total liberation and, on the other, the recognition of the safety and comfort of that connection.

In the case of the New Left in late 1968 and 1969, the song's ambivalence echoed how many would-be student militants framed their revolt against mainstream Japanese society as a rejection of the sticky affective ties of the bourgeois household as symbolized by the mother. The mother-child bond constituted a common theme in Terayama's various poems, plays, and films. Terayama, an avant-garde dramatist, film director, and poet very much at the center of the experimental theater and cultural scene of the 1960s in Tokyo, produced several works that featured extreme permutations on this relationship, from matricide to incest, and his oeuvre cannot easily be summarized. However, for Terayama as well as the Zenkyōtō students, the mother embodied the laws of society.

Terayama's words may have resonated with student activists, but he was cynical about the slogans of the University of Tokyo student movement in particular. Terayama compared the Komaba festival slogan—"Don't stop me, Mama"—to a wartime song for young male soldiers, although the University of Tokyo students had replaced *woman* with *Mama*. Terayama noted that, in attempting to affirm their potential for violence, University of Tokyo students expressed a rejection of any links to nurturing feminine relationships and thus replicated the tenor of militarist songs. Ultimately, however, Terayama suspected that the male romance of the University of Tokyo campus New Left would be short-lived: he imagined that the students involved would eventually wake from the "dream" of the "male University of Tokyo," end the strike, graduate, and take up the task for which they had been selected: "building Japan."[50]

University of Tokyo New Left slogans affirming masculinity confirmed to Terayama that activists also engaged in an existential battle against the social image of University of Tokyo students in particular as a coddled elite who enjoyed excessive protection as they transitioned from the safe space of their family to the space of the nation. Terayama argued that an urge to prove they were not brainy, physically weak, and overprotected informed the masculine assertions that characterized the University of Tokyo struggle. Terayama suspected that the graffiti remaining in the campus ruins that voiced sentiments about becoming male sought to affirm that the university's students could also act as masculine urban guerrillas, although the repression they faced was not as fierce as that on other campuses. As an example, Terayama recalled a roundtable between University of Tokyo and Nihon University student activists. The Nihon University students recounted how they had faced off against right-wing students armed with deadly weapons: one wielded a sword, and another even confronted them with a rifle. These activists, Terayama noted, did not need to invoke a "male Nihon University."[51]

Although Terayama acknowledged that the slogans of the University of Tokyo Zenkyōtō had quickly expanded to include broad social questions about the nature of the university in Japanese society, Terayama also noted that it was only because the University of Tokyo was incapacitated that he felt able to enter its grounds. Terayama, even as he became a celebrated creative and intellectual force, always remained aware of his origin in a backwater of Japan—an Aomori accent marked him as a son of isolated northern Tōhoku—and he was a college dropout to boot. He first entered the University of Tokyo campus when it was in ruins after the police siege in late January 1969, and he used the occasion to meditate on the institution's deep, metonymic relationship with the Japanese state. The university was built to make Japan modern, Terayama pointed out. And the fervor with which the average citizen greeted the University of Tokyo student movement's slogans, such as "Demolish the University of Tokyo," reflected, Terayama argued, "not only the issue of how the education system ought to be but also the citizens' [shimin] desire for revenge. It expresses the vigor of a personal grudge toward the University of Tokyo as the training school for bureaucrats, as a university that assigns class distinctions to brains, as a university that creates the ruling class."[52] Even as the general postwar social trend expanded higher education through waves of democratization, the University of Tokyo retained its elite standing; it remained the university of the state. Even as student activists at the University of Tokyo declared, "Demolish the University of Tokyo," their status as University of Tokyo students conferred celebrity status on their movement and their leaders.

When the University of Tokyo students invited Mishima Yukio to debate them on May 13, 1969, they demonstrated an awareness of the role of the mass media, and in framing their debate, they demonstrated an awareness of the Zenkyōtō brand, experimenting with the spectacle of their celebrity. No stranger to publicity himself, Mishima arrived at the debate with a cameraman and a stenographer from the publisher Shinchōsha in tow only to find that the Zenkyōtō students had already alerted journalists. The TV station TBS incorporated a segment on the debate into its evening prime-time news show, while the transcribed volume that Shinchōsha released a little over a month later became a minor bestseller.[53] Mishima and the students split the royalties.[54]

Debates like the one with Mishima were often undertaken as playful, but they contributed to a discourse of the New Left activist as a heterosexual male and fetishized a masculinist pose. The students who organized the discussion with Mishima were actually interested in the event as a kind of performance more in line with what situationists sought to stage, which was designed to reawaken authentic desires or feelings and thereby disrupt the power of capitalist spectacle, in which social life is replaced by its representation.

In projecting a swaggering image of the New Left male, however, they may have instead promoted the spectacular image of the New Left on the rise in the mass media at the time. Demonstrations' disruptions of the everyday life of the city, occupations' interruptions of business as usual at the universities, and Gewalt provocations of police violence all depended to a degree on appealing to nonparticipant observers. In 1969, however, the student New Left began to definitively lose the war for popular sympathy as the mass media image of the vulnerable activist became supplanted by the mass media image of the violent activist.

While many New Left students came to identify activist authenticity with a willingness to engage in masculinist violence, popular support for the postwar student New Left and its actions often depended on an ideal of student vulnerability. The deaths of student activists Kanba Michiko in 1960 and Yamazaki Hiroaki in 1967 marked high points in general sympathy toward the New Left. As Tsurumi Kazuko noted in 1970, students facing off against the riot police in the late 1960s won by losing: "The more violence on the part of the police the students can provoke, the more successful they consider themselves politically, notwithstanding military defeat."[55] So when students faced off against the better-armed riot police at Haneda Airport in the fall of 1967 and at Sasebo Bay in early 1968, popular opinion often sided with the gutsy student activists.[56]

This dynamic—political success through military defeat—can be found in other places and protest movements in the same period. Edward J. Escobar, writing about the Los Angeles Police Department's policing of the Chicano movement, calls this "the dialectics of repression."[57] Victoria Langland, writing about the student movement in 1960s Brazil, describes a similar situation, in which "increasing police violence aimed at silencing students became instead the central issue around which they organized and through which they earned public sympathy."[58] This was a shared dialectic, among protesters and police, in various places globally, although it depended heavily on how the mass media narrated confrontations.

The dialectics of repression cease to operate if activism that has been framed around vulnerability stops appearing vulnerable. When a social movement begins to appear threatening, policing and repression of the movement can become framed as protecting society against activist violence. The Zenkyōtō ethos of Gewalt sought to disrupt the growing conservative consensus that prioritized national economic strength as the goal for family and education, but it could also alienate popular sympathy when the targets of activism were no longer clearly authoritarian institutions. As Ulrike Meinhof pointed out in the case of the mass media in West Germany, popular descriptions of protest and the oppression of protest that began to blame activists for a general kind of "confusion" emphasized the vulnerability of order rather than the violence often involved in imposing order. Analyzing the language of many tabloid accounts of police violence against student protesters in 1967–1968, Meinhof outlines "strategies of concealment": (1) "petty bourgeois respectability as a value in itself"; (2) "the innocence of the system"; (3) "the order of things is in order; the others are confused"; and (4) "engagement—but of a different kind." These strategies conceal the violence of the state by calling for "decency" in debate (as determined by the powers that be), decrying police violence as "senseless" without linking the police with the system itself, placing blame for social and political disorder on "adolescent crazies," and calling for youth to engage politically but within the constraints of decency as defined by the existing political order.[59]

What became known as the Shinjuku riot of October 21, 1968, marked a turning point in the battle between New Left activists and the police for popular sympathy, and the defining of the mass protests as a riot invoked the kind of strategies of concealment that Meinhof noticed at work in West Germany. When protesters swarmed Shinjuku Station, a major transportation hub in Tokyo that also serviced tank cars transporting jet fuel to U.S. air bases, on the evening of October 21, 1968, accounts of the disruptive actions of the protesters displaced the message activists wanted to send about the link between this urban space and state violence. The protests were organized as a commemoration of the Antiwar Day protests of October 21, 1967, when demonstrators and U.S. marshals had clashed at an antiwar rally at the Pentagon in Washington, D.C.

In spite of Public Safety Commission prohibitions on public assemblies and demonstrations for the day, thousands of students gathered at the University of Tokyo, groups broke into the grounds of the Defense Agency and the Diet, and clashes between protesters and police—described by one Japanese military observer as synchronized "guerrilla warfare"—embroiled several Tokyo neighborhoods, from Roppongi to the Ginza.[60] The evening convergence of demonstrations at Shinjuku Station in particular, at which about a thousand students overran the railroad junction used to transport U.S. military supplies, induced the Metropolitan Police Department to invoke Article 106 of the Criminal Code, the law that defines "crimes of disturbance." In the most sweeping mass arrest in postwar Japan, police detained almost a thousand people nationwide, 450 of them in Tokyo alone.[61]

Although the events of the October 21, 1968, Antiwar Day entered public memory as a riot sparked by the violent actions of New Left students, there was a measure of popular sympathy and even participation by "ordinary citizens" during the event itself. Ōhara Kimiko described witnessing the hero's welcome given helmeted student activists when they arrived in Shinjuku on the evening of October 21: the assembled crowd, made up of all manner of young people—"student types, white-collar worker types, older brother types, vagabond types"—burst into cheers and applause.[62] The riot police often found themselves in danger of being overpowered by student activists joined by civilian sympathizers, who—far from remaining a neutral group of onlookers—frequently joined in throwing stones at the police.[63] Newspaper reports showed that bystanders often enthusiastically cheered on the student demonstrators, creating numbers that threatened to overwhelm the mobilized police force of twelve thousand.[64]

Such a display of civil defiance encouraged many New Left activists, but one intelligence officer for the Self-Defense Forces, Colonel Yamamoto Kiyokatsu, interpreted the events of October 1968 as more of a temporary carnival than an incipient revolution. Yamamoto didn't find the demonstrations deeply threatening to the status quo: "Even the masses in the demonstration return to their everyday life as commuters when the morning comes. Without broad sympathy, the battles of the Zenkyōtō, even as they seem to involve the masses, are struggles without roots in the space of everyday life."[65] Although, as discussed earlier, student activists designed their occupations and street actions to disrupt the everyday life of the state and capital, an authority like Yamamoto read the large-scale disturbance of the 1968 Antiwar Day protests as a temporally limited event. Yamamoto framed his lack of concern around his understanding that the New Left lacked more meaningful grassroots links and thus did not pose a real threat.

What the events of October 21, 1968, did offer state authorities was a backlash against the street actions of the New Left that the police were able to exploit. In April 1969 Columbia University's James W. Morely analyzed police strategy after the events of Sasebo as one in which they fell "back on the defense, hoping thereby that a public backlash would develop, enabling them to move out again forcibly later."[66] This hope was met, as Morely concluded in his report, since "repeated incidents of student violence, crescendoing to the riot at Shinjuku on October 21, have produced the backlash the police had hoped for."[67] While New Left radicals interpreted their close wins in street battles in fall and winter of 1968–1969 as incipient revolution, they actually began to lose the war for popular sympathy (figure 4.3).

Intensifying intersectarian battles between New Left groups and the Minsei affiliated with the Japanese Communist Party, and between competing New Left sects, also offered the public more and more images of student-initiated violence. Even sympathetic observers found the activist-on-activist rumbles childish, and undergraduate Ōhara Kimiko at the University of Tokyo dismissed as "boys" the participants on both sides of a fight she witnessed between New Left activists in front of the univer-

FIGURE 4.3 Clashes between students and an estimated two thousand riot police in Kanda on January 18, 1969. Students at Nihon University, Chuo University, and Meiji University built barricades in the street and threw chunks of pavement to protest the ousting of the University of Tokyo occupation in nearby Hongo. The "urban warfare" continued until night. Credit: *Kyodo tsūshin*.

sity library on November 12, 1968.[68] Ōhara herself was not categorically opposed to violence as a political strategy and admired Malcolm X over Martin Luther King Jr. However, she didn't see much point to the infighting of the campus New Left. Her impression of students pitting themselves against other students as juvenile masculinist play-fighting conveys how many came to see the New Left in the late 1960s as disconnected from more meaningful political battles.

From 1969 onward, instances of internal violence (uchigeba) between leftist sects also became more frequent and weakened student activists' framing of Gewalt as counterviolence disrupting the state's monopoly on force. As mentioned previously, such violence could have a gendered dimension, as male activists used sexual assault as a weapon against female activists in competing sects.

Police calculations put the number of those who died in uchigeba clashes between 1969 and 1976 at 46 and the number of those injured at

4,388.[69] The violence between the Chūkaku and Kakumaru sects was particularly brutal. Members of the two groups, which had both originated from the same organization (Kakumeiteki Kyōsanshugisha Dōmei, or Revolutionary Communist League), began to beat the other's members as they competed for control of university campuses and also, as they recruited young manufacturing and railway workers, for control of organizing labor in various industries.[70] The murder that transformed their brawls into a decades-long blood feud, however, was the 1970 death of Ebihara Toshio, a Kakumaru member and student at Tokyo University of Education. Ebihara's lifeless body was found early on the morning of August 4, 1970, at the entrance to a hospital in Shinjuku. The cause of death seemed to be shock following extensive pummeling with wooden staves and iron pipes. He also had stab wounds from what appeared to be a drill at twenty places on his body. According to the police investigation, Chūkaku activists captured Ebihara while he was collecting funds in front of the busy Ikebukuro Station, detained and tortured him at Hosei University, and finally dumped him outside the hospital the next day.[71]

The escalation of intersectarian violence drove many student activists away from the late 1960s student movement. Many narratives of the decline of student New Left activism blame young idealists for becoming complacent when they graduated and got a job. However, a 1994 survey of 563 former Zenkyōtō activists found that only 7.4 percent cited graduation, employment, or marriage as the reason they distanced themselves from the student movement. In contrast, close to one-fourth of them declared that uchigeba was the reason they ceased to be involved in activism, and an additional 16.9 percent named the United Red Army (URA) purge, in which a united sect had killed its own members, as the event that soured them on the student movement. The URA violence can also be seen as an instance of uchigeba, which means that uchigeba prompted 40 percent of the respondents to leave the student New Left.[72]

The viciousness of the series of internal purges that took place at the URA's training camp in the Japanese Alps in the winter of 1971 has undergone various interpretations, but there is no question that debates about the proper place for femininity in radical politics shaped the deadly "self-criticisms" members were forced to perform. Indeed, the killing of twelve members in the space of two months, including a woman eight months pregnant, may be read in part as an effort to purge what was perceived as feminine vulnerability from a revolutionary subjectivity.[73] All accounts of the events that took place in the mountain retreat point to the "Toyama incident" as the spark for the violence that followed. In this incident, the female leader Nagata Hiroko confronted Toyama Mieko about Toyama's maintenance of feminine rituals as she underwent guerrilla training: Toyama wore her hair long and wore a ring and makeup.

In some ways, the confrontation between the two women marked the uneasy alliance at the heart of the URA; the URA had formed in the summer of 1971 as a merger between a faction of the Japanese Red Army (JRA), under the leadership of Mori Tsuneo, and Kakusa (the Revolutionary Left Faction), led by Nagata Hiroko. Both groups were far left and operated underground by 1971. Members of the JRA had hijacked an airplane to North Korea in 1970, and other members had left Japan for Lebanon in 1971, where they linked up with the Popular Front for the Liberation of Palestine. The JRA also had money from a series of bank and post office robberies. Kakusa had weapons obtained by robbing a gun shop in 1971. The URA formed out of a mutual desire to pool these resources and wage armed revolution in Japan, but significant differences marked the two sects: differences of class (the JRA boasted mostly middle-class youth, while Kakusa attracted the working-class students of technical colleges), ideology (the internationalism of the JRA countered Kakusa's Maoism-inflected nationalism), and activist cultures.

Nagata based her criticism of Toyama on Kakusa's more explicit gender program, in which female members were to prioritize their identities as revolutionaries over their identities as women. In doing so, she touched on issues never discussed in the JRA. Toyama could not articulate a satisfactory response to Nagata, and Mori Tsuneo interpreted the incident as a call to ensure all members had overcome personal weaknesses and revolutionized from within.[74] This eventually escalated into the torture and death of twelve of the young people—four of them female—at the hands of their friends and comrades. Patricia Steinhoff has described the stages by which what began as a consciousness-raising exercise became a deadly endeavor in her scholarly effort to understand URA members as humans rather than the anomalous monsters the mass media made them out to be. In her account Mori bears a great deal of responsibility for the intensification of efforts to "communalize" URA members. Mori also clearly feared the difference that marked women's bodies, at one point declaring his disgust for menstruation.[75]

Like many women who came to hold leadership positions in New Left sects, Nagata Hiroko had taken the helm of Kakusa after its male leaders had been arrested.[76] Nagata herself had been raped by her comrade and sect leader Kawashima Tsuyoshi in 1969 and would ultimately conclude that her failure to attack the sexism of her male leaders and the leftist organization in general set the stage for her failure as a revolutionary leader. Writing in 1983, Nagata frames her penitence around her own lack of feminist consciousness: "If only I had had the independence to take on Kawashima's sexism in a structural way, our activism would have taken a different course. At the least, I think I might have avoided making such terrible mistakes as a leader."[77] This comment echoes the critiques female student activists launched in the early 1970s: that the New Left did not have a comprehensive theoretical tool for analyzing sexism in society or in the movement.

The URA members who assembled in the mountain lodge attempted to disrupt all kinship ties and literally attacked the body of the soon-to-be mother among them, discussing how to separate the eight-month-old fetus from its "unrevolutionary" mother to raise it as a child of the revolution.[78] Such grisly details emerged in the wake of the February 1972 standoff between five armed male URA members and over fifteen hundred riot police in what became a massive media spectacle named for the mountain lodge, Asama Sansō, in which they had holed up and taken a housewife hostage. When the police attempted to lure them out with appeals by the would-be revolutionaries' mothers, employing the logic of the Caramel Mama, one young man shot at his mother while she pleaded with him to surrender.[79]

These events demonstrated the power of the televised spectacle in Japan by 1972. If ever there was a single media event that unified the Japanese nation, this siege was it: "almost the entire nation" witnessed the final arrest of the radicals and rescue of the hostage as it was broadcast in real time on television.[80] This spectacular masculine stand against state authority offered the extreme fringe of the New Left maximum public exposure, definitively associating leftist activism with violence. But it was the news of the internal purge, which emerged in March 1972, that truly marked the death of popular support for the New Left in general. The actions of the URA also spoke to larger fears about the endgame of a radical politics that met any signs of human vulnerability with violence.

The blood feud between the far-left sects Kakumaru and Chūkaku lasted for decades but generally received less coverage than the actions of the URA. Part of this reflects the deep silence, sometimes forced on former activists with threats of violence, surrounding factional violence in the New Left after 1972. One former activist told me about menacing calls he received on his home phone for many years after he left a far-left sect.

He felt that they not only silenced his words but also prevented him from even being able to think about what had happened.[81] A traumatic knot still binds the issue of internecine violence in the New Left among former activists, and in many ways the police came to control the narrative by integrating policing into the everyday lives of local communities.

POLICING AS CARE WORK

While New Left activists embraced an ideal of invulnerable violent posturing in the late 1960s, the police conducted a campaign to woo the public in the early 1970s; they successfully contributed to a discourse about student activists as dangerous elements from which the police would protect citizens. The student movement's self-representation as aggressively masculine and violent in the late 1960s fed into police representations of social order as vulnerable to student activism. Policing strategies in Japan in the 1970s turned to focus on a grassroots connection to local residents, based around police boxes (*kōban*) and everyday communications between police officers and citizens.[82] Although from 1969 on police authorities responded to street protests and campus occupations through increasing their recruitment of new officers and controlling protest actions based on the 1952 Subversive Activities Prevention Law (Hakai katsudō bōshi hō), leaders at the National Police Agency also turned toward emphasizing the friendly activities of the local officer in a police box rather than the intimidating figure of the armor-clad riot police.

The kōban became important sites of casual contact between police and communities, and the National Police Agency encouraged officers to practice small acts of kindness. As an example of the character of these directives, one of the agency's 1970 campaigns went under the title "Humor and Police Officers."[83] Everyday interactions made police incredibly approachable; anyone could stop by a kōban to ask for directions or inquire after lost articles. Or they could also drop in to give anonymous tips about suspicious persons. Such tips led the police to locate many student radicals in 1970 and 1971.[84] This soft form of policing was conducted alongside more muscular efforts to root out activists and was based on lessons learned by many police forces as they countered contentious politics across the world.

Police experts in Japan understood that the challenges facing their police force with regard to protest were a problem they shared with police in other places. The National Police Agency in Japan embraced community relations influenced in part by strategies developing in the United States, most significantly as outlined in the work of Raymond Momboisse, an attorney with the California Department of Justice and an expert on policing demonstrations there in the late 1960s, whose writings were translated into Japanese by a National Police Agency officer.[85] An article in the January 1969 issue of *Keisatsu kenkyū*, a journal that featured research and opinion pieces by both policing scholars and police bureaucrats, discussed a big April 1968 conference on policing that had been held in Hiltrup, home of the German Police University. The author, Tsuchiya Sōzō, emphasized that policing "sudden lawless gatherings and demonstrations" was an "art," and he detailed various soft strategies, including employing undercover officers to watch activists and try to intercept radical elements.[86] Tsuchiya noted that while an event like the Shinjuku riot of October 1968 gave the police a public relations advantage, policing in the late 1960s also needed to develop new strategies to counter protest over the long term.

The police authorities in Japan in the 1970s also looked to new ways to tap into the rapidly changing communities of urban Japan; they sought out public relations companies, conducted surveys, and used new technologies alongside the old. Public relations companies gave police the same kind of demographic information about communities that they provided to corporations.[87] Local police departments polled opinions in their areas, asking questions that ranged from how well residents thought the police were doing at their jobs to what kind of impression police uniforms made.[88] In 1974 the Public Relations Office of the Cabinet Secretary published the results of an Opinion Survey on the Police, in which 49 percent of the interviewees responded that the police had improved because they had "become friendly." This increased amiability impressed even skeptical activists; one reported his confusion at the polite manner of a policeman.[89] Police were able to rebrand themselves as the nurturers, rather than the enforcers, of order against the spectacle of New Left disorder.

CONCLUSION

The Japanese New Left and the cultural products associated with its radicalism were not alone in conflating radical politics with male virility. Writing on the New Left in the United States and Western Europe, David Caute noted in 1988, "If one quality united the New Left with the underground arts—magazines, theatre, films, music—it was rampant male chauvinism."[90] In the United States, Marge Piercy penned an angry exposé of sexism in the New Left there in 1969 under the title *The Grand Coolie Damn*. She attacked the way female organizational labor was made invisible and noted how dominant definitions of masculinity defined who was heard and who was not heard in the movement: "Only a woman willing and able to act like a stereotyped American frontier male can make herself heard."[91] New Left movements may have responded to different cultural constellations associated with virile masculinity, but they often shared an overall trend toward romanticizing that vision of masculinity as a model of leadership and action.

Although barricades and organizing continued at various campuses in Japan, by early 1969 the confrontational relationship with the law and society in general became a focus for some prominent participants and for mass media accounts of spectacular New Left activism. The democratic access symbolized at earlier moments by female participation in the student movement gave way to the figure of the street-fighting militant, gendered male. The police contributed to the isolation of the New Left through more aggressive policing, and after the passage of the University Control Bill in early 1969, under which any school unable to end a campus conflict within six months would have to cede control to the Ministry of Education, universities were much more inclined to call in the riot police to quell campus disturbances. But the police also adopted a nurturing pose to appeal to citizens at the grassroots level. Even as student activists faced increasing police control, the figure of the student activist shifted from being represented as particularly vulnerable to state violence to presenting a violent threat to a vulnerable social order. In this context, the female student activist in the late 1960s also, ironically, became emblematic of the student movement's excesses. I turn to this story in the next chapter.

5 "Gewalt Rosas"

The Creation of the Terrifying, Titillating
Female Student Activist

In his 1993 memoir, *The Fall of the University of Tokyo Fortress*, National Police Agency security agent Sassa Atsuyuki opened with a scene that contrasted two generations of female students. He had recently seen a young woman dressed in a bridal gown on the steps of Yasuda Tower gushing to journalists upon her admission to the school that she was "marrying the University of Tokyo!"[1] This scene made him feel how dramatically the times had changed, since it contrasted sharply with his memories of a female student activist arrested in the same spot on January 19, 1969 (figure 5.1).

Sassa expressed nostalgia for the street fighting of the late 1960s, a nostalgia echoed by other right-wing activists who longed for the dramatic moments of romantic, masculine conflict made possible by battling the New Left in the 1960s.[2] But Sassa focused on the female student activist to illustrate the passing of the season of protest. Sassa recalled that only her long black hair, tangled beneath her helmet "like a bird's nest," and her "shrill protest cry" marked the otherwise androgynous young woman handcuffed outside Yasuda Tower in 1969 as female. Sassa was not the only one to notice her: the press surrounded her, urging her to look into their cameras, illuminating her face with their flash.[3] It might be an image of this very young woman that featured in an inset in a January 31, 1969, special report on the postsiege "ruins" of the University of Tokyo in the pages

FIGURE 5.1 The riot police entered the University of Tokyo Hongo campus to oust student occupiers on January 18, 1969. The most dramatic final confrontation occurred outside the campus's central Yasuda Tower. Employing water cannons and tear gas for two days straight, the police finally overwhelmed the occupying students. Credit: *Kyodo tsūshin*.

of the *Shūkan yomiuri*. In the coed revolution of the campus-based New Left, the female student participant became a particularly captivating figure for journalists.

Much like Sassa, who directed police countermeasures against student protests in the period, the mass media in the late 1960s fixated on the "Gewalt girls" of the New Left, who were by turns titillating and terrifying. The mass media used the figures of young women involved in radical politics to make sweeping statements about women in politics and the student movement. Through interpreting female student radicals' actions primarily through gendered ideas about behavior, the tabloids undermined young women's political positions. In many cases, the mass media also used the prominence of female student activists to challenge the political significance of the student movement in general, suggesting that female participation reflected rampant immaturity and irrationality in the movement as a whole.

In a sense, this journalistic interpretation of feminine political agency fit in with earlier formulations of a naive female student political subjectivity but emphasized what might be seen as the negative aspects of political naivete: emotionalism or even hysteria. The role of the mass media, an institution responsible in many cases for defining social facts, also demonstrated the gendered inequality of power between male-dominated institutions such as news journalism and female student activists, particularly in conveying the voices of activists to the wider public. Indeed, it was not until the 1985 Equal Employment Opportunity Law for Men and Women that newspaper and broadcasting companies began to hire women as regular full-time journalists.[4] In the late 1960s, when female participants in the student movement proved that women could also participate in radical politics, and also in violence, mass media reportage—written by male journalists—by turns emphasized the threat of female participation in a radical youth movement and also mitigated this perceived threat through characterizing it as feminine, emotional, and therefore (even comically) apolitical.

Female student activists confronted a journalistic scrutiny based on stereotyped expectations of feminine personalities and behaviors that their male comrades did not face. Mass media narratives overpowered the voices of female student activists targeted by such attention, who could rarely determine the social meaning of their activism. At the same time, comical fictional representations of female student activists channeled anxieties about what the press dubbed an ascendant "Era of Woman Superiority" into gendered categories that transformed what threatened to be a genuine shift in gender relations in a coed radical movement into harmless comedy.

Journalists in mainstream publications had enormous influence in producing representations of a threatening but exciting female activist, much as they had done in the 1920s with the forging of what Miriam Rom Silverberg identified as the media construct of the Modern Girl in prewar Japan. Silverberg argued that the Modern Girl was a media representation defined by her vigorous and strong body; her sexuality; her provocative behavior blurring the distinction between male and female, Western and Japanese; and "her real transgression: [that] she would not accept the division of labor that had placed her in the home."[5] This mass media creation, although ostensibly a figure devoted to play, was often read as militant. In turn, the mass media creation of the "Gewalt Rosa" often transformed women devoted to militancy into figures of play.

The 1969 case of "Kikuyabashi 101" demonstrated both what became interpreted in the mass media as the exceptional commitment of young women to radical politics and also the mass media's intervention in creating meaning out of female student activism and in affecting the legal outcomes of student activism. Kikuyabashi 101, a young woman, was one of 786 students the police arrested as they broke up the University of Tokyo campus occupations in January 1969. Of these almost 800 arrested students, 540 were indicted, and 469 of them elected a unified, rather than individual, trial. This request was refused, and many students and their lawyers boycotted the trials. Kikuyabashi 101 refused to disclose her name, a common strategy of legal resistance, so she was entered into the police records and referred to in the mass media by the number of her cell at Kikuyabashi Police Station.[6] She remained silent long after many other students had identified themselves, and her identity was not revealed until the tabloid *Yūkan fuji* ran her photograph on their front page on March 12, 1969. The women's magazine *Yangu redi* picked up the story, republishing the photo of Kikuyabashi 101 in April, and by May 1, 1969, *Yūkan fuji* was able to reveal details about her name and identity, again on the front page. For the Zenkyōtō (short for Zengaku kyōtō kaigi, or All-Campus Joint Struggle Committee) at the University of Tokyo, the tabloid's choice to run the photo of a heretofore-unidentified student activist—making her legally and personally vulnerable—reflected a deep alliance between mass media journalism and state authority. The University of Tokyo Zenkyōtō newspaper, *Shingeki*, employed the language of human rights to decry the actions of *Yūkan fuji* as violating the "basic human right" of Kikuyabashi 101 to maintain silence while under arrest.[7]

Although the student activists framed their opposition to the tabloid's publication of Kikuyabashi 101's photograph as a battle between the politics of the radical movement and "bourgeois journalism," *Yūkan fuji* made no ideological case for exposing Kikuyabashi 101. Instead, the publication simply reported on the "facts" of the case, while obscuring the greater legal and political meaning of its reportage. But in determining the facts of her case, the tabloid relied on the testimony of police authorities.

This pattern, in which mass media sources reported frequently impressionistic police accounts as expert opinions on student radicalism, demonstrated the deep links between the police and the mass media in defining student activism in the late 1960s. Both often parroted established gendered stereotypes. For example, the March 1969 *Yūkan fuji* article on Kikuyabashi 101 quoted a police officer's estimation that logic will break down male activists, but "once women are bent on something, they won't open their mouths for a while."[8] Thus, the police officer classified Kikuyabashi 101 as displaying a feminine commitment immune to logic. Within this feminine category, however, she struck him as rather extraordinary; she reportedly "brainwashed" a sex worker with whom she shared a cell, compelling her fellow inmate to use the language of human rights in subsequent interviews with police. Although some police reported finding Kikuyabashi 101 a little "creepy" because of her extreme refusal, another policeman relayed to the magazine *Young redi* his opinion that her loyalty to the cause demonstrated that she'd make a proper wife.[9] Her potential as a figure of terror (brainwashing presumably immoral and weaker-willed women) is mitigated by her demonstration of feminine loyalty (that, once domesticated, would make her a good wife).

The tabloids rapidly disseminated whatever private information they collected on Kikuyabashi 101. On 1 May 1, 1969, *Yūkan fuji* exposed Kikuyabashi 101's identity, giving not only her name but also her place of birth and current residence, the names of all the schools she had attended, and the names of her academic advisor and family members. In doing so, the tabloid demonstrated the power of the mass media to establish the facts about Kikuyabashi 101—named as Katō Hiroko, a young married graduate student at the University of Tokyo—and also their reach. *Yūkan fuji* sought out Katō's neighbors and colleagues, capturing the surprise of her various acquaintances and relations—including her father—at the news of her arrest.[10] The various interviews conveyed the sense that extreme political commitment might lurk underneath the quiet exterior of any "ordinary coed."

In her personal writings, Kikuyabashi 101 comes across as much less committed to radical extremism. In letters Kikuyabashi 101 wrote while in jail, published under her alias in an April 1969 volume of letters students wrote from jail, she wrote with a sense of wonder about how someone like herself who had been so "mild" had come to hate certain people and things. She described herself as experiencing conflicting feelings, unable to forgive what she tentatively called a "quasi-ruling class?" personality defined by fear of the unknown and an urge toward self-preservation: "Grappling with how to escape from this existence defined my whole history since entering college."[11] She interpreted her involvement in the leftist student movement as a process of questioning and working through conflicting feelings, rather than a compulsive commitment to the movement.

In the second letter of hers published in the same volume, dated March 11, 1969, she struggled in particular to counter interpretations of the confrontation between occupying students and the riot police at Yasuda Tower in January 1969 as a demonstration of extremism. Her interpretation opposed those, such as right-wing author Mishima Yukio, who felt unimpressed by the lack of student sacrifice at the University of Tokyo showdown. The stubborn fight of the occupying students, she argued, was by no means an attempt at self-sacrifice. She rejected any interpretation that would align the Zenkyōtō struggle with a "shattering jewel" (*gyokusai*), the euphemistic wartime term for patriotic suicide. For Kikuyabashi 101, a young woman described in the mass media as an example of extreme, feminine self-sacrifice, the more urgent matter remained one of building a collective. Writing almost two months after her arrest and before her identity was exposed, she described the siege as a "decision for a new collective." She identified an "oppressed everyday life" as the major obstacle to creating meaningful alternative communities.[12] Mass media portrayals of Kikuyabashi 101 and her silent refusal obscured her actual political convictions.

Although Kikuyabashi 101 did not see herself as particularly committed to the cause of the student movement, her protracted silence became a symbol of radical refusal for both the University of Tokyo Zenkyōtō and the tabloids.

KASHIWAZAKI CHIEKO AND FEMININE VIOLENCE

Kashiwazaki Chieko, another graduate student at the University of Tokyo, presented a case of a much more unambiguously radical female student activist. Nevertheless, the mass media's gendered analysis of her position mitigated her voice. Unlike Kikuyabashi 101, Kashiwazaki was a well-known and openly active member of the late 1960s student movement at the University of Tokyo, attracting media attention from early 1969 (figure 5.2). Similar to the treatment of Kikuyabashi 101, however, the mass media frequently interpreted Kashiwazaki's actions by explaining her behavior with gendered stereotypes. Such interpretations undermined Kashiwazaki's own attempts to define the social meaning of her activism.

FIGURE 5.2 A portrait of Kashiwazaki Chieko in the University of Tokyo Komaba barricades, taken by Watanabe Hitomi, probably in late December 1968. Credit: Watanabe Hitomi.

The term *Gewalt Rosa*, which rapidly became a generic term in the mass media for young women involved in the Zenkyōtō movement of the late 1960s, originated in a nickname attributed to Kashiwazaki Chieko, a member of the Student Front for Liberation (Gakusei kaihō sensen, SFL), which was part of the Maoist Marxist Leninist League (ML dōmei). The term drew on the German word *Gewalt* (violence) and the name of Rosa Luxemburg (1871–1919), the female Marxist theorist and revolutionary. Of Polish descent, Rosa Luxemburg became famous for her activism in Germany, and was murdered by the right-wing militarist Freikorps (Volunteer Corps) in their efforts to quell the revolutionary socialism for which she agitated. Kashiwazaki, a graduate student researching Polish history, embraced Rosa Luxemburg's revolutionary legacy with her nickname, which emblazoned the cover of the memoir she wrote while in jail in the spring of 1969. The title of the memoir itself—*Sun, Storm, and Liberty*—was from a letter Luxemburg had written while on vacation, where, she wrote, she had enjoyed, "sun, peace, and liberty—the finest things in life—except for sun, storm, and liberty."[13]

Kashiwazaki's book describes the pleasures available to both male and female students participating in the New Left, particularly a sense of purpose and community. Kashiwazaki details the exhilaration of demonstrations and the rewarding work of building barricades alongside comrades. It also details the anger that motivated her to devote so much time to activism.

Her descriptions of her influences give us a sense, although anecdotal, of some of the intellectual currents that also shaped the New Left. Kashiwazaki was raised in a Protestant "typical bourgeois home," as she put it, which made her part of a very small religious minority in Japan but a minority that was associated with both the middle-class intelligentsia and a longer radical tradition. Kanba Michiko had also grown up in a Christian household and often kept a Bible on her desk alongside the writings of Karl Marx, while Tokoro Mitsuko had admired the Christian-influenced thought of Simone Weil. Kashiwazaki described herself as growing up rather passionate about Christianity. She also recalled a deep interest in the heroes of the Warring States period in Japan (the sixteenth-century period of upheaval and conflict) and the biography of Marie Curie (which she wrote that she must have read over thirty times).

When Kashiwazaki entered university, she committed herself to reading the leftist classics: Lenin, Marx, Trotsky. Other books she cited as influential were John Reed's work on the Russian Revolution, Hugh Thomas on the Spanish Civil War, and the works of Georg Wilhelm Friedrich Hegel and Mao Zedong. Whenever she could get her hands on them, she also apparently loved to read the official newsletter of the Central Committee of the Cuban Communist Party (*Granma*), and that of the Chinese Communist Party, and to follow the activities of the Student Nonviolent Coordinating Committee in the United States.[14]

Kashiwazaki framed her personal narrative as one in which she shed her bourgeois background and sentimentality through revolutionary activism. This included shedding what she saw as a specifically feminine passivity and sentimentality. She related an incident in which she had once mooned over a boy, waiting for his attentions, reading German romantic poetry, and crying over a cup of coffee, listening to Beethoven in a Tokyo coffee shop.[15] In her account, she awoke from that haze and found herself in the New Left, where she could positively and actively affirm her selfhood through participating in something bigger and more important.

Although within her memoir Kashiwazaki attempted to reject any interpretations that made her participation as a woman a curiosity, her protestations had little effect on the memoir's advertising campaign, launched in mainstream newspapers. One such advertisement, which ran in the mainstream *Yomiuri shimbun*, described Kashiwazaki's voice as "the authentic cry of a female student!"[16] When the newspaper included her book as one of the standouts among the flood of new publications on University of Tokyo "Gewalt," the author deemed the work "very feminine."[17] Her memoir inspired gendered analyses in spite of her own protestations. As Kashiwazaki noted in the pages of her book, she reacted with hostility to a journalist who wanted to interview her "as a woman" in the movement. She noted, "Is it really so peculiar that a woman fights? In this struggle, I haven't been conscious of myself as a woman or as a wife at all."[18] Although Kashiwazaki rejected a gendered reading of her participation, those writing book reviews and ad copy sought out her words to gain insight into a specifically "coed" view on the movement. They did not share her assessment that in the struggle she was acting not as a woman but as a human.

At moments in her narrative, Kashiwazaki undermined her own willful rejection of a gendered subjectivity. In episodes that resonated with the experiences of many female student activists in the barricades, she described how young women cooked for the activists, making rice balls and boiled eggs to prepare for a battle against students affiliated with the Japanese Communist Party, or preparing a New Year's feast in the barricades.[19] While Kashiwazaki also occasionally cooked, she attempted to preempt gendered interpretations of that labor: "When I cook for my comrades in the barricades, it's because I really enjoy cooking and am concerned with everyone's health. It's absolutely not because I'm a woman."[20] However, she also affirmed her own worth as an activist when she succeeded in completing what might be considered men's work. In building the University of Tokyo barricades, she joined a men-only group and noted with satisfaction that she held her own.[21] Although Kashiwazaki declared that, for her, wielding a kitchen knife and brandishing a "Gewalt stave" were equally important, her own proclamations of overcoming her gender approached the individualist interpretations of extraordinary women from earlier generations, which Kanba Michiko had identified as an impediment to women's collective action.

Kashiwazaki, in rejecting completely the role of gendered labor in creating hierarchies of commitment in the movement, also obscured the fact that she was one of the few women to take up the Gewalt stave, something that some younger female students pointed out.[22] Street fighting remained the clearest rejection of the virtues of civil society, and participation in or abstention from violence became critical in student movement evaluations of activists' commitment. According to this system of appraisal, "wielding a knife" against a radish was considerably less revolutionary than using a stick against the police or "enemy" students.

In Kashiwazaki's personal narrative, she discussed the positive political implications of her female subjectivity only when describing her personal political awakening, which was linked to the 1960 death of Kanba Michiko. Her three elder brothers had participated as university students in the 1960 anti-Anpo protest.[23] She herself was a second-year high school student at the time and recalled her deep shock at Kanba's death on June 15, 1960. She felt that Kanba's death marked the end of a democratic ideal, for with that tragedy "postwar democracy was completely finished."[24] She located her early empathy with the dead female student as stemming from a sense of justice shared among women.[25] As was the case for many observers at the time, as we have seen, Kanba represented political purity and the potential of true postwar democracy for Kashiwazaki, even as Kashiwazaki stridently rejected her feminine subjectivity in the late 1960s student movement.

Much like the mass media reaction to Kanba, although with variation in the meanings created, the mass media of the late 1960s created popular images of Kashiwazaki the Gewalt Rosa that had little in common with Kashiwazaki the real person. Although the tabloids also published speculative articles on prominent male student activists such as the University of Tokyo's Yamamoto Yoshitaka and Nihon University's Akita Akehiro, the figures of female student activists provoked more emotive responses. A female student activist like Kashiwazaki drew dramatically contradictory responses, from articles that accused her of promoting hysterical violence to those that rejected her influence among student activists. As demonstrated in a March 1969 article in the *Yomiuri shimbun* on "Gewalt Rosas," the very prominence of a female student activist within the movement suggested that the movement as a whole could be dismissed as irrational. The author used Kashiwazaki's presence as evidence that the student movement "prioritizes women based on hysterical, infantile heroism." He also likened her relationship with student activists to that of "a mother to children studying for entrance exams," scolding and cheering them on.[26] In this way, the author reduced Kashiwazaki's claims to leadership to the very feminine role of the mother, and the "education mama" (*kyōiku mama*) in particular.

Associating a female activist leader with the figure of the "education mama" assumed that a woman's role in the student movement would replicate a feminine domestic role and also contributed to the generally negative image of the education mama then prominent in media discourse. As a female corollary of the emasculated *sarariiman* (salaryman), the wage slaves/soldiers of a rapidly growing national economy, the education mama was seen as a domineering woman who invested all of her self into ensuring her children's success in the increasingly competitive meritocratic system of entrance examinations.[27] She represented a kind of perversion of the prewar state-espoused ideal "wise mother" responsible for guiding learning in the home, even as she symbolized the massification of the bourgeois household and its values. Kashiwazaki, in her own writings, attacked the prominence of the figure of the bourgeois education mama as a representative of Japanese motherhood in the contemporary imagination, arguing that it obscured the actual existence of various socioeconomic classes in Japan.[28]

In the case of the student movement, projecting the education mama role onto a female student leader hinted at a threat of intensifying violence, as the presumed content of Kashiwazaki's teaching would include urging students to participate in increasingly dramatic confrontations. A goading feminine presence was thus cited as a threatening influence that could make the student movement more violent, even as the presence of a dominant female participant was also used to make the movement and its violence seem ridiculous.

Female student activists came across as both too earnest and too superficial. Sometimes the same young woman even received both treatments at once. A summer 1969 article on Kashiwazaki after her release from prison, published in *Shūkan yomiuri*, employed quotes from male student activists to dismiss her political ideas completely. The opinions of male students — many of them from competing sects — were presented as insider information, and their comments damned her variously as too passionate ("I acknowledge that she is genuine and pure. But in the real struggle she just gets mad too abruptly") or exceptionally trivial ("She had her hair cut at a salon especially for the meeting").[29] Within the article a source also compared Kashiwazaki unfavorably to the silent Kikuyabashi 101. Whether one or the other was truly more revolutionary is less crucial than which could more readily become a symbol for the movement. Kikuyabashi's silence was praised; her silence also meant that others could create meaning about her without the inconvenient intrusion of her own words.

Although the mass media had long controlled the meaning of images of vulnerability and threat on the part of student activists, tabloid articles from the mid-1960s responded to the increase in campus-based movements and in the participation of female students by relying on police as sources of insider knowledge. Tabloids quoted the police as expert witnesses of the dynamics of student protest. Some police assumed that young women were mere assistants to male activists, as did the officer interviewed by *Shūkan shinchō* in May 1968, who declared, "For me, the girls are not really an issue. In the end, what the girls do is just help the boys."[30] He regarded university student activists as an overprotected elite who had jumped into revolution as a rebellion after years at their mama's side. Then again, another officer described female activists as potentially more dangerous because they could smuggle weapons past police with feminine props. In retrospect, he recalled more women than men throwing bottle bombs, since they could easily conceal them in kimono sleeves and shopping bags.[31] It is unclear whether that was actually the case, or whether it was merely his impression, although at least one image of a young, kimono-clad woman busted carrying a suitcase filled with Molotov cocktails was distributed in the mass media at the time (figure 5.3).

Sometimes the danger was not only of violence but also of a blurring of the gendered categories that defined violence. A police officer quoted in a June 1966 *Shūkan shinchō* article on female student activists declared that a key aspect of the increasingly aggressive student movement was the participation of young women who not only dressed like men but also acted like the male students with whom they were protesting.[32]

These comments by the police, reported as expert opinions in the press, echoed themes previously articulated in the mid-1960s "Coeds Ruin the Nation" debates, discussed in chapter 2. The lack of intellectualism that supposedly made young women a poor fit for higher education institutions also made them irrational and potentially dangerous activists. It is thus fitting that *Shūkan shinchō* also consulted Teruoka Yasutaka, the Waseda professor who dreamed up the "Coeds Ruin the Nation Theory," for his opinion on female student activists. Teruoka declared that the young female activists were more dangerous than male student activists because they were irrational, perhaps even insane. Although Teruoka felt he could talk sense to male student activists in one-on-one conversations, he reacted differently to female activists: "It's like they are crazed. And they have eyes like

FIGURE 5.3 A young woman surrounded by police as she is arrested for carrying a suitcase full of Molotov cocktails on November 16, 1969. Credit: *Asahi shimbun.*

they've been possessed by foxes."[33] Much like tabloid interpretations of Ki-kuyabashi 101's long silence in jail, Teruoka read female student activism—in particular in its extreme variants—as rooted in feminine characteristics impenetrable to logic.

Assuming also that the inclusion of female bodies introduced rampant sexuality, tabloids relied on police conjectures as a main source of information for speculative articles on the kinds of sex that occurred as male and female students lived together in campus occupations. As student barricades became a key strategy of the campus-based student movements of the late 1960s, the presence of female bodies led mass media sources to suggest that the function of young women participants must be sexual release for the young men.[34] In publications such as *Shūkan shinchō* and *Shūkan pureibōi*, articles insinuated that coed campuses must be hotbeds of not only political but also sexual activity. Based on police gossip about literally hot beds—one officer reported feeling "the warmth of two bodies" on a futon in the barricades—the headlines of such articles included sensational terms like *free sex* (*furii sekusu*).[35] However, in quotes from the students, which articles buried between hypotheses and rumors, students both male and female not only denied that such salacious behavior occurred but also commonly expressed that student activists often sought to constrain sexual activity.

Students at several different schools reported that their movement's codes of conduct were rather strict. A Nihon University student elaborated on the custom in the campus barricades there, which was to assign a room to female students sleeping over and to have them lock the door from the inside. Citing the fear of popular opinion as the basis for this policy, he noted, "Some have complained that it's an exaggerated gesture, or that it's bourgeois, but it's our first struggle, so we don't want some silly mistake to become a weapon for our enemies."[36] A former activist at Hosei University repeated this fear that sexual activity could be used as a weapon against them, noting that the Hosei University barricades also attempted a strict management of sexual activities.[37] This seemed to be the case at other campuses as well.[38] In spite of student activists' care to avoid mass media accusations of unbridled sexuality, tabloid journalism equated the inclusion of female bodies with the introduction of sexuality. Again, the tabloids repeated the logic of the "Coeds Ruin the Nation Theory," in which female students sharing campus space with male students sexualized those spaces.

Periodicals that targeted young women often reflected a less dismissive view of female students in the New Left, although preoccupations with the potential for both titillating and terrifying encounters with activism also entered discussions of the student movement in women's magazines. The magazine *Josei jishin* included both celebratory and wary articles on female student activism.[39] Particularly in early 1968, in the context of broad popular support for the student movement, articles on admirable and strong-willed female students introduced the periodical's readership to stories of fortitude, passion, and self-discovery through female student activism.[40] Articles in *Josei jishin* rejected outright the idea that young men dragged young women into the movement and included bold headlines like "Goodbye, Good Wife and Wise Mother!" In late 1968, however, addressing readers' potential concerns about how to navigate the changing political scene at campuses, which included women's colleges, the magazine featured an article framed around "women's colleges without disputes."[41] Their analysis included not only which campuses were safe from unrest but also what opportunities to meet young men, participate in clubs, and take particular courses were offered by thirty schools. However, even while framing the article around schools without activism, the authors concluded by introducing their readers to key student movement terms, such as *Gewalt* and *nonpori* (nonsectarian activism). They also included anecdotes by female students at women's universities who described the excitement of their first awakening to student activism. In this way, even young women who were wary of campus disputes and the negative impact participation might have on their future marriage or employment became familiar with the vocabulary of the student movement.

A serial comic in *Josei jishin* demonstrated how the idea of the sexual availability of young female bodies in the student movement in particular captured the popular imagination. Ostensibly based on a young woman's real-life account of losing her virginity, the illustrated story—*The First Morning*—also drew on an "expert" on student issues for its claim to veracity.[42] Over the course of four installations running from November 18 to December 9, 1968, a wealthy young female student became estranged from her father, found camaraderie and excitement when she fell in with two male student activists, and eventually, provoked "by a maternal instinct," undressed and offered her body to them both in an act of selflessness and solidarity.[43] This narrative emphasized a sexualized ideal of the care work women could offer heterosexual male activists, comforting them with their bodies.[44] In this publication targeting young women, as in the tabloids that targeted a largely male readership, the idea of a politically awakened young woman often suggested an accompanying sexual awakening.

FEMALE ACTIVISM AS COMEDY

In some ways, the mass media's disproportionate fascination with the inclusion of female bodies in demonstrations and occupations continued social patterns set in the 1920s and 1930s, in which mass media political cartoons symbolized threats to political and social stability with female characters, whereas leftist and radical publications lacked representations of revolutionary female subjects.[45] The media formulation of a female student activist certainly followed a pattern created earlier around the figure of the Modern Girl, which Silverberg identified as "a highly commodified cultural construct."[46] The media representation of the Gewalt Rosa in many ways echoed the Modern Girl; she, too, was defined by her physical sensuality, her promiscuity, her liberation from gendered family obligations, and her visibility in public spaces. As noted earlier, student activists both male and female often ignored or actively sought to overcome feminine subjectivity in the student movement.

Although the campus-based student movement represented its ideal revolutionary subjectivity as a masculine street fighter, mass media representations of the radical shifts in what constituted a young female activist attracted more attention. For example, although the occasional cartoon would lampoon male student activists, two mainstream tabloid serial comics in the late 1960s featured a female student as the protagonist who exposed the twists and turns of the student movement. The earlier of the two was Sonoyama Shunji's *College Sister* (*Kareji neechan*), which ran in *Sunday mainichi* from September 1968 to July 1970, although the run of Sakurai Isamu's *Campus Kyanko* (*Kyanpasu Kyanko*), overlapped, running in *Shūkan yomiuri* from May 1969 through the end of 1970.[47] The fictional female protagonists of both series enjoyed vast appetites for food and men, expressing a corporeality marked by sensuality and sexual availability. Their creators often played their female title characters' brashness to comic effect, suggesting a kind of impossibility of integrating women into higher education; their bodies, drawn as busty and barelegged, always introduced sexuality. However, by including themes of radical activism, in which these female student characters participated, these two comic strips also highlighted female participation as a key characteristic of the late 1960s student movement and appealed to readers' attraction to and fear of the politicized subjectivity of the female student.

Although not all the weekly installments thrust these cartoon coeds into student activism, several episodes revealed the popular interest in such female student activists as Kashiwazaki Chieko and Kikuyabashi 101. At various points, both Gebako of *College Sister* and Kyanko of *Campus Kyanko* wielded Gewalt staves and wore helmets like the University of Tokyo's infamous Gewalt Rosa; both of them, like Kikuyabashi 101, claimed their right to remain silent when arrested (figure 5.4).[48] Of the two, Sonoyama's *College Sister* is more sympathetic to the student movement. In part, this may reflect the shift in journalistic sympathies away from the student movement in 1969; by the time Sakurai's *Campus Kyanko* began to run in May 1969, mass media reports of an increasingly violent and confrontational student movement meant the students no longer elicited the strong public sympathy they had enjoyed in 1968.

Although both Gebako and Kyanko represented sexually frank, modern young women, Kyanko embodied a more aggressive sexuality and a correspondingly more radical politics. In an early *Campus Kyanko* strip, from July 1969, Kyanko, rather than being scared off by a warning that her date is only out "for her body," vigorously drains the young man of all his resources, outdrinking him, ordering large amounts of food, and, finally, creating a barricaded "liberation zone" when the young man cannot afford a hotel room for the two of them. When Kyanko creates a barricade to facilitate a sexual encounter, her actions resonate with the tabloid speculations that the campus barricades of a mixed-sex movement represented a "liberation zone" for sexuality, namely, male heterosexuality and access to sex with female students.

Kyanko, a fictional campus radical as adept in mixing Molotov cocktails as she is in seducing men, also wields her sexual power as a political weapon. She lures not only a young man whom she is supposed to tutor but also the boy's father to the Zenkyōtō cause. While confirming tabloid fears about the role of young women in the student movement and the potential of female student leaders to goad others into violence, the author also took the popular idea to a comical extreme. In Kyanko's case, she influenced not only an impressionable high school student, but also his conservative father.

As in many tabloid discussions of female student participation in radical politics, the ideological motivations of both the fictional coed protagonists remained obscure in *College Sister* and *Campus Kyanko*. Their activ-

FIGURE 5.4 *College Sister's* Gebako observes her right to remain silent after her arrest. After asking for her name and school, the policeman speculates on her bust size. Credit: Sonoyama Shunji.

ism may have simply functioned as a way for the authors to comment on current events on campuses, and their politics were often undone by their desires. A running gag in both was their attraction to the manly riot police, for example. However, their creators also used the female students as a dramatic contrast to the men—and male activists—around them, as the young women responded with earnestness to matters of political radicalism and affirmed their own sexual and political agency. Kyanko, as just demonstrated, attracted men of various generations to her politics through her sexual allure. But Gebako in particular demonstrated a committed political subjectivity that exposed the hypocrisies of university authorities, police officers, and male students. For example, a fall 1969 installment contrasted the sincere commitment of Gebako with self-serving and careerist male students. In this strip, two male students discuss their desired jobs at the Ministry of Finance and the Bank of Japan and seek to ingratiate themselves with their professor to assure their future careers, while Gebako continues to collect wood to erect campus barricades. To please the professor, the male students interrupt her and restrain her with her materials. She cries out that she's been betrayed.

This strip reflected the perception of a more general gendered divide between young men who gave up student activism to take on careers and young women who found this a kind of betrayal; already by the spring of 1969, the *Asahi jaanaru* had begun to publish a series on male former student activists who had gone "from Gewalt stave to employment."[49] In a roundtable discussion with young men who until their recent employment had been involved in campus-based activism, topics such as what could be brought from the leftist movement to the workplace revealed how both the mass media and also former student activists built a narrative in which an elite white-collar career was not a break from radical activism. The term for this shift from activist to sarariiman was *employment conversion* (*shūshoku tenkō*), which alluded to a longer history of "ideological conversion" among prewar and wartime leftists who had abandoned their position of protest to embrace the nationalist project of Imperial Japan. In this late 1960s iteration, ideological conversion meant that leftist student activists turned from opposition to the structures of Japanese capital and industry to a cooperative stance in which they both built and benefited from Japan's powerful national economy. While in many ways this mass media discourse about conversion reflected normative wishful thinking that defined leftist activism as immaturity, many employers began to recruit by persuading male student activists that the skills they had acquired in the movement could serve them in employment.

This was a masculinist interpretation about how leadership and ambition developed, as a male activist could easily transfer to a new workplace context. Gebako's "betrayal" by her male comrades as they prepared to join the white-collar workforce demonstrated the young woman's greater commitment to continued activism; the humor of the betrayal lies in the knowledge, shared between the author and the reader, that Gebako should have known better than to trust those young men and their liberatory rhetoric in the first place.

As the campus-based student movement seemed to fade into irrelevance for the majority of people in 1970, Sonoyama's *College Sister* comic strip became an *Office Sister* series in the summer of 1970, while in the fall of that year, Sakurai's Kyanko dabbled in the women's liberation movement but ultimately became a shopgirl. Tensions between men and women remained a key theme for the tabloids in which these comic strips ran. A new catchphrase from mid-1969 characterized the moment as the "Era of Woman Superiority" (*Josei jōi jidai*), echoing strains of anxiety about the proper place of women but also often employed as a humorous slogan.

Several sarariiman-themed cartoons published in tabloids targeting a male readership used the idea of the "Era of Woman Superiority" to comic effect precisely because it seemed absurd that women would usurp men's roles. Such cartoons represented the "Era of Woman Superiority" as a complete swap in gender roles: men were demoted to feminine roles, serving women tea or keeping house.[50] These depictions allowed representations of women stepping into masculine social roles but required that men take on feminine roles, thus preserving a binary gender difference and differentiated labor performed by men and women.[51] These lampoons employed a kind of teasing that, because it insisted it was not to be taken seriously, was difficult to seriously critique, similar to the "politics of teasing" Yumiko Ehara has argued was used to discredit women's liberation activists of the 1970s through humor.[52]

Humor contained the potential threat that women like Gebako would enter the workplace as "office ladies" and headed off the demands of women's lib as well. Kyanko, when she marched with women behind a banner asking "What is femininity?" in a November 27, 1970, installment, drew the jeers of a male onlooker: "Women are superior! Embrace me! Hey, sister! Are you braless?" This prompted Kyanko to end the demonstration and return to campus, where her male student comrades asked her to pour the tea. She refused and excused herself to use the toilet, and one young man suggestively insisted she enter the men's room with him, in the name of equality. This comic strip in particular exposes the male framing of Kyanko and her various affiliations, both political and sexual. Namely, the source of Kyanko's meaning lies in her relationships with the heterosexual men around her, reflecting not only her male creator's view but also the logic of most of the tabloids, which continually defined the role of the female student activist in terms of her relationship with men and male society.

In the meantime, many young women were actually focusing on relationships among women and splintering off from the coed revolution to concentrate on the women's issues that had been ignored in New Left activism. The banner slogan questioning the meaning of femininity in *Cam-*

pus Kyanko referenced the banner under which a group of two hundred helmeted women marched in the October 21, 1970, Antiwar Day demonstration, in an event that many identify as the beginning of second-wave feminism in Japan.[53]

Even when many young women formed a women-only movement to counter not only hegemonic structures of sexism in the workplace and the home but also the sexism of the coed student movement in the late 1960s, the tabloids attempted to define a narrative of ideological conversion for female student activists as well. Unconcerned with the debates circulating among a new generation of self-proclaimed feminists about gender expectations, gendered labor, and reproductive labor, the mass media imagined how young women would transition from Gewalt Rosas to become wives and mothers. In some cases, this produced humorous situations. One cartoon featured a young couple out on a formal marriage interview. Although the young woman wears a kimono, her aggressive style and impeccable aim—perhaps honed through lobbing rocks at police—as she orders another juice by throwing a bottle at the waiter betray her activist background to her potential mate (figure 5.5). The strip offered humorous speculation on how these new politically active young women would integrate into established rituals of courtship and marriage. Although former female activists might prove a more aggressive breed of brides, it remained unthinkable that they would resist marriage altogether.

In a more earnest vein, although with similar effect, the July 5, 1971, issue of *Young Lady* placed female student radicals in the past in a feature on a young mother. The piece expressed admiration for the young woman's activism, introducing her story with the headline "My child, remember: Mama was once an incredible 'Gewalt Rosa' woman."[54] However, much like coverage on how young men could apply the lessons of past activism to their future career, the article characterized the young woman's activism as part of her past; motherhood defined her future.

THE NEW LEFT IS NO PLACE FOR A NICE GIRL

Although there had long been speculation on the propriety of young women participating in political activism, the increase in popular discourse about the violent excesses of the student New Left also strengthened narratives of the dangers faced by vulnerable and impressionable young women who were exposed to radicalism. A May 1971 article in *Shūkan gendai* introduced

FIGURE 5.5 Cartoon of a post–New Left formal marriage interview in which a young woman throws a bottle at the waiter to get his attention and order more juice. Credit: Suzuki Yoshiji.

a diary of a young female student at Ritsumeikan University, published in the wake of her June 1969 suicide. The writings of Takano Etsuko, another document that made public the private musings of a young woman, came out under the title *A Twenty-Year Old's Origin* in 1971 and quickly garnered a reputation as a document of the student movement. The *Shūkan gendai* piece on her diary appeared under the boldface sub-headline: "The Surging Wave of the Student Movement Was Too Intense for This Pure Coed." The author introduced excerpts of the text while speculating, "If there hadn't been campus unrest, perhaps Etsuko would not have died."[55]

It is strange that Takano's posthumously published journal became so strongly linked with the New Left, for while Takano certainly recounts how she compulsively followed the University of Tokyo struggle, she had limited interaction with activism. She wrote about envying the passion of those young people who lived in the barricades. She recorded that she had also felt a kind of camaraderie with other participants in her brief participation in campus demonstrations. Ultimately, however, Takano felt alienated from the student movement, and she lamented that while the students of the Zenkyōtō had agency and history, she felt that she had none and was merely a *kawaikko-chan* (cute little girl). In her journal, she details her self-mutilation: the cutting, burning, and strangulation that she experimented with before throwing herself in front of a train.

It is even stranger that commentators such as the one writing in *Shūkan yomiuri* framed Takano as a victim of the campus New Left in particular. Even in the excerpted bits of Takano's own writings there are other potential scapegoats; Takano describes, for example, the deep impression the nihilistic literature of Dazai Osamu made on her. In fact, reading Dazai made her feel her own discomfort with the social expectations that constrained her as a woman. As she wrote in her journal in February 1969, four months before her suicide, "I'm reading Dazai (Ozamu)'s works. I don't really understand him, but his world feels real. My world is—girls don't smoke cigarettes. Can't come home late. Wives manage the household to make it easy for husbands to work. . . . But, little by little, I'm becoming aware of how this world is mistaken."[56] Considering Takano's personal disgust with herself as a "cutie" and the vitriol with which she described the larger social circumstances faced by women in her journal, it's odd that the moral horror at her suicide focused entirely on the violence of the student movement and did not provoke a closer look at the gendered expectations faced by many young women.

By 1971, when Takano's diary was published, it seems that Takano and her personal narrative resonated with a larger discourse about how nice girls don't do radical activism. The corollary of that discursive conceit was that only bad girls were activists. This helps explain how two women in particular became symbolic of the New Left's violent excesses in the early 1970s: Nagata Hiroko of the United Red Army (URA) and Shigenobu Fusako of the Japanese Red Army (JRA).

Although by the early 1970s the proliferation of examples of sectarian violence represented the radicalization of the student movement to the Japanese public, no event symbolized the death of the New Left as dramatically and powerfully as the bloody internal purge waged by the URA in their mountain retreat, revealed to the nation via the mass media in early

1972. Nagata Hiroko, the young woman who shared power with the male leader, Mori Tsuneo, quickly became emblematic of the perversity of female participation in radical activism. More so than Mori, Nagata came to represent the group's extremist violence in the mass media.[57]

While, as I recount in the previous chapter, the male leader Mori played a key role in the URA's deadly internal purge, in contemporary journalistic reports no one came across as more monstrous than Nagata, who became a kind of confirmation that women were not to be trusted with power. What became known as the "Toyama incident" became in many cases a story of her female jealousy in which Nagata, described by journalists as ugly, manly, and—they speculated—infertile, attacked Toyama Mieko because Toyama represented a femininity unattainable to Nagata.[58]

As feminist contemporaries noted, male reporters gleefully seized on rumors of Nagata's "extreme emotions" and "cruelty that even men feared." One male commentator quoted in the mainstream *Asahi shimbun* even declared, "Women's participation in the movement is not only a problem for the URA, but a new problem today."[59] This followed earlier patterns of portraying female student activists—activists like Kikuyabashi 101 and Kashiwazaki Chieko—as agents of radicalization. With this violent incident, in which a young woman played a key role, both the New Left and the place of women in political movements faced crippling criticism.

This conflation of feminist activism with far-left terrorism challenged the goals of radical women's liberation activists worldwide in the 1970s. For example, a January 9, 1978, article in the *New York Times* paraphrased a female criminologist on the rise of women in far-left groups such as the Red Army Faction in West Germany, the Weather Underground in the United States, and the Popular Front for the Liberation of Palestine to interpret "terrorist activity as [a] deviant expression of feminism."[60] The article also mentioned not Nagata Hiroko but another Japanese woman involved in far-left extremism: Shigenobu Fusako. Shigenobu, arguably the most infamous export of the Japanese New Left, was a student activist involved in the Red Army when she left Japan to link up with the Popular Front for the Liberation of Palestine in 1971. She acted as a leader of the international JRA until her arrest in Japan in 2000.

Unlike the "ugly" Nagata, Shigenobu was attractive, but she was similarly terrifying, accused of luring young men to their deaths. On May 30, 1972, three young Japanese men opened fire in the baggage claim of Lod Airport in an attack organized with Shigenobu's help; this launched the JRA and Shigenobu into the international arena of violent spectacle and terrorist fame. Two of them blew themselves up on the spot. The JRA in the Middle East was careful to distance itself from the purge of the URA in 1972, and Shigenobu's public persona offered a dramatic contrast with Nagata's. Shigenobu was good-looking and feminine; the *Observer* described her in 1974 as "the lady terrorist with white gloves," less a "cold theoretician" than a "political tender heart."[61] The "pre-battle ceremony" conducted by the JRA under Shigenobu's guidance in the 1970s included a verbal oath delivered to a surrogate "mother and father" in a move that reformulated kinship ties rather than attempting to destroy them.[62] Shigenobu also portrayed herself as a manifestation of a self-consciously feminine revolutionary subjectivity. In her 1973 televised interview with Yamaguchi Yoshiko, Shigenobu spoke in unfailingly polite and feminine Japanese, brushing her long, straight hair back from her modestly smiling face.[63] The title of Shigenobu's 1974 memoir—the first of many she would publish—was *My Love, My Revolution*, which echoed the title of Tokoro Mitsuko's posthumously published essays: *My Love and Rebellion*.[64] Shigenobu's public persona attempted to tap into a radical politics of nurturing, but her prominence in a radical organization that organized bombings and hijackings also fed narratives about the dangers of women in politics.

The violence conducted by the women of the URA and the JRA under the leadership of women like Nagata Hiroko and Shigenobu Fusako threatened to smear all feminist activism in the 1970s. While many radical women's lib activists attempted to use the URA purge as an occasion to understand the potential for female violence, many more feminists in the 1970s distanced themselves from New Left violence and the figure of Nagata in particular.[65] Ueno Chizuko, who later became a professor at the University of Tokyo and a prominent academic feminist, described her reaction as a young woman to the news of the URA purge: it convinced her that collective action was impossible.[66] More conservative women intellectuals, dismissing the political gains of radical women's lib, continued to emphasize a completely nonconfrontational history of female activism.[67] Feminism never lost the taint of violence it gained in the early 1970s through associations both real and imaginary with groups like the URA. As Setsu Shigematsu points out, the mass media quickly exposed any ties between URA members and women's lib activists, suggesting that the feminist movement contained a deadly potential similar to that of the far-left sect.[68] In a context in which feminists risked popular condemnation for radical activism, which by the 1970s was a global discourse, the choice on the part of many women's groups to insist on an essentially nurturing feminine nature makes some strategic sense. In contemporary Japan, popular stereotypes of women's lib continue to define feminism as "radical and harsh" or "radical and overpowering."[69]

CONCLUSION

In the late 1960s and early 1970s, the mass media portrayed young women who participated in radical politics as both terrifying and titillating. The female student activist was terrifying in her potential to radically upset fixed gender roles, and she titillated by intimating more "liberated" sexual access to women's bodies in the coed revolution. Mass media reports emphasized the danger of her "hysterical" emotional politics but also diffused that threat through portraying her as ridiculous or as an extreme personality. The figure of the female student activist, and finally of the New Left femme fatale, became a warning away from radical activism for all good citizens but particularly for good women.

While female student activists were portrayed as dangerous, the actual female student activist was particularly vulnerable to salacious media reports. The press published identifying information on activists, which compromised many students' futures. But media reports also conflated women's political radicalism alongside men with increased sexual availability to men. This borrowed from older gendered formulations of what constituted a bad woman. Press reports of salacious female activist behavior, and imaginary representations of activist women, drowned out actual women's voices.

The popular fixation on deadly radical women also undergirds a powerful postwar narrative about the danger of emasculated men in Japan's postwar society. As Kiyoaki Murata, then the editor in chief of Japan's premier English-language newspaper, the *Japan Times*, put it in a 1971 article on women's lib, "There is little from which women of Japan need to be liberated. This has been, in fact, an age of 'female supremacy' and if anyone needs liberation, it is the downtrodden, browbeaten men of Japan." In his view, Mishima Yukio's suicide affirmed a kind of postwar "men's liberation": Mishima "died to restore masculinity for Japanese men."[70] Statements like this insist on the impossibility of actually incorporating women into the body politic by framing any political gains for women as an inherent threat to men.

Conclusion

Revolutionary Desire

This is not a history of a women's movement, but it does focus on women who moved into formerly all-male institutions of education, into street protests, and into campus barricades, and it explores the consequences of their movement. I identify female student participation as a site of particular tension for radical politics in Japan and beyond. My history illuminates the patterns of media coverage, policy reactions, and activist organization that defined what was politically possible for women in postwar Japan. What women could achieve in the student New Left movement was limited by larger social expectations about female political participation; their revolutionary desire was mediated by the desires projected onto them.

The coed female university student—a postwar middle-class subject position—demonstrates a key particularity that became embedded in the concept of the postwar citizen as it lives with us in contemporary Japan. Ethnic others were ousted from "the people" of postwar Japan in the transition from imperial subject to constitutional citizen. From the 1960s onward, with the dimming of a class-based political subjectivity and the idea of a fully middle-class citizenry, *women* became a primary signifier of difference in a people imagined as otherwise homogeneous. This demonstrates in many ways how relevant the "woman question"—a global set of issues about how to integrate women into modern societies and economies first articulated in Japan in the nineteenth century—remains in Japan today. What to do with women? Does their full integration into education and work "ruin the nation" or "fix the nation"? Both debates privilege the nation as the position from which to evaluate to what degree some people (that is, women) ought to participate as part of society, as the people.

In tracing the stories and receptions of women—from Kanba Michiko, who became a maiden martyr for postwar democracy with her 1960 death at a protest, to the deadly leftist femme fatales of campus Gewalt Rosas and Nagata Hiroko—I want to draw attention to how expectations about how women ought to participate in politics *as women* shape understandings about movements in which women take part. Such symbolic coed revolutionaries stepped into larger discourses about gendered participation in politics more generally, which ranged from the early 1960s embrace of young women as new democratic subjects to a late 1960s anxiety about women as political subjects with a potentially terrifying capacity for violence (both literal violence and also damage to accepted social relations and institutions). Women are not a fixed category with fixed political meanings. But many modern societies share a constellation of assumptions about women and vulnerability that frames the possibilities and the limits of women's political strategies if they want to be heard by society.

Vulnerability is often culturally coded as feminine. This was true in the "naive politics" framing of female student activism in the 1950s and early 1960s in Japan. As Judith Butler, Zeynep Gambetti, and Letizia Sabsay note, however, "There is always something both risky and true in claiming that women or other socially disadvantaged groups are especially vulnerable."[1] The truth is that women's voices are often disproportionately excluded, and women suffer unequally the effects of social problems like poverty. Women in Japan have long appealed to ideas about female vulnerability to legitimize their participation in politics and activism. Organizing women as wives and mothers has been a successful strategy to attract sympathetic media attention and influence political change. But it also reinforces ideas that women can intervene in politics only as protectors of children and the home, and it does not challenge the underlying assumption that there is a female domestic sphere separate from a public male economic and political sphere.

Also, as Setsu Shigematsu has pointed out while considering the case of women's lib in Japan, certain strands of feminism have tended to create a universalizing discourse of the victimhood of women, which can obscure women's capacity to wield power and commit violence.[2] We can see how this operated in the creation of a postwar discourse about female suffrage and the creation of Kanba Michiko the maiden sacrifice, as well as in Tokoro Mitsuko's ideas about an inherently nurturing "women's logic" based on women's complete victimization in war.

Assigning women the role of victims can quickly flip into a contrasting essentialist idea of female authority as a threat when women engage in behavior that does not fit ideas about female vulnerability. When women are expected to be natural nurturers, if they do not demonstrate nurturance—by taking on care work or supporting others emotionally—they are considered unnatural and potentially dangerous. This is the menace presented by the "Gewalt Rosa" female activist, and a common strategy to contain that threat was to frame it as laughable and as a temporary disruption of the natural order of things.

Culturally coding vulnerability as feminine also makes the construction of a masculine identity important to those who would claim invulnerability and strength. Butler, Gambetti, and Sabsay also consider how this can create ideas about the hypervulnerability of male honor, in which case women's behavior (political, economic, sexual) can take on threatening force.[3] The category of vulnerability, then, may help us understand why women can be seen as both particularly in need of protection and also as particularly dangerous.

The creation of a masculinist ideal of the New Left activist appeals to strength through tapping into the culturally available codes of rebel masculinity. That masculine image did convince many outside observers of the power of the student New Left, which ironically undermined any popular sympathy predicated on ideas about the student movement as particularly vulnerable to state authority. The role of state violence was a key debate in postwar Japan, as citizens worked through the militaristic implications of the recent past, and at many moments the New Left sought to provoke the ostensibly peaceful postwar state to reveal the force that sustained it. This put the radical student movement in a bind, where it seemed to win the most in terms of public goodwill when it "lost."

One of the most publicized legacies of the Japanese New Left is its violence, the dynamics of which remain little understood. As Patricia Steinhoff has noted, "A heavily negative view of the entire period has solidified in public collective memory through commemorative media presentations and films that recycle visual images of the protests into a blur of senseless violence without explanation of its causes."[4] Recent cinematic representations such as *United Red Army* (*Jitsuroku rengōsekigun Asama-sansō e no dōtei*) (2007) and *My Back Page* (*Mai bakku peeji*) (2011) replicate popular narratives of leftist good intentions turned bad.

These popular commemorations of a misguided and inherently terror-istic militarism obscure some of the more enduring legacies of New Left activism. Yamamoto Yoshitaka recently noted that the Sanpa (Three-Faction) Zengakuren did not pass without creating its own legacies, no-tably jail support infrastructure.[5] The Relief Support Contact Center (Kyūen renraku sentaa) was formed as a response to the mass arrests of students when riot police seized the University of Tokyo's main clock tower in January 1960 by many sympathetic volunteers and lawyers, many of them activists in women's groups like the Women's Democratic Club (Fujin minshu kurabu). Once the center was established, student activ-ists remembered the phone number (591-1301) through a mnemonic device that translated as "entering jail has many meanings" (*goku iri imi o-i*).[6] The center's support for arrested students made it possible for many to resist confessing and wage protracted legal battles, which gives us a window onto how, even as the mass media marginalized the New Left, many people still mobilized to support student activism. The center's activities continue to this day.

Yet the implosive violence of the Japanese New Left—the United Red Army purge and the ongoing blood feuds between factions—strength-ened the claims of the police's grassroots public relations campaign about the threat of activism, alienated a wide swath of the Japanese public from the early 1970s onward, and has discredited contentious politics in con-temporary Japan. Any demonstration that comes across as too aggressive risks setting off a whole chain of associations between dissent and extreme violence.

The disillusionment with radical politics in Japan today also has gen-dered nuances. Even today, female activists are particularly vulnerable to scrutiny and speculation if their politics seem too strident. This has dimin-ished the legacy of women who participated in the New Left, and also that of the radical women-only movement that emerged from the New Left in Japan. One of the founders of women's studies in Japan even declared that Japanese women gained their freedoms "quietly and unobtrusively, largely without the fanfare of an organized women's movement."[7] This isn't true, but its truthiness lies in the urge to distance whatever social reforms are deemed positive in postwar Japan from confrontational and radical protest cultures rooted in the New Left.

However, the New Left in Japan did not "fail" just because it lost a battle for popular appeal. Within the ostensibly hierarchy-free campus Zenkyōtō (All-Campus Joint Struggle Committee) movements, hierarchies formed, and these often reflected standard gendered roles and the values associated with those roles in mainstream society. While gender is a constantly negotiated system of hierarchical power relations, a study of the student movement in postwar Japan also must consider how, even as some value systems (e.g., related to violence) become renegotiated in small communities that form to dissent from the status quo, other value systems (in this case, regarding gender) can persist in organizing those alternative communities. The New Left's increasing insularity and stress on cultivating a street-combat subjectivity aligned with an emphasis on masculine homosociality that continues to dominate the political and corporate worlds in Japan.

What might it mean to think instead about how nurturing and care—Tokoro Mitsuko's "women's logic" but delinked from the societal expectations that define care as women's work—can figure in a movement that radically challenges the status quo? Rather than focus on spectacular confrontations, which can be effective in garnering public attention but can also become ends in and of themselves, what might it mean to live for the revolution? As Francis Beal, a founding member of the Student Nonviolent Coordinating Committee's Black Women's Liberation Committee, wrote in 1970, "We must begin to understand that a revolution entails not only the willingness to lay our lives on the firing line and get killed. In some ways, this is an easy commitment to make. To die for the revolution is a one-shot deal; to live for the revolution means taking on the more difficult commitment of changing our day-to-day life patterns."[8]

While my study does not integrate oral histories as fundamental sources, discussions with former student activists framed my research at several points and pointed me to how the very experience of the New Left could be based on different gendered expectations of what it meant to live for a revolution. My conversations followed distinct patterns based on the gender of my interlocutor, leading me to think about how the experience of postwar education, New Left activism, and postgraduate life "in society" differed for men and women in the baby boom generation that made up the postwar student movement. In particular, many former female student activists who fought in the late 1960s New Left impressed on me their lingering anger with male student activists. Such stories explain an aspect of the "Left-to-lib" narrative of the 1970s women's movement, which often distanced itself from the "male" New Left, but also reinforce the idea that the New Left was a movement and a moment that belonged only to men.

Female participation in a coed revolution in the 1960s influenced both activist and academic feminism, making it possible for former activists and for scholars of that activism, including me, to understand the gendered unevenness within the postwar student movement. Progressive and feminist presses like Inpakuto shuppankai and Shokado shoten have documented the New Left genealogies of second-wave feminism in Japan.[9] Ueno Chizuko, arguably the most famous gender scholar in Japan, was involved in Zenkyōtō activism at Kyoto University.[10] Her classmate and fellow activist, Itō Kimio, went on to found masculinity studies in Japan. He recalled his experiences in the New Left at Kyoto University—in particular, an instance in which female comrades demanded that the organizers of a striptease event perform a self-criticism—as providing the impetus to read more about women's studies and then think of gender in terms of analyzing masculinity as well.[11] Many male former student activists with whom I spoke were open to criticizing themselves for their own disregard of a culture of male chauvinism in the New Left.

However, many of the gendered codes employed to represent the 1960s coed revolution are still at work in Japan today. I was interested to read the 2014 news reports about the student-built barricades of the Umbrella Movement in Hong Kong, for example. One article in the *Tokyo shimbun* indicated its sympathy for the student activists by sharing the female face of the movement via a color photograph of a smiling young woman in front of a crowd with umbrellas, holding an iPad with the image of another young woman. The article emphasized that over one-quarter of the students in the campus barricades were female, "elegant and affable." The reporter added that it was almost "anticlimactic" how completely different these activists were from the "Japanese student movement that once clashed with riot police, wooden staves in hand." In describing the reporter's interviews with female student activists, the article included descriptions of young women playing with their long hair as they spoke.[12] The article both demonstrated the reporter's sympathy for the nonaggressive, nonideological Umbrella Movement in Hong Kong through drawing on ideas that linked young women with political moderation and social vulnerability and also made a historical comparison that confirmed a widespread view of the postwar Japanese student movement as masculine and violent.

At the same time, female activists in Japan today have noted that they are often subjected to sexist bashing by their opponents. Fukuda Wakako, a female leader of the group Students for Emergency Action for Liberal Democracy (SEALDs), which organized protests against Prime Minister Abe Shinzō in 2015 and 2016, noted in a 2016 interview that her fellow male activists didn't face the same kind of vitriol she and other female SEALDs did. Internet trolls would write sexually explicit messages to her and, for example, call her a "comfort woman" for contemporary Japan. Such abuse invokes the historical gendered violence of Japan's colonialism, nationalism, and war. It also suggests that, like women forcibly procured to provide sex to Japanese imperial soldiers, Fukuda's primary role in a movement or in society is to offer male sexual access to her body. Fukuda also recalled that women who were otherwise supportive of SEALDs would criticize how she dressed or spoke. She noted, "Up until this point I really hadn't been aware of 'woman' as a sex in public space. Through this experience, I realized that Japanese women are this oppressed."[13] The SEALDs group did not frame itself as radical in the same way as the New Left did; it focused on opposing specific policies rather than demanding widespread social revolution. However, SEALDs offered a young generation a taste of protest culture and exposed some of the deep-seated obstacles faced by activists in Japan, particularly female activists. Just like the young women of the 1960s New Left, young women today may not understand the depth of societal sexism until they participate in a movement. That female SEALDs members like Fukuda describe encountering many similar gendered expectations about female political participation to those faced by an earlier generation of "Gewalt girls" suggests that understanding the gendered reception of the New Left can also tell us a great deal about the social dynamics that shape contemporary activism as well.

The SEALDs group has been central to a recent rise in protest culture in response to the strong-arm tactics of Prime Minister Abe (the grandson of Kishi Nobusuke, prime minister during the 1960 Anpo), which has made it possible to revisit the history of protest in postwar Japan. And although an increasing number of memoirs documenting the 1960s generation of student activists open up some space to positively evaluate the actions of the New Left in postwar Japan, the nostalgia that defines many of those works poses the threat of a romantic rehabilitation that does not interrogate critical tensions—such as those around gendered hierarchies—that also undermined an earlier generation of activism. Fukuda and other female SEALDs have rejected the idea that women faced male chauvinism within the student organization. It will be interesting to see how they retrospectively evaluate their experiences and how that might inform other future activism, particularly if protest as students made them more aware of gendered dynamics in political life more generally.

However, the history I introduce here is about women who did not appeal for recognition within existing systems but called for a complete overhaul of existing socioeconomic systems that perpetuated inequalities within society and across the world. There are clear limits to a liberal feminism that makes more limited demands for gender equality while leaving economic structures unreformed. One example can be found in the second administration of Prime Minister Abe (2012–present), which has framed its policy of promoting female participation in business—a policy known as "womenomics"—as a win-win strategy of promoting women's advancement in the workplace and thus stimulating the stagnant Japanese economy. These policies are located within a broader global movement toward neoliberal market deregulation, which in many cases undermines social services and may actually contribute to more general labor precarity and aggravate a trend toward the feminization of poverty. The very language of womenomics does not challenge the historical context in which the Japanese economy became organized on a gendered division of labor, which I have outlined here and which has come to be seen as natural in Japan. We can actually observe, in real time, worrying cases that demonstrate an actual worsening of women's position in Japanese society in recent years, which speaks to a continual devaluation of care work and a fixation on the health of the national economy over that of living, breathing people.

Further, young women continue to occupy a particularly fraught position in contemporary Japanese society. Sharon Kinsella's recent work on schoolgirls traces how the "young girl" became both the most potentially vulnerable victim of exploitation (sexual, economic, or political) and also the most potentially threatening figure (preying on men's perceived sexual, economic, and political weaknesses) from the late 1990s on in Japan.[14] These trends mirror some of the dynamics at work in the 1960s, when coeds were accused of ruining the nation. But they take place in a new, more precarious context in which the national economy is stagnant, sparking new contestations over the proper role of women in the economy, the home, and the nation.

Femininity is also under attack as conservatives continue to blame social ills on a lack of paternal power. Tomiko Yoda has explored a "vogue of paternalism" that arose in the 1990s, in part as a response to "the destabilization of Japanese masculine identity in the wake of the nation's economic downturn since the early 1990s."[15] While mouthing an apparently feminist line about mobilizing more (middle-class) women in the workforce, Prime Minister Abe also seeks to simultaneously strengthen Japan's military and the patriarchal order of the Japanese family. Conservative proposals to revise the postwar constitution target two key sections: those limiting Japan's military powers *and* those guaranteeing greater rights to women within the family. This is a long-standing project, first initiated in the early 1950s under Kishi Nobusuke.[16] Women stand to lose the most from such attempts to bolster "traditional" patriarchal control in society, as projecting masculine might abroad also implicates reinforcing masculine power at home.[17] In the meantime, Japan consistently lags behind global standards for gender equality. In 2020 Japan ranked 121 out of 153 countries in the Global Gender Gap Index and remained the lowest-ranking of the Group of Seven industrialized nations.[18] This is mostly due to very low rates of political participation by women and to persistent wage gaps.

Ideas about young women as threatening agents are not limited to those who seek to protect "vulnerable" men and male authority. *Preliminary Materials for a Theory of the Young-Girl*, a 1999 work by a French collective of writers and activists writing under the name Tiqqun, analyzes the "Young-Girl" as a symbol of "the *model citizen* as redefined by consumer society since World War I, in *explicit* response to the revolutionary menace."[19] That is to say, the "Young-Girl" as theorized by Tiqqun mirrors the historical dynamics that shaped the reception of Kanba Michiko as a "model citizen" maiden in 1960 Japan and shut down her potential "revolutionary menace."

Tiqqun's text attacks the imaginary "young girl" as the model nonideological consumer citizen. In Japan Ōtsuka Eiji's studies of shōjo (young girl) folklore simultaneously champion serious analyses of the role of feminine cultures, while also arguing that this is important because of the role young women play as the ultimate consumers in an economy that has come to be organized around consumption; Ōtsuka understands Japan's shift from an industrial economy to a late-capital service economy as a "shōjo-ification" of Japanese society at large.[20] This fixes the image of the young female as inherently in collusion with late-capitalist spectacle and authority and necessarily antithetical to radical projects to undermine capitalism. I'm inclined to agree instead with Nina Power's critique, in which she notes that the Tiqqun text "both parodies and mirrors the misogyny that resonates at the heart of a culture that celebrates youth and beauty above all else while simultaneously denigrating the bearers—young women, overwhelmingly—of these purportedly desirable characteristics." Power wonders, "What, ultimately, would it mean to let the Young-Girl speak for herself and not through the categories imposed upon her by a culture that heralds her as the metaphysical apex of civilization while simultaneously denigrating her, or even the categories that Tiqqun mobilize to take her apart in a subtle way?"[21]

Desire *for* the young woman often eclipses discussions about what young women desire, particularly when it comes to radical politics. My work here is an attempt to describe the processes by which young women are given voice and are silenced, as icons of vulnerability and violence, in postwar Japan. That includes a silencing that insists on young women as representatives of a nonideological naive politics, and it also includes erasing the work of radical women, or undermining their demands through casting them as unnatural and dangerous, or eccentric and laughable. Young women's political desires were often mediated through assumptions about what women ought to desire or were understood in terms of male desire to access young women's bodies. What would it mean to allow young women to speak for themselves, particularly women in a coed revolution, who demand not only access to society and politics as they are but also radical change? Without understanding the social meanings that mediate young female activists' voices, we cannot understand how to listen to them. This is precisely the point made by the art collective Tomorrow Girls Troop, which brings together members of different nationalities and communicates in Japanese, Korean, and English to address gender inequality in both Japan and South Korea.[22] When I asked Tomorrow Girls Troop members why they chose to dub their "fourth-wave feminist social art collective" using the term *girl* (*shōjo* in Japanese and *sonyeo* in Korean), they noted that part of their project was a reappropriation or resignification of the very term *girl*, to create the girl as a site of subjectivity from which to speak and act artistically and politically, and to disrupt the processes by which *girl* often becomes an objectifying term of sexual desire or a term around which advertising campaigns stimulate consumer desire.[23]

In introducing readers here to radical female student activists' words, I hope we can also hear and begin to historicize how young women might speak for themselves. Kanba Michiko refused a liberal ideal of the individual citizen whose isolated actions would guarantee peace or democracy, insisting instead on identifying sources of conflict and organizing collectively. Tokoro Mitsuko insisted on love as the basis for a revolutionary project to challenge capitalism and urged activists to resist a mind-set that replicated the systems they fought against. An activist critique of the powers that be requires more than words; we can also see how the actions of female participants constituted the often invisible labor that made it possible for the New Left to claim spaces and continue their struggles. While many women were put in charge of care work by virtue of their sex, we don't need to replicate the sexist logic that privileges innovation over maintenance, leaders over organizers. As Tokoro Mitsuko put it: "Reject the superman, trust the ignorant. Don't wait on that singular Marx or Lenin. Let's begin to walk with our own legs. Change is our issue. If that doesn't preserve productivity, that's fine, isn't it?"[24] Here I've tried to disentangle the gendered patterns that obscured such voices and actions to allow for a feminist genealogy from within the New Left, because we need a leftist feminism and a feminist Left.

NOTES

INTRODUCTION

1. Yonezu, "Mizukara no SEX o mokuteki ishikitekini hikiukeru naka kara 70 nendai o bokki suru," 170.

2. Mori, "Shisō shūdan esu.ii.ekkusu soshikiron?," 172. Unless otherwise noted, all translations by the author.

3. Uno, "Death of 'Good Wife, Wise Mother'?," 307.

4. Draper, *1968 Mexico*, 128.

5. Scott, *Gender and the Politics of History*.

6. In this study I also include documents written by women at women's colleges, understanding these women as coeds in the sense that postwar education directives called for women to get the same education as men; also, many New Left events and networks allowed young men and women to organize together.

7. Gluck, "'End' of the Postwar."

8. Morris-Suzuki, *Re-inventing Japan*, 106–7.

9. Ando, *Japan's New Left Movements*.

10. Ando, *Japan's New Left Movements*.

11. Avenell, *Making Japanese Citizens*; Sasaki-Uemura, *Organizing the Spontaneous*.

12. Loftus, *Telling Lives*; Sasaki-Uemura, *Organizing the Spontaneous*.

13. Gerteis, *Gender Struggles*.

14. Andrews, *Dissenting Japan*; Oguma, *1968 (ge)*.

15. The high circulation rates of Japanese print media, as well as the high literacy rates of the population, were part of the legacy of the postwar high-growth period. Ishiyama, "Japan," 406.

16. Eades, Goodman, and Hada, *"Big Bang" in Japanese Higher Education*, 86.

17. Kelly, "At the Limits of New Middle Class Japan."

18. Nagai, *Nihon no daigaku*, 4.

19. Monbushō daijin kanbō chōsa tōkeika, *Gakkō kihon chōsa hōkokusho*, 5.

20. Zenkyōtō hakusho henshū iinkai, *Zenkyōtō hakusho*.

21. Oguma, *1968 (ge)*, 676.

22. Tanaka Mitsu, "Tanaka Mitsu 1968 o warau" [Tanaka Mitsu mocks 1968], *Shūkan kinyōbi*, December 25, 2009.

23. Suga, *1968-nen*, 16.

24. Suga, *Kakumeitekina, amari kakumeitekina*, 399–400.

25. Setsu Shigematsu's work offers such a close critical analysis of the texts and activism of the 1970s' *ūman ribu* (women's lib) in Japan. Shigematsu, *Scream from the Shadows*.

26. Onnatachi no ima o tō kai, *Zenkyōtō kara ribu e*; Mizonoguchi, Saeki, and Miki, *Shiryō ūman ribu shi I*.

27. Ueno, *Ueno Chizuko ga bungaku o shakaigaku suru*, 175.

28. Mackie, *Creating Socialist Women in Japan*, 26–33.

29. Mackie, *Creating Socialist Women in Japan*, 14.

30. E. Tsurumi, *Factory Girls*.

31. Mackie, *Creating Socialist Women in Japan*, 6.

32. Sturiano, "Community and Creativity," 26.

33. Haaland, *Emma Goldman*, 2.

34. Arruzza, *Dangerous Liaisons*.

35. Mori, "Shisō shūdan esu.ii.ekkusu soshikiron?," 170.

36. Mori, "Shisō shūdan esu.ii.ekkusu soshikiron?," 173.

37. Mori, "Shisō shūdan esu.ii.ekkusu soshikiron?," 174.

38. Marotti cites Kristin Ross's work on "May 1968" in France and Jacques Rancière's political philosophy as inspiration for his framing. Marotti, *Money, Trains, and Guillotines*, 2, 19.

39. Boggs, "Revolutionary Process," 359.

40. Breines, *Community and Organization*.

41. Polletta, *Freedom Is an Endless Meeting*.

42. Tokoro, *Waga ai to hangyaku*, 151.

43. Katō Mitsuko, "Tōdai zenkyōtō no naka de," 52–53.

44. Cohen and Frazier, "Talking Back to '68," 163.

45. Katō Mitsuko, "Tōdai zenkyōtō no naka de," 61–62.

46. Piercy, *Grand Coolie Damn*.

47. Piercy, *Grand Coolie Damn.*

48. Evans, "Sons, Daughters, and Patriarchy," 331.

49. Freeman, *Politics of Women's Liberation,* 203.

50. Springer, *Living for the Revolution,* 75; Shigematsu, *Scream from the Shadows.*

51. The term *excess of ethics* is from Ando, *Japan's New Left Movements,* 5.

1. NAIVE POLITICS

1. Kanba Michiko, *Hito shirezu hohoeman,* 133.

2. Simon Avenell has written of how a postwar idea of the *shimin* (citizen) harnessed a popular attachment to postwar affluence with a political stance of dissent in the 1960s. I want to point to how gendered ideas about political participation did not set the stage solely for the public reception of activism in this period. Avenell, *Making Japanese Citizens.*

3. Yoneyama, *Cold War Ruins,* 90.

4. Koikari, *Pedagogy of Democracy,* 49–50.

5. Dominant ideas about U.S. womanhood also figured in postwar formulations of ideal female participation in the political, domestic, and social spheres. That influence was both accepted and contested by many elite and middle-class Japanese women who shaped discussions in Japan. Koikari, *Pedagogy of Democracy;* Bardsley, *Women and Democracy.*

6. Pflugfelder, "'Fujin sanseiken' saikō."

7. Koikari, *Pedagogy of Democracy,* 47.

8. Garon, *Managing Japanese Minds,* 179.

9. Hane, *Reflections;* Hane, *Peasants, Rebels, Women, and Outcastes.*

10. Garon, "Women's Groups."

11. Koikari, *Pedagogy of Democracy,* 39.

12. Nakaya, *Sono "minshu" to wa dare nano ka,* 220.

13. Sasaki-Uemura, *Organizing the Spontaneous,* 112–18.

14. Loftus, *Telling Lives,* 53.

15. Quoted in Loftus, *Telling Lives,* 52.

16. Schieder, "Revolutionary Bodies."

17. Shimada, "Hōki seyo shōjo!"

18. Quoted in Shimada, "Hōki seyo shōjo!," 3.

19. Shakai mondai kenkyūkai, *Zengakuren kakuha,* 168.

20. Quoted in Matsunami, "Origins of Zengakuren," 48.

21. Ikeda, "Historical Background," 35; Koschmann, "Intellectuals and Politics," 397.

22. Shibata Shō's 1964 novel *Saredo warera ga hibi* focuses on this disappointed generation and includes a fictional account of a Communist student's conflicted personal relationship with violence and the JCP. The title is often translated as *Well, That's Our Lot*, but a more literal translation might be *Well, Those Were Our Days*.

23. Esashi, *Kanba Michiko*, 124–27.

24. Nikan rōdō tsūshinsha, *Zengakuren no jittai*.

25. As William Marotti notes, "Somewhat confusingly, 'Anpo' conventionally refers both to the Security Treaty and to the protests against it." Marotti, "Japan 1968," 98.

26. Sasaki-Uemura, *Organizing the Spontaneous*, 16.

27. Packard, *Protest in Tokyo*, 4. George Packard's account of the political events surrounding the 1960 treaty renewal is thorough enough to merit its position as a classic, although his paranoid anti-Communism marks it as a Cold War work. He generally describes the crisis as a public relations failure on the part of the ruling LDP and is dismissive of the political legitimacy of the mass civilian demonstrations.

28. Packard, *Protest in Tokyo*, 148.

29. Igarashi, *Bodies of Memory*, 136–37.

30. Kapur, *Japan at the Crossroads*, 25. Nick Kapur offers a thorough account of the timeline of the Security Treaty revision events and the protests they prompted.

31. Packard, *Protest in Tokyo*, 96.

32. Avenell, *Making Japanese Citizens*, 94–95.

33. Tanaka Sumie, "Senpai toshite, haha toshite," 69.

34. Quoted in Katō Katsuko et al., "Zadankai," 5:92–93.

35. Quoted in Katō Katsuko et al., "Zadankai," 5:97.

36. Quoted in Katō Katsuko et al., "Zadankai," 5:98.

37. House of Councillors, Committee on Judicial Affairs, Thirty-Fourth Diet Session, meeting no. 3, comment no. 50.

38. "Gurabia: Keikan to ikareru musumetachi" [Gravia: The police and the angry maiden], *Shūkan shinchō*, May 16, 1960.

39. Nakajima, *Zengakuren*, 2.

40. Packard, *Protest in Tokyo*, 229; Kim, "Moral Imperatives."

41. Hidaka Rokurō, "Kenryoku no bōryoku" [Violence by the authorities], *Tokyo daigaku shimbun*, July 11, 1960. At a study group of former Bund activists, many of whom were in the June 15, 1960, demonstration and recalled their physical locations with some precision, I was able to hear various participants' recollections of those events. Although everyone could recall that evening's events in a surprising amount

of detail, they all concluded that it was "hard to know what exactly had happened" to Kanba. Bund Study Group, interview with author, February 10, 2015.

42. Unno, *Rekishi e no shōgen*, 90–92.

43. "6.15 ryūketsu jiken no kiroku" [A record of the bloody events of June 15], *Asahi jaanaru*, July 3, 1960; Hidaka Rokurō, "Kenryoku no bōryoku" [Violence by the authorities], *Tokyo daigaku shimbun*, July 11, 1960.

44. Hirakawa, "Maiden Martyr.'"

45. Esashi, *Kanba Michiko*, 15.

46. Yamamoto Chie, "Anpo tōsō wa shuppatsu no toki," 5:120.

47. Kanba Michiko, *Hito shirezu hohoeman*, 45.

48. Kanba Michiko, *Hito shirezu hohoeman*, 187–97.

49. Kanba Michiko, *Hito shirezu hohoeman*, 196.

50. Kanba Michiko, *Hito shirezu hohoeman*, 189.

51. Kanba Michiko, *Hito shirezu hohoeman*, 194.

52. Kanba Michiko, *Hito shirezu hohoeman*, 197.

53. Esashi, *Kanba Michiko*, 37.

54. Esashi, *Kanba Michiko*, 43.

55. Kanba Michiko, *Hito shirezu hohoeman*, 56.

56. Kanba Michiko, *Hito shirezu hohoeman*, 56–57.

57. Kanba Toshio, "Arashi no gijidō ni kieta musume."

58. Kanba Toshio, "Zengakuren ni musume o ubawarete"; Kanba Toshio, "Arashi no gijidō ni kieta musume."

59. "'Kokumin no tame no gisei da' Kanba kyōju, kanashimi no taimen" ["A sacrifice for the people": Professor Kanba, confronting grief], *Yomiuri shimbun*, June 16, 1960.

60. Kanba Toshio, "Maegaki," 9–10.

61. Kanba Toshio, "Arashi no gijidō ni kieta musume," 492.

62. Kanba Toshio, "Arashi no gijidō ni kieta musume," 497–98.

63. Kanba Mitsuko, "Hontō ni yasashii ko" [Truly a sweet child], *Tokyo daigaku shimbun*, July 11, 1960; Kanba Mitsuko, "Tōku hanarete shimatta hoshi" [The star that drifted far away], *Shūkan Asahi*, July 3, 1960.

64. Mitsuko also appeared at activist events alongside Kashiwazaki Chieko, a female leader in the late 1960s, considered in detail in chapter 5.

65. Kanba Mitsuko, "Hontō ni yasashii ko" [Truly a sweet child], *Tokyo daigaku shimbun*, July 11, 1960.

66. Kanba Mitsuko, "Atogaki," 263.

67. Esashi, *Kanba Michiko*, 20.

68. Kuroiwa, "Anpo kara sanjūnen," 5:114.

69. Tsurumi Kazuko, "Seinen no chi o aganau mono," 110.

70. Tsurumi Kazuko, "Seinen no chi o aganau mono," 110.

71. Zen Kyōto shuppan iinkai, *Ashioto wa tayuru toki naku*. A worker described Kanba's death as "pure" (14), a worker and two citizens describe Kanba as a "maiden" (*otome*; 50, 157, 161), and in a worker's poem Kanba is described as "white-throated" (16).

72. Zen Kyōto shuppan iinkai, *Ashioto wa tayuru toki naku*, 17.

73. Zen Kyōto shuppan iinkai, *Ashioto wa tayuru toki naku*, 50.

74. Siniawer, "Befitting Bedfellows," 112.

75. Zen Kyōto shuppan iinkai, *Ashioto wa tayuru toki naku*, 9.

76. Kanba Toshio, "Arashi no gijidō ni kieta musume," 496.

77. Marx, *The Eighteenth Brumaire of Louis Bonaparte*, 15.

78. Kanba Michiko, *Hito shirezu hohoeman*, 67.

79. Kanba Toshio, "Maegaki," 14.

80. Quoted in Kanba Mitsuko, "Atogaki," 272.

81. Ozaki Moriteru, "Kanba-san no omoide" [Memories of Kanba], *Tokyo daigaku shimbun*, July 11, 1960.

2. "MY LOVE AND REBELLION"

1. Tokoro, *Waga ai to hangyaku*, 203.

2. Tokoro, *Waga ai to hangyaku*, 151.

3. Boggs, "Revolutionary Process."

4. Kapur, *Japan at the Crossroads*.

5. Ōhara, *Tokeidai wa takakatta*; interview with Project Inoshishikai, July 9, 2011.

6. Usami, "Micchan to Baabara," 197.

7. Usami, "Micchan to Baabara" 198.

8. Usami, "Micchan to Baabara," 199.

9. Tokoro, *Waga ai to hangyaku*, 188.

10. Tokoro, *Waga ai to hangyaku*, 187.

11. Tokoro, *Waga ai to hangyaku*, 188.

12. Tokoro, *Waga ai to hangyaku*, 190.

13. Yasko, "Japanese Student Movement," 18.

14. This translation is from Guy Yasko, based on Ōta Kyōko's recollections. Yasko, "Japanese Student Movement," 19; Ōta, "Onnatachi no Zenkyōtō undō," 76.

15. Sawara, "University Struggles," 139. Yukiko Sawara offers a detailed account of the University of Tokyo Zenkyōtō movement.

16. Tokoro, *Waga ai to hangyaku*, 141–60.

17. Yasko, "Japanese Student Movement," 19.

18. Yonezu, "Mizukara no SEX o mokuteki ishikitekini hikiukeru naka kara 70 nendai o bokki suru," 172.

19. Iijima, "Josei ni totte sabetsu towa nani ka"; Shigematsu, *Scream from the Shadows*.

20. Tokoro, *Waga ai to hangyaku*, 168–77.

21. Tokoro, *Waga ai to hangyaku*, 169.

22. Tokoro, *Waga ai to hangyaku*, 170.

23. Quoted in Tomano [Tokoro], "Onna wa dō aritai ka," in Tokoro, *Waga ai to hangyaku*, 168.

24. Tokoro, *Waga ai to hangyaku*, 168.

25. Tokoro, *Waga ai to hangyaku*, 169.

26. Yoneyama, *Hiroshima Traces*, 187–210.

27. Ryang, "Love and Colonialism," 18.

28. Ryang, "Love and Colonialism," 7.

29. Ryang, "Love and Colonialism," 12.

30. Kano, *Japanese Feminist Debates*, 113–14.

31. Yoneyama, *Hiroshima Traces*, 208–10.

32. Germer, "Feminist Thought."

33. K. Tsurumi, *Social Change*, 258–59.

34. The capitalization is Tokoro's; she uses the English word *man*MAN. Tokoro, *Waga ai to hangyaku*, 117.

35. Tokoro, *Waga ai to hangyaku*, 115.

36. Tokoro, *Waga ai to hangyaku*, 116.

37. Tokoro, *Waga ai to hangyaku*, 158–59.

38. Tokoro, *Waga ai to hangyaku*, 169.

39. Tokoro, *Waga ai to hangyaku*, 34–35.

40. Tokoro, *Waga ai to hangyaku*, 42.

41. Tokoro, *Waga ai to hangyaku*, 62.

42. This was also a question for many post-1968 thinkers in France. See Blanchot, *Unavowable Community*; Nancy, *Inoperative Community*.

43. Kōuchi, "Todai tōsō no sanakani," 8.

44. Kōuchi, "Todai tōsō no sanakani" 5.

45. Tokoro, *Waga ai to hangyaku*, 41.

46. Tokoro, *Waga ai to hangyaku*, 42.

47. The focus on democratic citizens was initiated by Occupation authorities, but quickly endorsed by Japanese progressives and the militant teachers' labor union (Nikkyōsō).

48. Takeda Haruhito, *Kōdō seichō*, 35.

49. Takeda Haruhito, *Kōdō seichō*, 36.

50. Park, "'Big Business' and Education Policy," 323–24. The translations of this and the following quotations are Park's.

51. Park, "'Big Business' and Education Policy," 317.

52. Park, "'Big Business' and Education Policy," 324.

53. Park, "'Big Business' and Education Policy," 325.

54. The number increased from 200,000 (160,000 entering universities, 40,000 entering junior colleges) in 1960 to 400,000 (290,000 entering universities, 110,000 entering junior colleges) in 1965. Higher Education Bureau, Ministry of Education, Culture, Sports, Science and Technology, "Higher Education in Japan," 5.

55. Ono, "Training the Nation's Elite," 5.

56. Takeda Haruhito, *Kōdō seichō*, 166.

57. Shorrock, "Prewar Legacy," 87.

58. Kitamura, "Mass Higher Education," 67.

59. Young women made up 54 percent of junior college students in 1955. Ministry of Internal Affairs and Communications, Statistics Bureau, Director-General for Policy Planning and Statistical Research and Training Institute, "Chapter 25-11."

60. Kagawa and Kawamura, *Josei to kōtō kyōiku*.

61. Already in 1960, almost 70 percent of the junior college student population was female (67.5 percent). In the same period, junior colleges increased the number of female instructors they employed, although at a much more gradual rate. Still, the percentage increase in female faculty at junior colleges was greatest in the period 1950–1955. There was very little change between 1965 and 1990, when the percentage of female instructors hovered at a little under 40 percent. Ministry of Internal Affairs and Communications, Statistics Bureau, Director-General for Policy Planning and Statistical Research and Training Institute, "Chapter 25-11."

62. Women went from 7.7 percent of the student population in 1950 to 12.4 percent in 1955. Ministry of Internal Affairs and Communications, Statistics Bureau, Director-General for Policy Planning and Statistical Research and Training Institute, "Chapter 25-11."

63. Ministry of Internal Affairs and Communications, Statistics Bureau, Director-General for Policy Planning and Statistical Research and Training Institute, "Chapter 25-11." The percentage of female students at universities in 1970 was 18 percent. It still only hit 21.2 percent five years later.

64. Hori Hideo, "Danjo gakusei kōsai no rūru" [Social rules for male and female students], *Yomiuri shimbun*, May 26, 1959.

65. Kanba Michiko, *Hito shirezu hohoeman*, 181–82.

66. Kanba Michiko, *Hito shirezu hohoeman*, 182.

67. Kanba Michiko, *Hito shirezu hohoeman*, 183. This point was not lost on Japanese unions, either. See Christopher Gerteis on how unions in Japan in the 1950s marginalized women to a support role to guarantee "breadwinning" wages for male union members. Gerteis, *Gender Struggles*. For a theoretical argument that both mass unemployment and the impossibility of full employment of women are two of the absolute limits of capitalism, see Mészáros, *Beyond Capital*.

68. Tokoro, *Waga ai to hangyaku*, 11.

69. Uno, "Death of 'Good Wife, Wise Mother'?"

70. Kōseishō jidō kateikyoku, *Jidō fukushi sanjūnen no ayumi*, 55.

71. Buckley, "Altered States," 351.

72. See the chapter "The Housewife Debate of 1955." in Bardsley, *Women and Democracy*, 45–73.

73. Hiroko Takeda, *Political Economy*, 195.

74. Uno, "Death of 'Good Wife, Wise Mother'?," 305.

75. Ministry of Education Japan, *Educational Developments*, 24. As for the role of women as educators outside the home, in the schools, their position as hired labor was still marked by potential motherhood. The "status and conditions" of women were declared "fundamentally equal to men's," but special provisions were also granted to women teachers "as the bearers of children:": six weeks' maternity leave, breaks to nurse an infant, and menstruation leave. Ministry of Education Japan, *Educational Developments*, 6.

76. Bullock, "'Female Students Ruining the Nation.'"

77. From the mid-1950s, the Ministry of Education worked closely with the Department of Economic Planning to increase studies in science and technology. See Narita, *Systems of Higher Education*, 13–16.

78. Koyama Shizuko notes that even before this article, Teruoka had suggested in the major newspaper *Asahi shimbun* in early 1961 that the rise in female students was an "issue/problem." Koyama, *Sengo kyōiku no jendā chitsujo*, 188.

79. "Waseda kokubunka no bijin no kurasumeeto" [The beautiful Waseda literature classmate], *Shūkan shinchō*, March 5, 1962, 92.

80. Marshall, *Learning to Be Modern*, 193.

81. Tokoro, *Waga ai to hangyaku*, 178.

82. Tokoro, *Waga ai to hangyaku*, 178.

83. Tokoro, *Waga ai to hangyaku*, 177.

84. Tokoro, *Waga ai to hangyaku*, 179.

85. Quoted in Katō Katsuko et al., "Zadankai," 5:104.

86. Yamamoto Chie, "Anpo tōsō wa shuppatsu no toki," 5:120.

87. Maruyama, "Joshi gakusei taisaku shikan," 79–82.

88. Maruyama, "Joshi gakusei taisaku shikan," 82.

89. Maruyama "Joshi gakusei taisaku shikan," 82.

90. Maruyama "Joshi gakusei taisaku shikan," 82.

91. Buckley, "Altered States," 351.

92. Uno, "Death of 'Good Wife, Wise Mother'?," 306.

3. IS THE PERSONAL POLITICAL?

1. Nonpori hansen shūdan [Nonpolitical antiwar group], "Nonpori no gakuyū ni uttaeru" [Appeal to nonpolitical school friends], July 2, 1968, Todai tōsō shiryo shū [University of Tokyo struggle collection], National Diet Library, Tokyo.

2. Lefebvre, *Critique of Everyday Life*; Tosaka, *Tosaka Jun zenshū dai 4 kan*; Bronson, *One Hundred Million Philosophers*.

3. Unoda et al., *"Saakuru jidai" o yomu*; Marotti, *Money, Trains, and Guillotines*.

4. Ando, *Japan's New Left Movements*, 11.

5. Havens, *Fire across the Sea*, 18.

6. For example, Kishi Nobusuke, who had been prime minister during the forced revision of the U.S.-Japan Security Treaty, had been a member of the wartime Tōjō Cabinet.

7. Oguma, *1968 (jō)*; 10.8 Yamazaki Hiroaki Project, *Katsute 10.8 Haneda tōsō ga atta*, 8.

8. 10.8 Yamazaki Hiroaki Project, *Katsute 10.8 Haneda tōsō ga atta*, 18.

9. Zen nihon igakusei rengō chūō shikkō iinkai [Central executive committee of the national medical student union], "Yamazaki Hiroaki-kun gyakusatsu kōgi!" [In protest against the murder of Yamazaki Hiroaki!], October 1967, Todai tōsō shiryo shū [University of Tokyo struggle collection].

10. Ōhara, *Tokeidai wa takakatta*, 10–11. Other accounts of the influence of Yamazaki's death include Murakami, "Jiko hitei wa tsurai iyashi michi e," 110; Katō Mitsuko, "Tōdai zenkyōtō no naka de," 27.

11. Kashiwazaki, *Taiyō to arashi to jiyū o*, 92–93.

12. As William Marotti notes in his study of artist activists in the 1960s, it was a marker of the "paradigmatic activist experience during the global moment of the 1960s" that daily life felt "bound up with issues of political protest and violence, law and the Constitution, state authority and legitimacy, the cold war, American hegemony, neoimperialism, and Fordist capitalism." Marotti, *Money, Trains, and Guillotines*, 3.

13. Yoshihara, "Tōsō no seishun ni ikite," 114–15.

14. Aoyama, "Erosu no hangyaku," 180.

15. Havens, *Fire across the Sea*, 188. For more on how Japan was a key beneficiary of U.S. policies to keep Southeast Asian markets "free" and open to Japanese imports, see pp. 84–106.

16. Yamamoto Yoshitaka, *Chisei no hanran*, 83.

17. Yamamoto Yoshitaka, *Chisei no hanran*, 84–85.

18. Yamamoto Yoshitaka, *Chisei no hanran*, 94.

19. Yamamoto Yoshitaka, *Chisei no hanran*, 92.

20. Sawara, "University Struggles," 139. Yukiko Sawara offers a detailed account of the University of Tokyo Zenkyōtō movement.

21. Sawara, "University Struggles," 140–41.

22. Kosugi Ryōko describes some of the issues facing a historian when trying to portray the diversity of the student movement in the 1960s in Japan. Kosugi, "Nihon no 1960-nendai gakusei undō ni okeru tagensei."

23. Nagai, *Nihon no daigaku*, 4.

24. Eades, Goodman, and Hada, *"Big Bang" in Japanese Higher Education*, 86.

25. Takeda Haruhito, *Kōdō seichō*.

26. "A Statement on the Current Difficulties at the University of California Study Center, Mitaka-Tokyo, Japan," November 10, 1969, box 22, folder 22, Hans H. Baerwald Papers, 1945–1991, University of California, Los Angeles, Library Special Collections.

27. Sawara, "University Struggles," 138.

28. Takazawa, Takagi, and Kurata, *Shinsayoku nijūnenshi*, 117.

29. Sawara, "University Struggles," 165.

30. Hoshino Chieko, a student at Hosei University, noted in retrospect that most university Zenkyōtō were not truly nonsectarian, as she understood those at the University of Tokyo and at Nihon University to be. Hoshino, "Kamonegi shôjo no sanjû nen," 90.

31. Sawara, "University Struggles," 165.

32. Kashiwazaki, *Taiyō to arashi to jiyū o*, 96–97.

33. Kida, "Nichidai kōka wo utainagara misakishō wo yuragasu demotai," 91.

34. Tarōra Jōji (former Nihon University student activist), interview with author, August 27, 2011.

35. Kida, "Nichidai kōka wo utainagara misakishō wo yuragasu demotai," 94.

36. Takazawa, Takagi, and Kurata, *Shinsayoku nijūnenshi*, 114.

37. Quoted in Takazawa, Takagi, and Kurata, *Shinsayoku nijūnenshi*, 114.

38. Sawara, "University Struggles," 158.

39. Kida, "Nichidai kōka wo utainagara misakishō wo yuragasu demotai," 92–93.

40. Takazawa, Takagi, and Kurata, *Shinsayoku nijūnenshi*, 118–22.

41. Nonpori hansen shūdan, "Nonpori no gakuyū ni uttaeru."

42. Marotti, "Japan 1968," 98.

43. Ōhara, *Tokeidai wa takakatta*, 72.

44. "Kō, kenchiku jishu karikyuramu (3nen)" [Request: Architecture self-directed curriculum (3rd year)], July 5, 1968, Todai tōsō shiryo shū [University of Tokyo struggle collection]; Tō C zengaku tōsō iinkai [University of Tokyo C All-Campus Struggle Commission], "Jishu kōza kara warera no te ni naru aratana daigaku no sōzō wo" [Imagining a new university ourselves through self-directed courses], July 10, 1968, Todai tōsō shiryo shū [University of Tokyo struggle collection].

45. "Gakuyū no minasan! Tachi noborō! Tento mura ni sanka shiyō!" [To all school comrades! Stand up! Get involved in the tent village!], July 1968, Todai tōsō shiryo shū [University of Tokyo struggle collection].

46. "Tokeidai jishu zemi: Kayō kōza 7-gatsu 30-nichi pm 4-ji" [Clock tower self-directed seminar: Tuesday course July 30th, 4pm], July 26, 1968, vol. 4, Todai tōsō shiryo shū [University of Tokyo struggle collection].

47. "Tokeidai jishu zemi."

48. Ōhara, *Tokeidai wa takakatta*, 13–16.

49. Ōhara, *Tokeidai wa takakatta*, 98–99.

50. Ōhara, *Tokeidai wa takakatta*, 101–3.

51. Project Inoshishikai. Interview with author, July 9, 2011. For more on Sanpa Zengakuren, see Ando, *Japan's New Left Movements*, 54.

52. As Francesca Polletta argues, participatory democracy can be an effective strategy for groups, not just an inherently temporary and inefficient political experiment. Polletta, *Freedom Is an Endless Meeting*.

53. Tokuyama, "Watashi ga ugokeba yo no naka ga hitori bun ugoku to iu jikkan," 85.

54. Shigenobu, *Nihon sekigun shishi*, 20–22.

55. Yonezu, "Barikeedo wo kugutte," 121.

56. Katō Mitsuko, "Tōdai zenkyōtō no naka de," 54.

57. Katō Mitsuko, "Tōdai zenkyōtō no naka de," 51.

58. Kuwabara, "Watashi wa nigerarenai," 90.

59. Kuwabara, "Watashi wa nigerarenai," 91.

60. Katō Mitsuko, "Tōdai zenkyōtō no naka de," 52.

61. Mihashi Toshiaki. Interview with author. August 27, 2011.

62. Tokuyama, "Watashi ga ugokeba yo no naka ga hitori bun ugoku to iu jikkan," 88; Ōhara, *Tokeidai wa takakatta*.

63. This gendered labor, symbolized by the rice ball, was not necessarily new: Shima Hiroko, the wife of 1960 Bund leader Shima Shigeo, wrote retrospectively about her experiences as a "rice ball [*onigiri*] wife" involved behind the scenes of the "mainly male" Bund. Shima Hiroko, "Onigiri nyōbō."

64. Mori, "'Otoko narabi onna' kara ribu e," 166.

65. Inamura, "Nagare nagarete," 105.

66. Katō Mitsuko, "Tōdai zenkyōtō no naka de," 29.

67. Adam Bronson writes at length about the German idealist thought that shaped many understandings of what constituted culture and education among an influential segment of intellectual elites in Japan. Bronson, *One Hundred Million Philosophers*, 21–47.

68. The Gewalt staves were apparently originally employed in sectarian battles and only later came to be used in clashes with the police. Marotti, "Japan 1968," 103n19. I discuss how Gewalt figured into the masculinist culture of the New Left in chapter 4.

69. Katō Mitsuko, "Tōdai zenkyōtō no naka de," 43.

70. Ōhara, *Tokeidai wa takakatta*, 143–45.

71. Sakai, "Onna to iu mainoriti o mitsukete," 101.

72. Murakami, "Jiko hitei wa tsurai iyashi michi e," 112.

73. Horie, "'Joshi daisei' 'nyūkan tōsō,'" 118.

74. Banba, "Zenkyōtō undō no toppakō toshite no 'seisaken' sōsetsu," 115.

75. Ōta, "Onnatachi no Zenkyōtō undō," 78.

76. Katō Mitsuko describes such a meeting in March 1969 at the University of Tokyo. Katō Mitsuko, "Tōdai zenkyōtō no naka de," 21–22.

77. See the excellent collected writings of various women's liberation groups in Miki, Mizonoguchi, and Saeki, *Shiryō ūman ribu shi I*; Mizonoguchi, Saeki, and Miki, *Shiryō ūman ribu shi II*. For an English analysis, see Shigematsu, *Scream from the Shadows*.

78. Imai, "Bunto to feminizum."

79. Shima Hiroko, "Onigiri nyōbō," 222–23.

80. Kanō and Kanō, *Omae no 1960-nendai o, shinu mae ni shabettoke*; Mihashi, *Rojō no Zenkyōtō 1968*; Takahashi, *Tsuwamono-domo ga yume no saki*; Onnatachi no ima o tō kai, *Zenkyōtō kara ribu e*.

81. Kondō Keiko. Interview with author, May 10, 2013.

4. "WHEN YOU FUCK A VANGUARD GIRL . . . "

1. Toritsudai Zenkyōtō yajiuma gundan, *Tōsei gakusei undō zareutashū*, 20. The song's lyrics seem like a play on the lyrics of a song also featured in director Ōshima Nagisa's 1967 film *Sing a Song of Sex* (*Nihon shunka kō*). On the general popularity of the parody song, see Dorsey, "Breaking Records," 99.

2. Mizonoguchi, Saeki, and Miki, *Shiryō ūman ribu shi I*; Onnatachi no ima o tō kai, *Zenkyōtō kara ribu e*; Shigematsu, *Scream from the Shadows*.

3. Katō Mitsuko, "Tōdai zenkyōtō no naka de," 45.

4. Quoted in Okamoto and Murao, *Daigaku gerira no uta*, 112.

5. Quoted in Okamoto and Murao, *Daigaku gerira no uta*, 115

6. Nihon daigaku bunri gakubu tōsō iinkai shokikyoku, *Hangyaku no barikeedo*, 115.

7. Okamoto and Murao, *Daigaku gerira no uta*, 114.

8. Tokuyama, "Watashi ga ugokeba yo no naka ga hitori bun ugoku to iu jikkan," 87–88.

9. Osamu Hashimoto, 19th Tokyo University Komaba Festival Poster, 1968, in Konno Tetsuo, "Hashimoto Osamu wa 'atama' yori saki ni 'karada' ga aru hito datta."

10. Shima Taizō, *Yasuda kōdō, 1968–1969*, 146–47; Inuhiko, *Hai skuuru 1968*, 65.

11. Kanayama and Gurupu 69, *Zenkyōtō imajineishon*, 23; Katō Tokiko, "Hito ga kokoro ni omou koto," 115.

12. Aoyama, "Erosu no hangyaku," 198–99.

13. Tanaka Mitsu, "Benjō kara no kaihō," 59.

14. The Japanese expression using the transliterated English word *lynch* refers to any kind of beating inflicted as punishment.

15. Oguma, *1968 (ge)*, 685.

16. Oguma, *1968 (ge)*, 686.

17. Ōshima, "Sexual Poverty," 240.

18. Furuhata, *Cinema of Actuality*, 94.

19. Quoted in McKnight, "At the Source (Code)," 273.

20. Yonezu, "Mizukara no SEX o mokuteki ishikitekini hikiukeru naka kara 70 nendai o bokki suru," 170.

21. Shigematsu, *Scream from the Shadows*, 66–67.

22. Okazawa Sumie, "Zengakuren dai-30 kai teiki zenkoku taikai de no sei no sabetsu = haigaishugi to tatakau katsui hyōmei," 105.

23. Mishima, Todai zengaku kyōtō kaigi, and Komaba kyōtō funsai iinkai, *Tōron Mishima Yukio vs. Todai Zenkyōtō*.

24. Mishima, Todai zengaku kyōtō kaigi, and Komaba kyōtō funsai iinkai, *Tōron Mishima Yukio vs. Todai Zenkyōtō*, 7–12.

25. Kosaka, *Shisō toshite no Zenkyōtō sedai*, 107. Members of Mishima's Shield Society actually slipped into the auditorium just in case Mishima needed protection from the "violent" students of the Zenkyōtō. Hosaka, *Yūkoku no ronri*.

26. One such case was the eight-day confinement of Professor Hayashi Kentarō at the University of Tokyo by the Faculty of Literature Zenkyōtō, from November 4 to November 12, 1968.

27. Mishima, Todai zengaku kyōtō kaigi, and Komaba kyōtō funsai iinkai, *Tōron Mishima Yukio vs. Todai Zenkyōtō*, 19.

28. Mishima, Todai zengaku kyōtō kaigi, and Komaba kyōtō funsai iinkai, *Tōron Mishima Yukio vs. Todai Zenkyōtō*, 15–17.

29. Mishima, "Tōdai o dōbutsuen ni shiro."

30. Inose and Sato, *Persona*, 488. Actor Mifune Toshirō took second place, and Ishihara Shintarō took fourth. Mushiake Aromu gleefully commented, "Yukio Mishima has said 'I don't want to be a dandy, and I don't think I am one either.' But he got the highest vote. This is ironic. This is exciting." Quoted in Inoue and Sato, *Persona*, 488.

31. Inose and Sato, *Persona*, 314.

32. Guy Yasko locates the Mishima-versus-Zenkyōtō debate at a "turning point in Japanese intellectual history in that left and right had begun to converge." Both the Left and the Right challenged postwar rationalism in particular, and Yasko marks the debate as an opportunity for the Zenkyōtō to articulate how it differed from the romantic Right, as represented by Mishima. Yasko, "Japanese Student Movement," 157.

33. Inose and Sato, *Persona*, 619.

34. Quoted in Inose and Sato, *Persona*, 493.

35. Mishima, "Tōdai o dōbutsuen ni shiro," 2:664–65.

36. Tōdai 1.18, 19 Tōsō saiban bōtō chinjutsusho [Opening statements for the University of Tokyo January 18, 19 struggle trial], n.d., folder 68, Takazawa Collection, University of Hawai'i at Mānoa Library.

37. Shima Taizō, *Yasuda kōdō*, 178–80.

38. Inose and Sato, *Persona*, 590.

39. Mishima, Todai zengaku kyōtō kaigi, and Komaba kyōtō funsai iinkai, *Tōron Mishima Yukio vs. Todai Zenkyōtō*, 90–93.

40. Mishima, Todai zengaku kyōtō kaigi, and Komaba kyōtō funsai iinkai, *Tōron Mishima Yukio vs. Todai Zenkyōtō*, 21–22.

41. *Constitution of Japan*. Chapter II, Article 9.

42. Quoted in Inose and Sato, *Persona*, 536.

43. Yamada, "Ronsō."

44. Yamada, "Ronsō," 140.

45. Okamoto and Murao, "Haha o koeyo," 88–89.

46. Okamoto and Murao, "Haha o koeyo," 87.

47. Ōhara, *Tokeidai wa takakatta*, 157.

48. Ōsawa, "Barikeedo no naka no <haha - watashi>," 304.

49. Takahashi, *Tsuwamono-domo ga yume no saki*, 58.

50. Terayama, "Kibō to iu byōki," 4:480.

51. Terayama, "Kibō to iu byōki," 4:480.

52. Terayama, "Kibō to iu byōki," 4:478–79.

53. Inose and Sato, *Persona*, 622–23.

54. Yasko, "Japanese Student Movement," 157.

55. K. Tsurumi, "Some Comments," 109.

56. Kanayama and Gurupu 69, *Zenkyōtō imajineishon*, 22.

57. Escobar, "Dialectics of Repression."

58. Langland, *Speaking of Flowers*, 109.

59. Meinhof, "Water Cannons," 215–19.

60. Yamamoto Kiyokatsu, *Mishima Yukio*, 134.

61. Yamamoto Kiyokatsu, *Mishima Yukio*, 134.

62. Ōhara, *Tokeidai wa takakatta*, 123–25.

63. Inose and Sato, *Persona*, 541–42.

64. Inose and Sato, *Persona*, 585–90.

65. Yamamoto Kiyokatsu, *Mishima Yukio*, 136.

66. Marotti, "Japan 1968," 130.

67. Quoted in Marotti, "Japan 1968," 134.

68. Ōhara, *Tokeidai wa takakatta*, 136.

69. Ministry of Justice, "Shōwa 52-nen han hanzai hakusho."

70. For a narrative account of the rivalry in English, see Andrews, *Dissenting Japan*, 148–59.

71. Tachibana, *Chūkaku vs. Kakumaru*, 160.

72. However, 52.9 percent responded that they left for "other reasons," which makes it difficult to make an overarching statement about why young people abandoned activism. Zenkyōtō hakusho henshū iinkai, *Zenkyōtō hakusho*, 413.

73. Ōtsuka, *"Kanojotachi" no rengō sekigun*.

74. Steinhoff, "Death by Defeatism," 199.

75. Nagata, *Jūroku no bohyō*, 2:128.

76. Steinhoff, "Three Women Who Loved the Left."

77. Nagata, *Hyōkai*, 65.

78. Igarashi, "Dead Bodies and Living Guns," 134.

79. Ōizumi, *Asama Sansō jūgekisen no shinsō*, 2:100.

80. Shigematsu, *Scream from the Shadows*, 142.

81. Kanō Akihiro (former University of Tokyo activist), interview with author, July 28, 2011.

82. Ando, *Japan's New Left Movements*, 87.

83. Ando, *Japan's New Left Movements*, 95.

84. Bayley, *Forces of Order*, 86.

85. Ando, *Japan's New Left Movements*, 108.

86. Tsuchiya, "Jii undō sono ta taishū kōdō no shochi," 24.

87. Ando, *Japan's New Left Movements*, 89.

88. Ministry of Justice, "Shōwa 50-nen han hanzai hakusho."

89. Ando, *Japan's New Left Movements*, 95–96.

90. Caute, *Sixty-Eight*, 234.

91. Piercy, "Grand Coolie Damn."

5. "GEWALT ROSAS"

1. Sassa, *Tōdai rakujō*, 10–11.

2. Suzuki, *Ganbare!! Shinsayoku*.

3. Sassa, *Tōdai rakujō*, 10–11.

4. Ishiyama, "Japan."

5. Silverberg, *Erotic Grotesque Nonsense*, 57.

6. Sawara, "University Struggles," 162–63.

7. "'Hōdō no jiyū' de mokuhi ken assatsu" [Crushing the right to remain silent with "freedom of information"], *Shingeki*, May 14, 1969.

8. "'Mokuhi shimasu' itten bari" [Single-mindedly "I remain silent"], *Yūkan fuji*, March 12, 1969.

9. "Uwa! Geba geba josei" [Whoa! Gewalt women], *Yangu redi*, April 21, 1969.

10. "Doro numa ureu shufu gakusei" [Housewife student concerned about a quagmire], *Yūkan fuji*, May 1, 1969.

11. Kikuyabashi 101, letter 1, n.d., in Gokuchū shokan hakkan iinkai, *Tōdai tōsō gokuchū shokanshū*, 14.

12. Kikuyabashi 101, letter 2, March 11, 1969, in Gokuchū shokan hakkan iinkai, *Tōdai tōsō gokuchū shokanshū*, 15.

13. Quoted in Fröhlick, *Rosa Luxemburg*, 130.

14. Kashiwazaki, *Taiyō to arashi to jiyū o*, 117–18.

15. Kashiwazaki, *Taiyō to arashi to jiyū o*, 84–88.

16. *Yomiuri shimbun*, July 15, 1969.

17. "Tōdai gebaruto" [University of Tokyo Gewalt] *Yomiuri shimbun*, July 11, 1969.

18. Kashiwazaki, *Taiyō to arashi to jiyū o*, 268–69.

19. Kashiwazaki, *Taiyō to arashi to jiyū o*, 249.

20. Kashiwazaki, *Taiyō to arashi to jiyū o*, 268–69.

21. Kashiwazaki, *Taiyō to arashi to jiyū o*, 207–10.

22. Katō Mitsuko, "Tōdai zenkyōtō no naka de," 42–43.

23. Kashiwazaki, *Taiyō to arashi to jiyū o*, 80.

24. Kashiwazaki, *Taiyō to arashi to jiyū o*, 72.

25. Kashiwazaki, *Taiyō to arashi to jiyū o*, 64–68.

26. "Yomiuri sunpyō" [Yomiuri brief review], *Yomiuri shimbun*, March 23, 1969.

27. Thorsten, "A Few Bad Women."

28. Kashiwazaki, *Taiyō to arashi to jiyū o*, 333–34.

29. "Kono atsukute nagai natsu yasumi" [This hot and long summer vacation], *Shūkan yomiuri*, August 8, 1969.

30. "Akatsuki no teire to hachinin no joshigakusei" [Crackdown at dawn and eight co-eds], *Shūkan shinchō*, May 11, 1968.

31. Harada, *Aru keisatsukan no shōwa sesō shi*, 145–46.

32. "'Zengakuren' joshigakusei no senpai kōhai" ["Zengakuren" coeds, senior and junior], *Shūkan shinchō*, June 18, 1966.

33. Quoted in "Akatsuki no teire to hachinin no joshigakusei."

34. "'Zengakuren' kago danjo gakusei wa nani wo shiteiru?" [What are male and female students doing in the "Zengakuren" cage?], *Shūkan pureibōi*, August 20, 1968.

35. "Akatsuki no teire to hachinin no joshigakusei."

36. "'Zengakuren' kago danjo gakusei wa nani wo shiteiru?"

37. Umezawa Tadashi (former Hosei University student activist), interview with author, July 25, 2011.

38. Shirakawa, "Watashi wa 'tataku zenkōren' no shōjo riidaa."

39. Although the magazine's name suggested female autonomy (meaning, roughly, "Woman herself"), the editorial staff featured male leadership.

40. "Sasebo e itta shachō reijō Shinoda Reiko-san no baai" [The case of Shinoda Reiko, the CEO's daughter who went to Sasebo], *Josei jishin*, January 29, 1968, 26–29.

41. "Funsō no nai joshidai wa koko!" [Here are women's colleges without campus disputes!], *Josei jishin*, December 23, 1968.

42. The illustrator of *The First Morning*, Satō Masa'aki, went on to publish an eighteen-volume manga in the 1980s, *Bōkō* [Rape].

43. Satō Masa'aki, *Hajimete no asa* [The first morning], *Josei jishin*, November 18, 25, December 2, 9, 1968.

44. In this case, *comfort* indicates the same kind of sexual access expected by male soldiers during wartime in Japan at "comfort stations" that institutionalized sexual slavery to "comfort" male troops. Argibay, "Sexual Slavery."

45. Mackie, "Picturing Political Space."

46. Silverberg, *Erotic Grotesque Nonsense*, 51.

47. The *neechan* in *Kareji Neechan* could be translated as "girl," but in light of student activists' casual practice of calling young women "sister" in the anglophone world in the same period, I translate *neechan* as "sister."

48. Gebako declared her silence under arrest in a strip on November 11, 1968, while Kyanko did so a year later, on November 28, 1969. Both these strips most likely responded to the rash of student arrests in the October 21 Antiwar Day demonstrations of both 1968 and 1969. Both names are not actually existing women's names in Japanese. *Gebako* uses the term *geba* from *Gewalt*, and the *kyan* in *Kyanko* means "tomboy."

49. "Gebabō kara shūshoku e no dōtei" [The journey from Gewalt stave to employment], *Asahi jaanaru*, April 6, 1969.

50. Santa Puro and Satō Sanpei, "Warera sarariiman tō" [We, the salaryman faction], *Yūkan fuji*, March 7, 1969.

51. As E. Ann Kaplan noted in the case of cinema in the United States in the 1970s and early 1980s, "as a result of the recent women's movement, women have been permitted in representation to assume (step into) the position defined as masculine, as long as the man then steps into *her* position, so as to keep the whole structure intact." Kaplan, "Is the Gaze Male?" 29.

52. Ehara, "Politics of Teasing."

53. Ueno, "Forty Years of Japanese Feminism."

54. "Bōya, oboeteoide: Mama wa mukashi 'Gebaruto Rōza' to iu sugoi onna deshita" [My child, remember: Mama was once an incredible "Gewalt Rosa" woman], *Yangu leedi*, July 5, 1971.

55. Komatsu, "Zenkyōtō joshigakusei hatachi no shi," 120.

56. Quoted in Komatsu, "Zenkyōtō joshigakusei hatachi no shi," 123.

57. Steinhoff, "Three Women Who Loved the Left," 311.

58. Director Wakamatsu Kōji's 2007 film *United Red Army* (*Rengō sekigun*), replicates this dynamic. Wakamatsu, famous for his leftist convictions and vast directorial experience in soft-core pornography, portrays Nagata as a particularly brutal villainess fit for a horror film.

59. Quoted in Shigematsu, *Scream from the Shadows*, 145.

60. Judy Klemesrud, "A Criminologist's View of Women Terrorists," *New York Times*, January 9, 1978.

61. Mark Frankland, "The Lady Terrorist in White Gloves," *Observer* (London), February 10, 1974.

62. Sam Jameson, "Woman Leader Tells Ritual," *Los Angeles Times*, August 9, 1975.

63. Yamaguchi Yoshiko became famous as a star of Manchuria Film Productions as Li Xianglan (Ri Kōran) and had performed in the United States as Shirley Yamaguchi before she embarked on her career as a television journalist. "Shigenobu Fusako: Nikkōki haijakku no shinsō kataru" [Shigenobu Fusako: Telling the truth of the Japan Airlines flight hijacking], *3-ji no anata*, Fuji terebi, August 14, 1973.

64. Shigenobu, *Waga ai waga kakumei*.

65. For more on the complicated reception of URA violence by women's lib activists, see Shigematsu, *Scream from the Shadows*, in particular chapter 5, "*Ribu's* Response to the United Red Army."

66. Ueno, *Onna tachi no sabaibaru sakusen*, 126.

67. Iwao, *Japanese Woman*, 15.

68. Shigematsu, *Scream from the Shadows*, 149.

69. Dales, *Feminist Movements in Contemporary Japan*, 61.

70. Kiyoaki Murata, "Liberate Whom? Women's Lib Movement Unlikely to Take Roots in Japan," *Japan Times*, February 5, 1971.

CONCLUSION

1. Butler, Gambetti, and Sabsay, "Introduction," 2.

2. Shigematsu, *Scream from the Shadows*.

3. Butler, Gambetti, and Sabsay, "Introduction," 4.

4. Steinhoff, "Memories of New Left Protest," 127.

5. Yamamoto Yoshitaka quoted in Katō and Yamanaka, "Kyūen Renraku Sentaa no gojū nen," 143.

6. Murakami, "Jiko hitei wa tsurai iyashi michi e," 111–12.

7. Iwao, *Japanese Woman*, 2.

8. Quoted in Springer, *Living for the Revolution*, 1.

9. Onnatachi no ima o tō kai, *Zenkyōtō kara ribu e*; Mizonoguchi, Saeki, and Miki, *Shiryō ūman ribu shi I*.

10. Ueno, "Hitori ni naru koto."

11. Itō, *Danseigaku nyūmon*, 342–57.

12. "Watashi wa reisei, anshin shite" [I am calm and at peace], *Tokyo shimbun*, November 13, 2014.

13. Fukuda, "Tokubetsu intabyū."

14. Kinsella, *Schoolgirls, Money and Rebellion*.

15. Yoda, "Rise and Fall of Maternal Society," 866.

16. Sasaki-Uemura, *Organizing the Spontaneous*, 114.

17. Schieder, "Blood Ties"; Schieder, "Womenomics vs. Women."

18. World Economic Forum, "Global Gender Gap Report 2020," 9.

19. Tiqqun (Collective), *Preliminary Materials*, 15.

20. Ōtsuka, *Shōjo minzokugaku*.

21. Power, "She's Just Not That into You."

22. Tomorrow Girls Troop website, accessed July 27, 2019, https://tomorrowgirlstroop .com/.

23. Midori and Myeongsoon, interview with author, July 10, 2019.

24. Tokoro, *Waga ai to hangyaku*, 159.

BIBLIOGRAPHY

MANUSCRIPT COLLECTIONS

Baerwald, Hans H., Papers, 1945–1991. University of California, Los Angeles, Library Special Collections.

Masaki Motoi Collection of Japanese Student Movement Materials, 1959–2003. David M. Rubenstein Rare Book and Manuscript Library, Duke University, Durham, North Carolina.

Takazawa Collection. University of Hawai'i at Mānoa Library.

Todai tōsō shiryo shū [University of Tokyo struggle collection]. National Diet Library, Tokyo, Japan.

INTERVIEWS

All interviews conducted by the author in Tokyo.

Bund Study Group, February 10, 2015.

Project Inoshishikai, July 9, 2011.

Kanō Akihiro, July 28, 2011.

Kondō Keiko, May 10, 2013.

Midori and Myeongsoon (founders of Tomorrow Girls Troop), July 10, 2019.

Mihashi Toshiaki, August 27, 2011.

Tarōra Jōji, August 27, 2011.

Umezawa Tadashi, July 25, 2011.

OTHER SOURCES

Ando, Takemasa. *Japan's New Left Movements: Legacies for Civil Society*. New York: Routledge, 2013.

Andrews, William. *Dissenting Japan: A History of Japanese Radicalism and Counterculture, from 1945 to Fukushima*. London: Hurst, 2016.

Aoyama Michiko. "Erosu no hangyaku" [The revolt of eros]. In Yoshihara et al., *Joshi Zengakuren gonin no shuki*, 163–206.

Argibay, Carmen M. "Sexual Slavery and the Comfort Women of World War II." *Berkeley Journal of International Law* 21, no. 1 (2003): 375–89.

Arruzza, Cinzia. *Dangerous Liaisons: The Marriages and Divorces of Marxism and Feminism*. Translated by Penelope Duggan. Ponty-pool, UK: Merlin, 2013.

Avenell, Simon. *Making Japanese Citizens: Civil Society and the Mythology of the Shimin in Postwar Japan*. Berkeley: University of California Press, 2010.

Banba Tomoko. "Zenkyōtō undō no toppakō toshite no 'seisaken' sōsetsu" [The Zenkyōtō movement as a breakthrough for the foundation of "research on sexism"]. In Onnatachi no ima o tō kai, *Zenkyōtō kara ribu e*, 113–19.

Bardsley, Jan. *Women and Democracy in Cold War Japan*. SOAS Studies in Modern and Contemporary Japan. London: Bloomsbury, 2014.

Bayley, David H. *Forces of Order: Police Behavior in Japan and the U.S.* New ed. Berkeley: University of California Press, 1978.

Blanchot, Maurice. *The Unavowable Community*. Translated by Jeffrey Mehlman. Barrytown, NY: Station Hill, 1988.

Boggs, Carl, Jr. "Revolutionary Process, Political Strategy, and the Dilemma of Power." *Theory and Society* 4, no. 3 (September 1977): 359–93.

Breines, Wini. *Community and Organization in the New Left*. New Brunswick, NJ: Rutgers University Press, 1989.

Bronson, Adam. *One Hundred Million Philosophers: Science of Thought and the Culture of Democracy in Postwar Japan*. Honolulu: University of Hawai'i Press, 2016.

Buckley, Sandra. "Altered States: The Body Politics of 'Being-Woman.'" In Gordon, *Postwar Japan as History*, 347–72.

Bullock, Julia C. "'Female Students Ruining the Nation': The Debate over Coeducation in Postwar Japan." *U.S.-Japan Women's Journal*, no. 46 (2014): 3–23.

Bungei shunjū. "*Bungei shunjū*" ni miru shōwa shi [Shōwa history as seen by "Bungei shunjū"]. 4 vols. Tokyo: Bungei shunjū, 1988.

Butler, Judith, Zeynep Gambetti, and Letizia Sabsay. Introduction to *Vulnerability in Resistance,* edited by Judith Butler, Zeynep Gambette, and Letizia Sabsay, 1–11. Durham, NC: Duke University Press, 2016.

Caute, David. *Sixty-Eight: The Year of the Barricades*. London: Hamilton, 1988.

Cohen, Deborah, and Lessie Jo Frazier. "Talking Back to '68: Gendered Narratives, Participatory Spaces, and Political Cultures." In *Gender and Sexuality in 1968: Transformative Politics in the Cultural Imagination,* edited by Deborah Cohen and Lessie Jo Frazier, 145–72. New York: Palgrave Macmillan, 2009.

Constitution of Japan. November 3, 1946. Accessed June 1, 2020. https://www.refworld.org/docid/3ae6b4ee38.html.

Dales, Laura. *Feminist Movements in Contemporary Japan*. London: Routledge, 2009.

Dorsey, James. "Breaking Records: Media Censorship, and the Folk Song Movement of Japan's 1960s." In *Asian Popular Culture: New, Hybrid, and Alternate Media*, edited by John A. Lent. 79–108. Lanham, MD: Lexington Books, 2013.

Dowsey, Stuart J., ed. *Zengakuren: Japan's Revolutionary Students.* Berkeley, CA: Ishi, 1970.

Draper, Susana. *1968 Mexico: Constellations of Freedom and Democracy.* Durham, NC: Duke University Press, 2018.

Eades, Jeremy Seymour, Roger Goodman, and Yumiko Hada, eds. *The "Big Bang" in Japanese Higher Education: The 2004 Reforms and the Dynamics of Change.* Melbourne, Australia: Trans Pacific Press, 2005.

Ehara, Yumiko. "The Politics of Teasing." In *Contemporary Japanese Thought,* edited by Richard F. Calichman, 43–70. New York: Columbia University Press, 2005.

Esashi Akiko. *Kanba Michiko: Seishōjo densetsu* [Kanba Michiko: The legend of a sacred maiden]. Tokyo: Bungei shunjū, 2010.

Escobar, Edward J. "The Dialectics of Repression: The Los Angeles Police Department and the Chicano Movement, 1968–1971." *Journal of American History* 79, no. 4 (March 1993): 1483–1514.

Evans, Sara M. "Sons, Daughters, and Patriarchy: Gender and the 1968 Generation." *American Historical Review* 114, no. 2 (2009): 331–47.

Freeman, Jo. *The Politics of Women's Liberation: A Case Study of an Emerging Social Movement and Its Relation to the Policy Process.* Philadelphia: David McKay, 1975.

Fröhlick, Paul. *Rosa Luxemburg: Ideas in Action.* London: Pluto, 1972.

Fukuda Wakako. "Tokubetsu intabyū: SEALDs menbaa Fukuda Wakako-san intabyū" [Special interview: Interview with SEALDs member Fukuda Wakako]. *Daily AJWRC* (blog), Asia-Japan Women's Resource Center, February 29, 2016. http:// ajwrc.blog102.fc2.com/blog-entry-1034.html.

Furuhata, Yuriko. *Cinema of Actuality: Japanese Avant-Garde Filmmaking in the Season of Image Politics.* Durham, NC: Duke University Press, 2013.

Garon, Sheldon. *Managing Japanese Minds: The State in Everyday Life.* Princeton, NJ: Princeton University Press, 1997.

Garon, Sheldon. "Women's Groups and the Japanese State: Contending Approaches to Political Integration, 1890–1945." *Journal of Japanese Studies* 19, no. 1 (1993): 5–41.

Germer, Andrea. "Feminist Thought and Women's History in Japan: The Case of Takamure Itsue." In *Historical Consciousness, Historiography, and Modern Japanese Values,* edited by J. Baxter, 247–61. Kyoto: International Research Center for Japanese Studies, 2006.

Gerteis, Christopher. *Gender Struggles: Wage-Earning Women and Male-Dominated Unions in Postwar Japan.* Cambridge, MA: Harvard University Asia Center, 2010.

Gluck, Carol. "The 'End' of the Postwar: Japan at the Turn of the Millennium." *Public Culture* 10, no. 1 (1997): 1–23.

Gokuchū shokan hakkan iinkai [Prison letters publishing committee]. *Tōdai tōsō gokuchū shokanshū* [The collected prison letters of the University of Tokyo struggle]. Vol. 1. 7 vols. Tokyo: San'ichi shobō, 1969.

Gordon, Andrew, ed. *Postwar Japan as History.* Berkeley: University of California Press, 1993.

Gordon, Andrew. *The Wages of Affluence: Labor and Management in Postwar Japan.* Cambridge, MA: Harvard University Press, 1998.

Haaland, Bonnie. *Emma Goldman: Sexuality and the Impurity of the State.* Montreal: Black Rose Books, 1993.

Hane, Mikiso. *Peasants, Rebels, Women, and Outcastes: The Underside of Modern Japan.* Lanham, MD: Rowman and Littlefield, 2003.

Hane, Mikiso. *Reflections on the Way to the Gallows: Rebel Women in Prewar Japan.* Berkeley: University of California Press, 1988.

Harada Hiroshi. *Aru keisatsukan no shōwa sesō shi* [One policeman's history of Shōwa society]. Tokyo: Soshisha, 2011.

Havens, Thomas. *Fire across the Sea: The Vietnam War and Japan, 1965–1975.* Princeton, NJ: Princeton University Press, 1987.

Higher Education Bureau, Ministry of Education, Culture, Sports, Science and Technology. "Higher Education in Japan." 2012. Accessed May 1, 2017. https://www .mext.go.jp/en/policy/education/highered/title03/detail03/__icsFiles/afieldfile /2012/06/19/1302653_1.pdf.

Hirakawa, Hiroko. "Maiden Martyr for 'New Japan': The 1960 Ampo and the Rhetoric of the Other Michiko." *U.S.-Japan Women's Journal*, no. 23 (December 2002): 92–109.

Horie Setsuko. "'Joshi daisei' 'nyūkan tōsō'" ["College coeds'" "entrance struggle"]. In *Onnatachi no ima o tō kai, Zenkyōtō kara ribu e*, 117–20.

Hosaka Masayuki. *Yūkoku no ronri: Mishima Yukio to Tate no Kai jiken* [The logic of patriotism: Mishima Yukio and the Shield Society incident]. Tokyo: Kodansha, 1980.

Hoshino Chieko. "Kamonegi shōjo no sanjū nen" [Thirty years as a naive maiden]. In *Onnatachi no ima o tō kai, Zenkyōtō kara ribu e*, 89–91.

House of Councillors, Committee on Judicial Affairs. Thirty-Fourth Diet Session, Meeting no. 3, February 16, 1960 (committee hearing transcript). In "Kokkai kaigi kiroku shisutomu" [Diet Debate Records System]." Accessed March 13, 2015. https://kokkai.ndl.go.jp/#/detail?minId=103415206X00319600216&current=1.

Igarashi, Yoshikuni. *Bodies of Memory: Narratives of War in Postwar Japanese Culture, 1945–1970.* Princeton, NJ: Princeton University Press, 2000.

Igarashi, Yoshikuni. "Dead Bodies and Living Guns: The United Red Army and Its Deadly Pursuit of Revolution, 1971–1972." *Japanese Studies* 27, no. 2 (September 2007): 119–37.

Iijima Aiko. "Josei ni totte sabetsu towa nani ka" [What is discrimination to women?]. In Mizonoguchi, Saeki, and Miki, *Shiryō ūman ribu shi I*, 1:47–53.

Ikeda, Kazuo. "Historical Background." In Dowsey, *Zengakuren*, 9–41.

Imai Yasuko. "Bunto to feminizumu" [Bund and feminism]. In *60-nen Anpo to Bunto o yomu* [Reading 1960 Anpo and the Bund], edited by Shima Shigeo kinen bunshū kankō kai [Shigeo Shima Memorial Proceedings Publishing Association], 74–75. Tokyo: Jōkyō shuppan, 2002.

Inamura Kyōko. "Nagare nagarete" [Flowing]. In Onnatachi no ima o tō kai, *Zenkyōtō kara ribu e*, 103–6.

Inose, Naoki, and Hiroaki Sato. *Persona: A Biography of Yukio Mishima*. Berkeley, CA: Stone Bridge, 2012.

Inuhiko Yomota. *Hai skuuru 1968* [High school 1968]. Tokyo: Shinchō bunko, n.d.

Ishiyama, Reiko. "Japan: Why So Few Women Journalists?" In *The Palgrave International Handbook of Women and Journalism*, edited by Carolyn Byerly, 404–18. London: Palgrave Macmillan, 2013.

Itō Kimio. *Danseigaku nyūmon* [Introduction to men's studies]. Tokyo: Sakuhinsha, 1996.

Iwao, Sumiko. *The Japanese Woman: Traditional Image and Changing Reality*. New York: Free Press, 1993.

Kagawa Setsuko and Kawamura Sadae. *Josei to kōtō kyōiku: Kikai kakuchō to shakaiteki sōkoku* [Women and higher education: Expanding opportunities and social rivalry]. Kyoto: Shōwadō, 2008.

Kanayama Toshiaki and Gurupu 69 [Group 69], ed. *Zenkyōtō imajineishon* [Zenkyōtō imagination]. Tokyo: Gendai shorin, 1984.

Kanba Michiko. *Hito shirezu hohoeman: Kanba Michiko ikō shū* [The smile nobody knows: Kanba Michiko's collected writings]. Kyoto: San'ichi Shinsho, 1960.

Kanba Mitsuko. "Atogaku" [Afterword]. In Kanba Michiko, *Hito shirezu hohoeman*, 263–72.

Kanba Toshio. "Arashi no gijidō ni kieta musume" [The daughter who disappeared in the tempest at the Diet]. In Bungei shunjū, *"Bungei shunjū" ni miru shōwa shi*, 2:491–98.

Kanba Toshio. "Maegaki" [Preface]. In Kanba Michiko, *Hito shirezu hohoeman*, 7–14.

Kanba Toshio, "Zengakuren ni musume o ubawarete" [Zengakuren stole my daughter]. *Bungei shunjū* 38, no. 3 (March 1960): 204–09.

Kanō Akihiro and Kanō Kenta. *Omae no 1960-nendai o, shinu mae ni shabettoke* [Tell me your 1960s before you die!]. Tokyo: Potto shuppan, 2010.

Kano, Ayako. *Japanese Feminist Debates: A Century of Contention on Sex, Love, and Labor*. Honolulu: University of Hawai'i Press, 2016.

Kaplan, E. Ann. "Is the Gaze Male?" In *Women and Film: Both Sides of the Camera*, 23–35. New York: Methuen, 1983.

Kapur, Nick. *Japan at the Crossroads: Conflict and Compromise after Anpo*. Cambridge, MA: Harvard University Press, 2018.

Kashiwazaki Chieko. *Taiyō to arashi to jiyū o: Gebaruto Rōza tōsō no shuki* [Sun, storm, and liberty: A journal of a Gewalt Rosa struggle]. Tokyo: Noberu shobō, 1969.

Katō Katsuko, Kida Hiroko, Terakura Ikuko, Matsumoto Sachiko, Minagawa Kanae, and Yamamoto Miwa. "Zadankai: Joshi gakusei no anpo tōsō" [Roundtable: Female students' Anpo struggle]. In Onnatachi no ima o tō kai, *Onnatachi no 60-nen anpo*, 5:92–110.

Katō Kei and Yamanaka Yukio. "Kyūen Renraku Sentaa no gojū nen: Gekidō no hassoku toki" [50 years of the Relief Support Contact Center: Inaugurated in a time of upheaval]. *Jōkyō* [Situation], Autumn 2018, 143–60.

Katō Mitsuko. "Tōdai zenkyōtō no naka de" [In the middle of the University of Tokyo Zenkyōtō]. In Yoshihara et al., *Joshi Zengakuren gonin no shuki*, 16–67.

Katō Tokiko. "Hito ga kokoro ni omou koto" [What people think with their hearts]. *Eureka*, February 2015, 114–24.

Kelly, William. "At the Limits of New Middle Class Japan: Beyond 'Mainstream Consciousness.'" In *Social Contracts under Stress: The Middle Classes of America, Europe, and Japan at the Turn of the Century*, edited by Olivier Zunz, Leonard J. Schoppa, and Nobuhiro Hiwatari, 232–54. New York: Russell Sage Foundation, 2002.

Kida Midori. "Nichidai kōka wo utainagara misakishō wo yuragasu demotai" [Shaking Misaki town while singing the Nihon University school song]. In Onnatachi no ima o tō kai, *Zenkyōtō kara ribu e*, 91–95.

Kim, Charles. "Moral Imperatives: South Korean Studenthood and April 19th." *Journal of Asian Studies* 71, no. 2 (May 2012): 399–422.

Kinsella, Sharon. *Schoolgirls, Money and Rebellion in Japan*. New York: Routledge, 2014.

Kitamura, Kazuyuki. "Mass Higher Education." In *Changes in the Japanese University: A Comparative Perspective*, edited by William K. Cummings, 64–82. Praeger Special Studies Series in Comparative Education. New York: Praeger, 1979.

Kiyoshi Inoue, *Nihon josei shi* [Japanese women's history]. Kyoto: San'ichi shobō, 1949.

Koikari, Mire. *Pedagogy of Democracy: Feminism and the Cold War in the U.S. Occupation of Japan*. Philadelphia: Temple University Press, 2008.

Komatsu Shinroku. "Zenkyōtō joshigakusei hatachi no shi" [Zenkyōtō coed's death at twenty]. *Shūkan gendai*, May 1971. 120–26.

Konno Tetsuo. "Hashimoto Osamu wa 'atama' yori saki ni 'karada' ga aru hito datta [Hashimoto Osamu was a person who prioritized 'body' over 'mind']." *Webronza .asahi.com*. February 19, 2019. Accessed June 1, 2020. https://webronza.asahi.com /culture/articles/2018021800011.html.

Kosaka Shūhei. *Shisō toshite no Zenkyōtō sedai* [The Zenkyōtō generation as philosophy]. Tokyo: Chikuma shobō, 2006.

Koschmann, Victor J. "Intellectuals and Politics." In Gordon, *Postwar Japan as History*, 395–423.

Kōseishō jidō kateikyoku [Ministry of Health and Welfare Children and Home Affairs Bureau]. *Jidō fukushi sanjūnen no ayumi* [Thirty years of advancements in child welfare]. Tokyo: Nihon jidō mondai chōsakai, 1978.

Kosugi Ryōko. "Nihon no 1960-nendai gakusei undō ni okeru tagensei: Bunkateki apurōchi ni yoru jirei bunseki kara" [Plurality in the 1960s student movement in Japan: A case study using a cultural approach]. *Shakaigaku Kenkyū* [Sociology research] 96 (July 2015): 165–91.

Kōuchi Saburō. "Todai tōsō no sanakani" [Right in the middle of the University of Tokyo struggle]. In Tokoro, *Waga ai to hangyaku*, 1–9.

Koyama Shizuko. *Sengo kyōiku no jendā chitsujo* [The gender order of postwar education]. Tokyo: Keisō shobō, 2009.

Kuroiwa Chizuko. "Anpo kara sanjūnen" [Thirty years since Anpo]. In Onnatachi no ima o tō kai, *Onnatachi no 60-nen anpo*, 5:111–16.

Kuwabara Yōko. "Watashi wa nigerarenai" [I can't escape]. In Yoshihara et al., *Joshi Zengakuren gonin no shuki*, 70–106.

Langland, Victoria. *Speaking of Flowers: Student Movements and the Making and Remembering of 1968 in Military Brazil*. Durham, NC: Duke University Press, 2013.

Lefebvre, Henri. *Critique of Everyday Life: The Three-Volume Text*. Translated by John Moore and Gregory Elliott. London: Verso, 2014.

Loftus, Ronald. *Telling Lives: Women's Self-Writing in Modern Japan*. Honolulu: University of Hawai'i Press, 2013.

Mackie, Vera. *Creating Socialist Women in Japan: Gender, Labour and Activism, 1900–1937*. Cambridge: Cambridge University Press, 2003.

Mackie, Vera. *Feminism in Modern Japan: Citizenship, Embodiment and Sexuality*. Cambridge: Cambridge University Press, 2003.

Mackie, Vera. "Picturing Political Space in 1920s and 1930s Japan." In *Nation and Nationalism in Japan*, edited by Sandra Wilson, 38–54. London: Routledge Curzon, 2002.

Marotti, William. "Japan 1968: The Performance of Violence and the Theater of Protest." *American Historical Review* 114, no. 1 (February 2009): 97–135.

Marotti, William. *Money, Trains, and Guillotines: Art and Revolution in 1960s Japan*. Durham, NC: Duke University Press, 2013.

Marshall, Byron K. *Learning to Be Modern*. Boulder, CO: Westview, 1994.

Maruyama Kunio. "Joshi gakusei taisaku shikan" [A personal impression on female student countermeasures]. *Shisō no kagaku* [Science of thought], April 1966, 79–82.

Marx, Karl. *The Eighteenth Brumaire of Louis Bonaparte*. New York: International Publishers, 1990.

Matsunami, Michihiro. "Origins of Zengakuren." In Dowsey, *Zengakuren*, 42–74.

McKnight, Anne. "At the Source (Code)." In *Media Theory in Japan*, edited by Marc Steinberg and Alexander Zahlten, 250–84. Durham, NC: Duke University Press, 2017.

Meinhof, Ulrike. "Water Cannons, against Women, Too." In *Everybody Talks about the Weather . . . We Don't*, edited by Karin Bauer, translated by Luise von Flotow, 214–23. New York: Seven Stories, 2008.

Mészáros, István. *Beyond Capital: Toward a Theory of Transition*. New York: Monthly Review Press, 1995.

Mihashi Toshiaki. *Rojō no Zenkyōtō 1968* [Zenkyoto 1968 on the streets]. Tokyo: Kawde bukkusu, 2010.

Ministry of Education Japan. *Educational Developments in 1965–66: Report Presented at the XXVIIIth International Conference on Public Education, Geneva*. Tokyo: Ministry of Education, 1966.

Ministry of Internal Affairs and Communications, Statistics Bureau, Director-General for Policy Planning and Statistical Research and Training Institute. "Chapter 25-11: Share of Female Teachers, Pupils and Students by Kind of School

(1950–2005)." Historical Statistics of Japan, 2012. Accessed January 12, 2014. http://www.stat.go.jp/english/data/chouki/25.html.

Ministry of Justice. "Shōwa 50-nen han hanzai hakusho" [1975 edition white paper on crime]. National Police Agency, vol. 3, chapter 2, section 3. Accessed February 12, 2019. http://hakusyo1.moj.go.jp/jp/16/nfm/mokuji.html.

Ministry of Justice. "Shōwa 52-nen han hanzai hakusho" [1977 edition white paper on crime]. National Police Agency, vol. 1, chapter 1, section 4. Accessed June 3, 2019. http://hakusyo1.moj.go.jp/jp/18/nfm/mokuji.html.

Mishima Yukio. "Tōdai o dōbutsuen ni shiro" [Make the University of Tokyo a zoo]. In Bungei shunjū, "Bungei shunjū" ni miru shōwa shi, 2:657–66.

Mishima Yukio, Todai zengaku kyōtō kaigi [University of Tokyo All-Campus Joint Struggle Committee], and Komaba kyōtō funsai iinkai [Komaba Campus Joint Struggle Demolition Board]. Tōron Mishima Yukio vs. Todai Zenkyōtō: Bi to kyōdōtai to Todai tōsō [Mishima vs. University of Tokyo Zenkyōtō: Beauty and community and the University of Tokyo struggle]. Tokyo: Shinchōsha, 1969.

Mizonoguchi Akiyo, Saeki Yōko, and Miki Sōko, eds. Shiryō ūman ribu shi I [A documentary history of women's lib, vol. 1]. Tokyo: Shōkadō shoten, 1992.

Mizonoguchi Akiyo, Saeki Yōko, and Miki Sōko, eds. Shiryō ūman ribu shi II [A documentary history of women's lib, vol. 2]. Kyoto: Shōkadō shoten, 1994.

Monbushō daijin kanbō chōsa tōkeika [Ministry of Education Secretariat Survey Statistics Division]. Gakkō kihon chōsa hōkokusho: Shōwa 44 nendo dai 2 bunsatsu [Department of Education basic survey report: Shōwa 44, vol. 2]. Tokyo: Monbushō daijin kanbō chōsa tōkeika [Ministry of Education Secretariat Survey Statistics Division], 1969.

Mori Setsuko. "'Otoko narabi onna' kara ribu e" [From a "woman in the men's ranks" to lib]. In Onnatachi no ima o tō kai, Zenkyōtō kara ribu e, 164–71.

Mori Setsuko. "Shisō shūdan esu.ii.ekkusu soshikiron? Josetsu" [An organizational theory for Thought Group S.E.X.? Introduction]. In Mizonoguchi, Saeki, and Miki, Shiryō ūman ribu shi I, 171–75.

Morris-Suzuki, Tessa. Re-inventing Japan: Time, Space, Nation. Armonk, NY: Sharpe, 1998.

Murakami Kyōko. "Jiko hitei wa tsurai iyashi michi e" [Self-negation is a hard road to comfort]. In Onnatachi no ima o tō kai, Zenkyōtō kara ribu e, 109–13.

Nagai Michio. Nihon no daigaku: Sangyō shakai ni hatatsu yakuwari [Japan's universities: The role in developing industrial society]. Tokyo: Chūkō shinsho, 1965.

Nagata Hiroko. Hyōkai: Onna no jiritsu o motomete [Melting: Wish for woman's independence]. Tokyo: Kōdansha, 1983.

Nagata Hiroko. Jūroku no bohyō [Sixteen headstones]. Vol. 2. 2 vols. Tokyo: Sairyūsha, 1983.

Nakajima Makoto. Zengakuren. Tokyo: San'ichi shobō, 1968.

Nakaya Izumi. Sono "minshu" to wa dare nano ka: Jendaa, kaikyū, aidentiti [Who are "the people"? Gender, class, identity]. Tokyo: Seikyusha, 2013.

Nancy, Jean-Luc. *The Inoperative Community*. Edited by Peter Connor. Translated by Peter Connor, Lisa Garbus, Michael Holland, and Simona Sawhney. Minneapolis: University of Minnesota Press, 1991.

Narita, Katsuya. *Systems of Higher Education: Japan*. New York: International Council for Educational Development, 1978.

Nihon daigaku bunri gakubu tōsō iinkai shokikyoku [Nihon University College of Arts and Sciences Struggle Committee Secretariat], ed. *Hangyaku no barikeedo: Nichidai tōsō no kiroku* [Barricades of revolt: A record of the Nihon University struggle]. Tokyo: San'ichi shobō, 2008.

Nikkan rōdō tsūshinsha [Nikkan Labor News Agency], ed. *Zengakuren no jittai: Sono habatsu o chūshin to shite* [The actual state of Zengakuren: Focusing on those factions]. Tokyo: Nikan rōdō tsūshinsha, 1959.

Oguma Eiji. *1968 (ge): Hanran no shūen to sono isan* [1968 (vol. 2): The uprising's demise and its legacies]. Tokyo: Shinyōsha, 2009.

Oguma Eiji. *1968 (jō): Wakamono tachi no hanran to sono haikei* [1968 (vol. 1): The young people's revolt and its background]. Tokyo: Shinyōsha, 2009.

Ōhara Kimiko. *Tokeidai wa takakatta* [The clock tower was tall]. Tokyo: San'ichi shobō, 1969.

Ōizumi Yasuo. *Asama Sansō jūgekisen no shinsō* [Depths of the firefight at the Asama lodge]. Vol. 2. 2 vols. Tokyo: Kodansha, 2012.

Okamoto Masami and Murao Kōichi, eds. *Daigaku gerira no uta: Rakugaki tōdai tōsō* [University guerrilla songs: University of Tokyo struggle in graffiti]. Tokyo: Sanseido, 1969.

Okamoto Masami and Murao Kōichi. "Haha o koeyo" [Overcome mama]. In Okamoto and Murao, *Daigaku gerira no uta*, 87–89.

Okazawa Sumie. "Zengakuren dai-30 kai teiki zenkoku taikai de no sei no sabetsu = haigaishugi to tatakau katsui hyōmei" [Declaration to fight sexism and xenophobia made at the 30th National Zengakuren Assembly]." In *Ribu to feminizumu* [Lib and feminism], edited by Amano Masako, Itō Kimio, Itō Ruri, Inoue Teruko, Ueno Chizuko, Ehara Yumiko, Ōsawa Mari, and Kanō Mikiyo, 96–107. Nihon no feminizumu 1 [Japanese feminism 1]. Tokyo: Iwanami shoten, 2009.

Onnatachi no ima o tō kai [Association to question women's present]. *Onnatachi no 60-nen anpo* [Women's 1960 Anpo]. Jūgoshi nōto sengohen [Notes from the front lines, postwar edition]. 8 vols. Kawasaki: Inpakuto shuppankai, 1990.

Onnatachi no ima o tō kai [Association to question women's present]. *Zenkyōtō kara ribu e* [From Zenkyōtō to lib]. Jūgoshi nōto sengohen [Notes from the front lines, postwar edition]. Kawasaki: Inpakuto shuppankai, 1996.

Ono, Hiroshi. "Training the Nation's Elite: National—Private Sector Differences in Japanese University Education." Working Paper No. 96. Stockholm: European Institute of Japanese Studies, June 2000.

Ōsawa Toshirō. "Barikeedo no naka no <haha - watashi>" ["Mother and me" in the barricades]. In *Nihon no okaasan tachi* [Mothers of Japan], edited by Shibata Michiko, 299–312. Tokyo: Perikansha, 1972.

Ōshima, Nagisa. "Sexual Poverty." In *Cinema, Censorship, and the State: The Writings of Nagisa Oshima*, edited by Annette Michelson, translated by Dawn Larson, 240–48. Cambridge, MA: MIT Press, 1992.

Ōta Kyōko. "Onnatachi no Zenkyōtō undō" [Women's Zenkyōtō movement]. In Onnatachi no ima o tō kai, *Zenkyōtō kara ribu e*, 71–79.

Ōtsuka Eiji. *"Kanojotachi" no rengō sekigun: Sabukaruchaa to sengo minshushugi* ["Her" United Red Army: Subcultures and postwar democracies]. Tokyo: Bungei shunjū, 1996.

Ōtsuka Eiji. *Shōjo minzokugaku: Seikimatsu no shinwa o tsumugu "miko no matsuei"* [Young girl folkloristics: "Descendants of shine maidens" in myth at the end of the century]. Tokyo: Kōbunsha, 1989.

Packard, George. *Protest in Tokyo: The Security Treaty Crisis of 1960*. 1st ed. Princeton, NJ: Princeton University Press, 1966.

Park, Yung H. "'Big Business' and Education Policy in Japan." *Asian Survey* 22, no. 3 (March 1982): 315–36.

Pflugfelder, Gregory M. "'Fujin sanseiken' saikō: Senzen seiji bunka no jendaaka" [Reconsidering "women's suffrage": Gendering prewar political culture]. In *Iwanami Kōza Kindai Nihon no bunkashi 6: Kakudaisuru modaniti* [Iwanami course on modern Japanese history, vol. 6: Expanding modernity], edited by Komori Yōichi, et al., 63–114. Tokyo: Iwanami shoten, 2002.

Piercy, Marge. "The Grand Coolie Damn." Chicago Women's Liberation Union Herstory Project. Accessed May 20, 2020. https://www.cwluherstory.org/classic -feminist-writings-articles/the-grand-coolie-damn?rq=grand%20coolie%20damn.

Polletta, Francesca. *Freedom Is an Endless Meeting: Democracy in American Social Movements*. Chicago: University of Chicago Press, 2002.

Power, Nina. "She's Just Not That into You." *Radical Philosophy* 177 (January–February 2013). Accessed July 15, 2020. https://www.radicalphilosophy.com/reviews /individual-reviews/rp177-shes-just-not-that-into-you.

Ryang, Sonia. "Love and Colonialism in Takamure Itsue's Feminism: A Postcolonial Critique." *Feminist Review* 60 (Autumn 1998): 1–32.

Sakai Kazuko. "Onna to iu mainoriti o mitsukete" [Discovering a minority called woman]. In Onnatachi no ima o tō kai, *Zenkyōtō kara ribu e*, 99–103.

Sasaki-Uemura, Wesley. *Organizing the Spontaneous: Citizen Protest in Postwar Japan*. Honolulu: University of Hawai'i Press, 2001.

Sassa Atsuyuki. *Tōdai rakujō: Yasuda kōdō kōbō shichijūnijikan* [The fall of the University of Tokyo fortress: Seventy-two hours of defense and offense at the Yasuda clock tower]. Tokyo: Bungei shunjū, 1993.

Sawara, Yukiko. "The University Struggles." In Dowsey, *Zengakuren*, 136–92.

Schieder, Chelsea Szendi. "Blood Ties: Intimate Violence in Shinzō Abe's Japan." *World Policy Journal* 34, no. 2 (2017): 28–35.

Schieder, Chelsea Szendi. "Revolutionary Bodies: The Female Student Activist in the 'Student Fiction' of Ōe Kenzaburō and Kurahashi Yumiko." *Gengotai*, March 2016, 67–75.

Schieder, Chelsea Szendi. "Womenomics vs. Women: Neoliberal Cooptation of Feminism in Japan." *Meiji Journal of Political Science and Economics* 3 (2014): 53–60.

Scott, Joan Wallach. *Gender and the Politics of History.* New York City: Columbia University Press, 1999.

Shakai mondai kenkyūkai [Social issues study group]. *Zengakuren kakuha: Gakusei undō jiten* [Zengakuren sects: A student movement dictionary]. Tokyo: Futabasha, 1969.

Shibata Shō. *Saredo warera ga hibi* [Well, that's our lot]. Tokyo: Bungei shunjū shinsha, 1964.

Shigematsu, Setsu. *Scream from the Shadows: The Women's Liberation Movement in Japan.* Minneapolis: University of Minnesota Press, 2012.

Shigenobu Fusako. *Nihon sekigun shishi: Paresuchina to tomoni* [A personal history of the Japan Red Army: With Palestine]. Tokyo: Kawade shobō shinsha, 2009.

Shigenobu Fusako. *Waga ai waga kakumei* [My love, my revolution]. Tokyo: Kodansha, 1974.

Shima Hiroko. "Onigiri nyōbō" [A rice-ball wife]. In *Bunto Shishi: Seishun no gyōshoku sareta nama no hibi tomoni tatakatta yūjintachi e* [A personal history of Bund: To the friends who fought toegther during the condensed and raw days of youth], Shima Shigeo and Shima Hiroko, 222–62. Tokyo: Hihyōsha, 2010.

Shima Taizō. *Yasuda kōdō, 1968–1969* [Yasuda tower, 1968–1969]. Tokyo: Chūō kōron shinsha, 2005.

Shimada Yoshiko. "Hōki seyo shōjo! Seifuku shōjo o kaitai suru" [Rise up, girl! Dismantling the uniformed girl]. *Aida,* no. 220 (April 2015): 2–8.

Shirakawa Yoshiko. "Watashi wa 'tatakau zenkōren' no shōjo riidaa" [I'm a maiden leader of the "fighting all–high school alliance"]. *Gendai,* January 1969, 84–91.

Shorrock, Hallam C., Jr. "The Prewar Legacy and Postwar Epiphany of International Christian University." *Japan Christian Review* 59 (1993): 79–91.

Silverberg, Miriam Rom. *Erotic Grotesque Nonsense: The Mass Culture of Japanese Modern Times.* Berkeley: University of California Press, 2006.

Siniawer, Eiko Maruko. "Befitting Bedfellows." In *The Hidden History of Crime, Corruption, and State,* edited by Renate Bridenthal, 98–122. New York: Berghahn Books, 2013. Cartoon originally published in *Sekai,* August 1960, 261.

Springer, Kimberly. *Living for the Revolution.* Durham, NC: Duke University Press, 2005.

Steinhoff, Patricia. "Death by Defeatism and Other Fables: The Social Dynamics of the Rengō Sekigun Purge." In *Japanese Social Organization,* edited by Takie Sugiyama Lebra, 195–224. Honolulu: University of Hawai'i Press, 1992.

Steinhoff, Patricia. "Memories of New Left Protest." *Contemporary Japan* 25, no. 2 (2013): 127–65.

Steinhoff, Patricia. "Three Women Who Loved the Left: Radical Women Leaders in the Japanese Red Army Movement." In *Re-imaging Japanese Women,* edited by Anne Imamura, 301–22. Berkeley: University of California Press, 1996.

Sturiano, Joanna. "Community and Creativity in the 'Revival of Writing by Women' in

Modern Japan: Mapping an Early Shōwa Literary Network." PhD diss., Stanford University, 2014.

Suga Hidemi. *1968-nen* [Year 1968]. Tokyo: Chikuma shinsho, 2006.

Suga Hidemi. *Kakumeitekina, amari kakumeitekina: "1968-nen no kakumei" shiron* [Revolutionary, too revolutionary: Historical essays on "the 1968 revolution"]. Tokyo: Chikuma gakugei bunko, 2018.

Suzuki Kunio. *Ganbare!! Shinsayoku: "Waga teki, waga tomo" kagekiha saiki e no eeru* [C'mon!! New Left: "My enemy, my friend," cheering on a comeback of extremist sects]. Nishinomiya, Hyōgo: Esueru shuppankai, 1989.

Tachibana Takashi. *Chūkaku vs. Kakumaru*. Tokyo: Kodansha, 1983.

Takahashi Hiroshi. *Tsuwamono-domo ga yume no saki* [The rank and file has surpassed the dream]. Tokyo: Wayts, 2010.

Takamure Itsue. *Josei no rekishi* [Women's history]. Tokyo: Kodansha, 1954–58.

Takamure Itsue. *Takamure Itsue zenshū* [Collected writings of Takamure Itsue]. Edited by Hashimoto Kenzō. Tokyo: Rironsha, 1966–67.

Takano Etsuko. *Hatachi no genten* [A twenty-year-old's origin]. Tokyo: Shinchosha, 1971.

Takazawa Kōji, Takagi Masayuki, and Kurata Kazunari. *Shinsayoku nijūnenshi: Hanran no kiseki* [A twenty-year history of the New Left: The wonder of revolt]. Tokyo: Shinsensha, 1981.

Takeda Haruhito. *Kōdo seichō* [High growth]. Shiriizu Nihon kingendai shi 8 [Series modern and contemporary Japanese history 8]. Tokyo: Iwanami shinsho, 2008.

Takeda, Hiroko. *The Political Economy of Reproduction in Japan: Between Nation-State and Everyday Life*. London: Routledge Curzon, 2005.

Tanaka Mitsu. "Benjō kara no kaihō" [Liberation from the toilet]. In *Ribu to feminizumu* [Lib and feminism], edited by Amano Masako, Itō Kimio, Itō Ruri, Inoue Teruko, Ueno Chizuko, Ehara Yumiko, Ōsawa Mari, and Kanō Mikiyo, 55–71. Nihon no feminizumu 1 [Japanese feminism 1]. Tokyo: Iwanami shoten, 2003.

Tanaka Sumie. "Senpai toshite, haha toshite" [As an elder, as a mother]. *Fujin kōron* [Ladies' review], February 1960, 67–69.

10.8 Yamazaki Hiroaki Project. *Katsute 10.8 Haneda tōsō ga atta* [Once there was the 10.8 Haneda struggle]. Tokyo: Gōdō foresuto shuppan, 2018.

Terayama Shūji. "Kibō to iu byōki: Tokyo daigaku ron" [The sickness called hope: On the University of Tokyo]. In *Terayama Shūji chosakushū* [Terayama Shūji's collected works], 4:477–85. Tokyo: Quintessence, 2009.

Thorsten, Marie. "A Few Bad Women: Manufacturing 'Education Mamas' in Postwar Japan." *International Journal of Politics, Culture, and Society* 10, no. 1 (Fall 1996): 51–71.

Tiqqun (Collective). *Preliminary Materials for a Theory of the Young-Girl*. Translated by Ariana Reines. Los Angeles: Semiotext(e), 2012.

Tocco, Martha Caroline. *School Bound: Women's Higher Education in Nineteenth-Century Japan*. Stanford, CA: Stanford University, 1994.

Tokoro Mitsuko. *Waga ai to hangyaku* [My love and rebellion]. Tokyo: Zeneisha, 1969.

Tokuyama Haruko. "Watashi ga ugokeba yo no naka ga hitori bun ugoku to iu jikkan" [The feeling that if I move one more person in the world is moving]. In Onnatachi no ima o tō kai, *Zenkyōtō kara ribu e*, 82–89.

Toritsudai Zenkyōtō yajiuma gundan [Tokyo Metropolitan University Zenkyōtō rubbernecker corps], *Tōsei gakusei undō zareutashū* [Collection of play songs from the current student movement generation]. Tokyo: Toritsu Zenkyōtō yajiuma gundan, 1969.

Tosaka Jun. *Tosaka Jun zenshū dai 4 kan* [Tosaka Jun: Collected works, vol. 4]. Tokyo: Keisō shobō, 1966.

Tsuchiya Sōzō. "Jii undō sono ta taishū kōdō no shochi" [Measures for demonstrations and other mass mobilizations]. *Keisatsu kenkyū* [Police studies] 40, no. 1 (January 1969): 23–42.

Tsurumi, E. Patricia. *Factory Girls: Women in the Thread Mills of Meiji Japan*. Princeton, NJ: Princeton University Press, 1992.

Tsurumi Kazuko. "Seinen no chi o aganau mono" [Atoning for a youth's blood]. *Shisō no kagaku* [Science of thought], July 1960, 110–12.

Tsurumi, Kazuko. *Social Change and the Individual: Japan before and after Defeat in World War II*. Princeton, NJ: Princeton University Press, 1970.

Tsurumi, Kazuko. "Some Comments on the Japanese Student Movement in the Sixties." *Journal of Contemporary History* 5, no. 1 (1970): 104–12.

Ueno Chizuko. "Forty Years of Japanese Feminism: What It Has Achieved . . . and What It Has Not." Lecture, Najita Distinguished Lecture in Japanese Studies series, University of Chicago, April 22, 2013.

Ueno Chizuko. "Hitori ni naru koto" [Becoming alone]. In Onnatachi no ima o tō kai, *Zenkyōtō kara ribu e*, 126–27.

Ueno Chizuko. *Onna tachi no sabaibaru sakusen* [Women's survival strategies]. Tokyo: Bungei shinsho, 2013.

Ueno Chizuko. *Ueno Chizuko ga bungaku o shakaigaku suru* [Ueno Chizuko sociologizes literature]. Tokyo: Asahi shinbun sha, 2000.

Unno Shinkichi. *Rekishi e no shōgen: 6.15 no dokyumento* [Testimony for history: Documents from June 15]. Tokyo: Nihon hyōron shinsha, 1960.

Uno, Kathleen. "The Death of 'Good Wife, Wise Mother'?" In Gordon, *Postwar Japan as History*, 293–322.

Unoda Shōya, Kawaguchi Takayuki, Sakaguchi Hiroshi, Toba Kōji, and Nakaya Izumi, eds. *"Saakuru jidai" o yomu: Sengo bunka undō kenkyū e no shōtai* [Reading the "Circle Period": An invitation to postwar cultural movement research]. Tokyo: Kage shobō, 2016.

Usami Shō. "Micchan to Baabara" [Miss Mitsuko and Barbara]. In Tokoro, *Waga ai to hangyaku*, 197–200.

World Economic Forum. "The Global Gender Gap Report 2020." 2019. http://www3 .weforum.org/docs/WEF_GGGR_2020.pdf.

Yamada Masahiro. "Ronsō: Zenkyōtō joshigakusei to uyoku seinen" [Debate: Zenkyōtō coed and right-wing youth]. *Shokun!* [Everyone!], November 1969, 134–57.

Yamamoto Chie. "Anpo tōsō wa shuppatsu no toki" [When the Anpo struggle was the start]. In Onnatachi no ima o tō kai, *Onnatachi no 60-nen anpo*, 5:119–21.

Yamamoto Kiyokatsu. *Mishima Yukio: Yūmon no sokoku bōeifu* [Mishima Yukio: Rhapsody on defending the anguished homeland]. Tokyo: Nihon bungeisha, 1980.

Yamamoto, Yoshitaka. *Chisei no hanran: Tōdai kaitai made* [Revolt of the intellect: Until the University of Tokyo is demolished]. Tokyo: Zeneisha kanna shobō, 1969.

Yasko, Guy. "The Japanese Student Movement, 1968–1970: The Zenkyoto Uprising." PhD diss., Cornell University, 1997.

Yoda, Tomiko. "The Rise and Fall of Maternal Society: Gender, Labor, and Capital in Contemporary Japan." *South Atlantic Quarterly* 99, no. 4 (Fall 2000): 865–902.

Yoneyama, Lisa. *Cold War Ruins: Transpacific Critique of American Justice and Japanese War Crimes*. Durham, NC: Duke University Press, 2016.

Yoneyama, Lisa. *Hiroshima Traces: Time, Space, and the Dialectics of Memory*. Berkeley: University of California Press, 1999.

Yonezu Tomoko. "Barikeedo wo kugutte" [Passing through the barricades]. In Onnatachi no ima o tō kai, *Zenkyōtō kara ribu e*, 120–23.

Yonezu Tomoko. "Mizukara no SEX o mokuteki ishikitekini hikiukeru naka kara 70 nendai o bokki suru" [Take on your own SEX with purpose and consciousness and erect the 1970s]. In Mizonoguchi, Saeki, and Miki *Shiryō ūman ribu shi I*, 170–71.

Yoshihara Isami. "Tōsō no seishun ni ikite" [Living youth in the struggle]. In Yoshihara et al., *Joshi Zengakuren gonin no shuki*, 107–71.

Yoshihara Isami, Kuwabara Yōko, Katō Mitsuko, and Aoyama Michiko. *Joshi Zengakuren gonin no shuki* [A journal of five female Zengakuren]. Tokyo: Jiyū kokuminsha, 1970.

Zenkyōtō hakusho henshū iinkai [Zenkyōtō white paper editorial board], ed. *Zenkyōtō hakusho* [White paper on the Zenkyōtō]. Tokyo: Shinchosha, 1994.

Zen Kyōto shuppan iinkai [All-Kyoto publishing committee], ed. *Ashioto wa tayuru toki naku: Kanba Michiko tsuitō shishū* [Unending footsteps: Collection of Kanba Michiko memorial poems]. Kyoto: Shirakawa Shoin, 1960.

INDEX

Page references in italics indicate illustrations.

Abe Shinzō, 163–66
Akita Akehiro, 87–88, 141
All-Campus Joint Struggle Committees.
    See Zenkyōtō (Zengaku kyōtō kaigi; All-
    Campus Joint Struggle Committees)
Ando, Takemasa, 5–6
Anpo struggle, 55, 66, 85, 90, 172n25, 178n6;
    activism after, 54; activists injured in, *38*;
    as antiwar and anti-Kishi, 30–31, 57; lack
    of change following, 56; media coverage
    of, 33, *34–35*, 36; Packard on, 172n27; po-
    litical season of, 53, 67; scope of, 30–31;
    state force in, 36–37; Tokoro in, 49, 55–56;
    women and, 32–33, *34–35*, 36; Zengakuren
    in, 30–32, 44. *See also* Kanba Michiko
Antiwar Day protests: in Japan (1968–70),
    123–24, 151–52, 187n48; in Washington,
    D.C. (1967), 123
Aoyama Michiko, 108
Arruzza, Cinzia, 11
Asahi jaanaru, 37, 55–56, 150
Asahi shimbun, 155
Asakura Toshihiro, 97, *98*
Asama Sansō siege, 128
Avenell, Simon, 171n2

barricades, student-run: codes of conduct at,
    145; creation of, 78, 85; daily life/studies
    within, 19, 91–92, *92*; and gender, 14, 16,
    18–19, 79, 97–100, *98*, 102, 140, 181n63; goals
    of, 83; graffiti in, 106; hierarchies within, 19,

93, 100; riot police at, *88*, 88–89; scope of,
    85; sexism within, 79, 97, 99; social func-
    tions of, 95–96; women and, 1–2 , 96–97
Beal, Francis, 162
Bloody May Day (1952), 36
Boggs, Carl, Jr., 12, 52
Breines, Wini, 12–13
"Brumaire" (Kanba Michiko), 46–47
Buckley, Sandra, 76
Bund, 29, 51, 54, 58, 172–73n41, 181n63
Butler, Judith, 159–60

Campus Kyanko (Sakurai), 147–52, 187n48
capitalism: and everyday life, 80, 82–83, 179n12;
    gendered equality under, 70–71; masculine
    logic of, 51; rationalization of, 13, 65
Caramel Mamas, 117–18, *118*
care work: as bourgeois, 16; devaluation of, 165;
    family dependence on, 71–72; as gendered,
    14; versus intellectual production, 64; New
    Left and, 17, 79, 102–3; policing as, 129–30;
    postwar economy undergirded by, 53
Caute, David, 130–31
Central Child Welfare Commission, 71
Chūkaku (the National Committee of the
    Revolutionary Communist League, Nu-
    cleus Faction), 58, 94, 108, 126, 128
citizens and citizenship, 171n2; education and,
    176n47; female student activists and, 33,
    36; versus imperial subjects, 158; liberalism
    and, 40

coal miners' strike (Kyushu), 53, 66

"Coeds Ruin the Nation Theory" (Teruoka), 73–75, 178n78

coeducation: as threat, 50–51, 73–76, 106–7, 178n78; percentages of, 69, 176n59, 176n61, 177nn62–63; and sexual activity, 145; and universal human liberation, 100; use of *coed*, 5, 169n6. See also education; higher education; universities

Cohen, Deborah, 14

College Sister (Sonoyama), 147–50, *149*, 187nn47–48

Combahee River Collective, 17

comfort stations/women, 164, 187n44

communism, 11, 29

Communist League (Kyōsanshugisha dōmei), 29

Complete Works of Takamure Itsue (Takamure), 63–64

Dazai Osamu, 154

democracy: and family system, 71; liberal, 40, 48; participatory, 93–94, 181n52; in postwar Japan, 22

Department of Economic Planning, 177n77

dialectics of repression, 122

Draper, Susana, 3, 9

Ebihara Toshio, 126

economic and scientific rationalism, 49–51, 60, 65–66

Economic Deliberative Council, 72

education: and democratic citizens, 66–67, 176n47; female, 71–72; humanitarian approach to, 69; in humanities, 73–74, 177n77; industry and, 66–68. See also coeducation; higher education; universities

education mama (*kyōiku mama*), 141–42

Ehara, Yumiko, 151

Eighteenth Brumaire of Louis Bonaparte, The (Marx), 46

Equal Employment Opportunity Law for Men and Women (1985), 134

Era of Woman Superiority (*Josei jōi jidai*), 151

Escobar, Edward J., 122

Evans, Sara M., 16–17

everyday life, 78–103, 179n12

Fall of the University of Tokyo Fortress, The (Sassa), 132

far right, 105, 110–17, *111*

Federation of Housewives (Shufuren), 25

female student activists: as angry maidens, 33, *34–35*, 36; in Anpo, 32–33, *34–35*, 36; as dangerous, 47–48; focus on, 5–10; as good citizens, 33, 36; legacy of, 161; masculinist attitudes critiqued by, 109–10; middle-class identity of, 5; police aggression toward, 33, *34–35*, 36; in postwar Japanese politics, 27; and rape/sexual assault, 108–9, 125, 127–28; and social customs, 26–27; and violence, 7; at women's universities, 99–100. See also Gewalt Rosas (Violent Rosas); Kanba Michiko; Nagata Hiroko; Tokoro Mitsuko

femininity: attacks on, 165–67; and memory, 62

feminism: and activism, 155–57, 162–63; dismissal/criticism of, 8–9; multiplicity of, 76; New Left and, 8–9, 20, 60, 102; and pornography, 109; second-wave, 151–52, 163; Takamure and, 62–63; on victimhood, 159–60; and violence, 20. See also women's liberation movement

First Morning, The, 146–47, 187n42

Frazier, Lessie Jo, 14

Freeman, Jo, 17

free sex/sexual liberation, 105, 107–9, 114, 145, 148

Free Speech Movement (University of California, Berkeley), 55–57

Freikorps (Volunteer Corps, Germany), 138

French Revolution, 46

Fujin kōron, 72–73

Fujita Mizue, 115–16

Fukuda Wakako, 163–64

Gambetti, Zeynep, 159–60

Garden of Women (Kinoshita), 26

Garson, Barbara, 55–57

gender equality, 24, 70–71, 76, 165–66

Gewalt, 98–99, 106, 122, 125, 181n68

Gewalt Rosas (Violent Rosas), 132–57, 160; comedic interpretations of, 134, 147–52, *149*, *153*, 157; critiques of, 20, 132–37, 141–43, 145, 147–52, 157; ideological conversion of,

152; Kikuyabashi 101, 135–37, 142, 148, 155; and the Modern Girl, 134, 147; and radical politics, 135–37; and sexual availability, 145–47, 157, 187n44; Shigenobu Fusako, 95–96, 154–56; and URA purge, 126–28, 154–56, 161; and violence, 143, *144*, 155–56; and women in politics, 152–57; at Yasuda Tower, 132. *See also* Kashiwazaki Chieko; Nagata Hiroko

Global Gender Gap Index, 166

Goldman, Emma, 11

Grand Coolie Damn, The (Piercy), 15–16, 131

Greater East Asian Co-Prosperity Sphere, 61

Greater Japan National Defense Women's Association (Dai Nippon kokubo fujinkai), 24

Great Principle (*taigi*), 115

Guevara, Che, 82

Haneda Airport protests, 33, 42, 48, 54, 81, 122

Hayashi Fumiko, 101

Hayashi Kentarō, 183n26

Hegel, Georg Wilhelm Friedrich, 46

Heibon panchi, 113

Heiminsha (Commoners' Society), 10

higher education: diversification of, 67–68; mass, 7–8; number of institutions, 85 ; rationalization of, 51, 59, 69, 74, 85; women at junior colleges, 69, 176n59, 176n61; women at universities, 69, 177nn62–63. *See also* coeducation; education; universities

Hirabayashi Taiko, 11, 101

Hirohito, Emperor, 60–61

Hosei University, 145

Hoshino Chieko, 180n30

Housewife Debates, 72, 76

"How Do Women Want to Be?" (Tokoro [Tomano Mimie]), 60–61, 65

Ichikawa Fusae, 24

Iida Momo, 55

Ikeda Hayato, 53, 57, 67

Ikejima Shinpei, 116

Imai Yasuko, 101

Inpakuto shuppankai, 163

instrumental politics, 12–13

International Christian University (Tokyo), 68–69

Ishigaki Ayako, 72

Itō Kimio, 163

Itō Noe, 24

Japan: Allied occupation, 23, 25, 30; Koreans in, 91–92; militarism of, 31, 43, 62; postwar, 15, 22, 115, 166, 169n15; sexism in, 15, 101, 163–64; South Korea and, 54, 57, 80; United States and, 53; and war, 80–81, 178n6; women in, 165–67

Japanese Communist Party (JCP), 2, 13, 28–29, 51–52, 56–59, 66, 93, 124, 172n22. See also *shinsayoku* (leftist factions)

Japanese Red Army (JRA), 127, 154–56

Japanese Socialist Party, 2, 51

Japanese Women's History (Kiyoshi), 63

Japan Times, 157

Japan Trotskyist League (Nihon Torotsukisuto renmei; Toro-ren), 29

Japan–United States Productivity Conference (Nichibei seisansei kyōgikai), 66–67

Japan Women's University, 32–33

JCP (Japanese Communist Party), 2, 13, 28–29, 51–52, 56–59, 66, 93, 124, 172n22. See also *shinsayoku* (leftist factions)

jichikai (student self-governance associations), 27–28, 59. *See also* Zengakuren (Zen Nihon gakusei jichikai sōrengō; All-Japan General Alliance of Student Self-Governing Associations)

Josei jishin, 86, 146–47, 187n39

Joshibi University of Art and Design and Ochanomizu University, 32

joshigakusei (female student), 5

JRA (Japanese Red Army), 127, 154–56

Kagoshima University, 68

Kakumaru (Nihon kakumeiteki kyōsanshugisha dōmei kakumeiteki marukusu shugi-ha; Japanese Revolutionary Communist League Revolutionary Marxist Faction), 94–95, 106, 108, 126, 128

Kakusa, 127–28

Kanba Michiko, 7, 167; and Anpo, 22; in Bund, 29; death, 21–22, 37, 43, 45, 172–73n41; on equality, 70–71; on history, 40–41; as "Japan's best daughter," 42–44;

Kanba Michiko (*continued*)
and Kashiwazaki, 141; on Kishi, 22; on
liberal democracy, 40, 48; and New Left,
122; as radical political activist, 18, 22,
36–43, 47–48; and postwar democracy, 18,
22–23, 37–39, 42–43, 45–48, 55, 159–60,
166, 174n71; upbringing of, 39–40, 139;
writings/influence of, 39, 43, 46–47; and
Yamazaki's death, 81
Kanba Mitsuko, 39, 43, 47, 173n64
Kanba Toshio, 42–43, 46–47
Kaneko Fumiko, 24
Kanno Suga, 24
Kaplan, E. Ann, 188n51
Kashiwazaki Chieko, 81–82, 137–42, 148, 155,
173n64
Katō Hiroko. *See* Kikuyabashi 101 (Katō Hiroko)
Katō Ichirō, 83
Katō Katsuko, 75
Katō Mitsuko, 14–15, 96–97, 99, 105
Kawashima Tsuyoshi, 127–28
Keidanren (Japan Business Federation), 66–67
Keisatsu kenkyū, 130
Keizai dōyūkai (Japan Association of Corpo-
rate Executives), 66–67
Khrushchev, Nikita, 29
Kikuyabashi 101 (Katō Hiroko), 135–37, 142,
148, 155
Kinjiki (Mishima), 112
Kin Kirō (Kwon Hyi-ro) incident, 91
Kinoshita Keisuke, 26
Kishi Nobusuke, 22, 30–31, 36–37, 53, 57, 67,
164, 166, 178n6
Kiyoaki Murata, 157
Kiyose Ichirō, 31
Kiyoshi Inoue, 63
Komaba Festival poster and slogan (Univer-
sity of Tokyo), 107, 117–19, *118*
Komatsu Sakyō, 60–61
Korea-Japan Security Pact, 54, 57, 80
Korean War, 30
Kōuchi Saburō, 66
Koyama Shizuko, 178n78
Kropotkin, Pyotr, 11
Kurahashi Yumiko, 26–27
Kuwabara Yōko, 96
Kyoto University, 97, *98*

LDP (Liberal Democratic Party), 22, 30–31,
53, 172n27
Lefebvre, Henri, 80
leftist student movement. *See* female student
activists; New Left (Japan); radical movements (1960s)
Liberal Democratic Party (LDP), 22, 30–31,
53, 172n27
liberalism, 40, 48, 104–6, 110–12
liberation struggles, 2, 68
logic of love, 62–63, 65–66
Luxemburg, Rosa, 138–39
lynching, 181n14

MacArthur, Douglas, 23
MacBird! (Garson), 55
Mainichi shimbun, 37
Maki, Carmen, 119
Marotti, William, 12, 90, 170n38, 172n25,
179n12
Maruyama Kunio, 75
Maruyama Masao, 75–76, 112
Marx, Karl, 46
Marxist Leninist League (ML dōmei), 81–82,
138
masculinity. *See* New Left (Japan), and
masculinity
mass media (1960s): circulation rates, 169n15;
on employment conversion, 150; and gen-
dered meaning, 143, 145–47; influence of, 7;
and student activism, 135–36; on URA ties
with feminists, 156
Meiji era (1868–1912), 101
Meiji University, 95–96
Meinhof, Ulrike, 122–23
men's liberation, 157
Minagawa Kanae, 32–33
minikomi (minicommunications), 7, 104
Ministry of Education, 67, 72, 76, 177n77
Minsei, 58, 93–95, 124
Mishima Yukio, 110–15, *111*, 121, 137, 157, 183n25,
183n30, 183n32; *Kinjiki*, 112
Mitsui Miike Coal Mine (Kyushu), 53, 66
ML dōmei (Marxist Leninist League), 81–82,
138
Modern Girl, 134, 147
Momboisse, Raymond, 130

Morely, James W., 124
Morisaki Kazue, 9
Mori Setsuko, 97, 109
Mori Tsuneo, 127, 155
Morris-Suzuki, Tessa, 5
mothers, 116–19, *118*, 141–42
My Back Page, 160
My Love and Rebellion (Tokoro), 49, 55

Nagata Hiroko, 7, 20, 127–28, 154–56, 159
naive politics, 21–48. *See also* Anpo struggle;
    female student activists; Kanba Michiko;
    vulnerability
Nakamura Hiroshi, 27, *118*
National Police Agency, 129–30
New Left (global), 5–6, 12–20, 55–56; and
    masculinity, 104–31, 160–61, 182n1
New Left (Japan), 5–6: after Anpo, 54; *Asahi
    jaanaru* on, 55–56; care work in, 17, 79,
    102–3; versus establishment Left, 2, 51;
    establishment of, 29; on everyday life, 80;
    factions (*ha*), 54–55; feminists on, 8–9, 20,
    102; and gender, 1, 3, 8–9, 19–20, 60, 97–98,
    101–3, 109, 162–63; police clashes, 113–14;
    sexism within, 6, 9, 100–101, 106, 109–10,
    115, 130–31, 163–64; and student activism,
    6, 126, 185n72; Tokoro's influence on, 51,
    54–55, 58, 77; versus U.S. New Left, 55–56;
    and violence (*Gewalt/gebaruto*), 20, 108, 111,
    160–61, 163, 183n26; women and , 2–4, 12,
    16–17, 158; Yamazaki and, 81–82. *See also* fe-
    male student activists; Gewalt Rosas (Vio-
    lent Rosas); Tokoro Mitsuko
Newsweek, 113
New York Times, 155
Nichibei anzen hoshō jōyaku. *See* Anpo
    struggle
Nihon University, 59, 85, 87–89, 120, 145,
    180n30
Nikkeiren (Japan Federation of Employers'
    Associations), 66–67
Nishida Sawako, 21
Nishimura Shogorō, 109
Nisshō (Japan Chamber of Commerce and
    Industry), 66–67
nurturing (women's logic), 18–19, 50–53,
    59–65, 74, 77, 102, 159–60, 162

Observer, 156
Ochanomizu University, 55
Oda Makoto, 55, 82
Ōe Kenzaburō, 26–27
Office Sister (Sonoyama), 150–51
Oguma Eiji, 8–9
Ōhara Kimiko, 93–94, 97, 99, 117, 123–25
Okinawa, 30, 82
Ōkōchi Kazuo, 83
Ono Tōsaburō, 45
Opinion Survey on the Police, 130
Osana tsuma no kokuhaku (Nishimura), 109
Ōsawa Toshirō, 119
Ōshima Nagisa, 108–9, 182n1
Ōta Kyōko, 100
Ōtsuka Eiji, 166

Packard, George, 31, 172n27
paternalism/patriarchy, 165–66
Patriotic Women's Association (Aikoku
    fujinkai), 24
peasant rebellions (*ikki*), 87
Piercy, Marge, 15–16, 131
police: care work by, 129–30; community out-
    reach by, 20; criticisms of, 45; and New Left,
    113–14; and organized crime, 45; and the
    press, 143, 145; and student activism, 85; at
    University of Tokyo, *88*, 88–91, *133*; and vio-
    lence, 122–28, *125*; and women, 33, *34–35*, 36
police boxes (*kōban*), 129
Police Duties Bill (Keishoku hō; Japan), 29–31
Polletta, Francesca, 13, 181n52
Popular Front for the Liberation of Palestine,
    127, 155
pornography, 109
Power, Nina, 166–67
prefigurative politics, 12–13
*Preliminary Materials for a Theory of the Young-
    Girl* (Tiqqun), 166–67
Protest in Tokyo (Packard), 172n27
Public Relations Office of the Cabinet Secre-
    tary, 130

radical movements (1960s): sexism within,
    3–4, 100–101; and social meaning, 6;
    and violence, 17; women-only, 16–17, 60,
    99–102, 152, 161. *See also* New Left (Japan)

Rancière, Jacques, 12, 170n38
rape/sexual assault, 108–9, 125, 127–28
rationalism: economic and scientific, 49–51, 60, 65–66
Red Army Faction (West Germany), 155
Relief Support Contact Center (Kyūen renraku sentaa), 161
Revolutionary Communist League (Nihon kakumeiteki kyōsanshugisha dōmei; Kakukyōdō), 29
Ribu Shinjuku Center, 109
rice balls, 97, 98, 99, 181n63
the Right, 105, 110–17, 111
Rise Up, Girl! (Nakamura), 27
Ross, Kristen, 12, 170n38
Russian Revolution, 11
Ryang, Sonia, 62–63

Sabsay, Letizia, 159–60
Sakurai Isamu, 147–52, 187n48
Sanpa (Three Factions), 58, 94, 161
sarariiman (salaryman), 142, 150–51
Saredo warera ga hibi (Shibata), 172n22
Sasaki-Uemura, Wesley, 25
Sasebo protests (1968), 57–58, 124
Sassa Atsuyuki, 132, 133
Satō Eisaku, 76, 81
Satō Masa'aki, 187n42
scientific and economic rationalism, 49–51, 60, 65–66
SEALDS (Students for Emergency Action for Liberal Democracy), 163–64
sexual liberation/free sex, 105, 107–9, 114, 145, 148
SFL (Student Front for Liberation; Gakusei kaihō sensen), 138
Shagakudō (Shakai shugi gakusei dōmei; Socialist Students League), 58
Shaseidō Kaihō (Liberation Group of the Socialist Youth League), 58, 94
Shibata Shō, 172n22
Shidehara Kijūrō, 23
Shield Society, 113, 183n25
Shigematsu, Setsu, 17, 156, 159, 170n25
Shigenobu Fusako, 95–96, 154–56
Shima Hiroko, 101–2, 181n63
Shima Shigeo, 101, 181n63

shimin (citizen), 171n2
Shinchōsha, 121
Shingeki, 117, 135
Shinjuku Lib Center, 17
Shinjuku Station riot (1968), 123–24, 130
shinsayoku (leftist factions), 5–6, 56, 95
Shisō no kagaku, 44, 60, 80
Shōda Michiko, 112–13
shōjo (young girl) folklore, 166
Shokado shoten, 163
Shokun!, 115–16
Shūkan gendai, 152–53
Shūkan pureibōi, 145
Shūkan shinchō, 33, 34–35, 36, 143, 145
Shūkan yomiuri, 118, 132–33, 147, 154
Silverberg, Miriam Rom, 134, 147
Sing a Song of Sex (Ōshima), 182n1
Smile Nobody Knows, The (Kanba Michiko), 39
socialist movement, 11–13
"Sometimes Like a Motherless Child" (Maki and Terayama), 119
Sonoyama Shunji, 147–51, 187nn47–48
South Korea, 54, 57, 80
Soviet Union, 11, 29–30, 57
Springer, Kimberly, 17
Stalinism, 2, 29
Steinhoff, Patricia, 127, 160
strikes, 27–28
student (campus-based) activism (1968–69): abandonment of, 126, 185n72; arrested students, 161; everyday life of, 90–93, 92; issues protested, 68–69, 80, 82, 94–95; men and, 150; militancy (Gewalt) of, 98–99, 122, 181n68; mothers and, 117–19, 118; of nonpori (nonpolitical) students, 78, 82, 90–91, 94; scope of, 85, 86; symbolic power of, 114; women and, 79, 109. See also barricades, student-run; Zenkyōtō (Zengaku kyōtō kaigi; All-Campus Joint Struggle Committees)
Student Front for Liberation (Gakusei kaihō sensen; SFL), 138
student self-governance associations (jichikai), 27–28, 59. See also Zengakuren (Zen Nihon gakusei jichikai sōrengō; All-Japan General Alliance of Student Self-Governing Associations)

Students for Emergency Action for Liberal Democracy (SEALDS), 163–64
student strikes, 27–28. *See also* Zengakuren (Zen Nihon gakusei jichikai sōrengō; All-Japan General Alliance of Student Self-Governing Associations)
Subversive Activities Prevention Law (Hakai katsudō bōshi hō; 1952), 129
Suga Hidemi, 9
Sun, Storm, and Liberty (Kashiwazaki), 138–41
Sunday mainichi, 147
Suzuki Shin'ichi, 115–16

Tachikawa Air Base protests, 29
Takada Nahoko, 33, 36
Takakura Ken, 107
Takamine Hideko, 26
Takamure Itsue, 60, 62–66
Takano Etsuko, 152–54
Takeda, Hiroko, 72
Tanaka Mitsu, 9
Tanaka Sumie, 32, 108
Terayama Shūji, 119, 120–21
Teruoka Yasutaka, 73–75, 143, 145, 178n78
Thought Group S.E.X., 1, 109
Tiqqun, 166–67
Toei Studios, 107
Tokoro Mitsuko, 49–77, *50*, 167–68; activism of, 49, 54–58, 60, 66; in Anpo, 49, 55–56; on capitalist rationalization, 13, 65; on co-education, 74; death of, 49, 57, 58; on economic and scientific rationalism, 49–51, 60, 65–66; and Garson, 55–57; "How Do Women Want to Be?" 60–61, 65; influence of, 18, 51, 54–55, 58, 60, 77; on the JCP, 13, 51–52, 57, 66; *My Love and Rebellion*, 49, 55; and New Left, 54–57; Takamure's influence on, 60, 62–66; "Toward the Coming Organization," 59, 65; on war, 61–62, 65–66; Weil's influence on, 60, 139; on women's logic (nurturing), 18–19, 50–53, 59–65, 74, 77, 102, 159–60, 162; writings of, 49, 52, 54–55, 60–61, 65, 77; and Yamamoto Yoshitaka, 54–55, 58, 82–83; and Zenkyōtō, 57–65, 59
Tokuyama Haruko, 94–95
Tokyo shimbun, 163

Tokyo Women's University, 99–100
Tomano Mimie. *See* Tokoro Mitsuko
Tomorrow Girls Troop, 167
Tosaka Jun, 80
"Toward the Coming Organization" (Tokoro [Tomano Mimie]), 59, 65
Toyama Mieko, 126–27, 155
Treaty of Mutual Cooperation and Security (U.S.-Japan Security Treaty), 30–31, 53. *See also* Anpo struggle
Tsuchiya Sōzō, 130
Tsurumi Kazuko, 44, 122
Tsurumi Shunsuke, 55
Twenty-Year Old's Origin, A (Takano), 152–54

Ueno Chizuko, 10, 156, 163
Ueno Gakuen High School protests, 27
Umbrella Movement (Hong Kong), 163
Unending Footsteps, 45
unions, 177n67
United Red Army, 126–28, 154–56, 161
United Red Army (Wakamatsu), 160, 187n58
United States, 30, 53, 66–67, 113. *See also* Anpo struggle
universities: and academic freedom, 89; number of students, 68, 176n54; rationalization of, 53; women's history courses at, 74–75. *See also* coeducation; education; higher education; Nihon University; University of Tokyo
University Control Bill (1969), 131
University of Tokyo: activism at, 52, 57, 87–89, 120; elite standing of, 120–21; National Diet Building, 21, 31–33, 36, 42, 45–46, *46*, 89, 123; News Research Center, 54; riot police at, 88–91, 133; student strikes at, 57, 83, 90–91; Yasuda Tower, *84*, 87, 89–91, 93, 114, 132, *133*, 137, 161
University of Tokyo Zenkyōtō: gendered division of labor in, 93; influence of, 58–59; and masculinity, 106, 120; and Mishima debate, 110–12, *111*, 183n25; on mothers, 117; as nonsectarian, 87, 180n30; origins of, 58, 83; prominence of, 85, 87; slogans of, 120; and the university, 82–83, 90–91; violence of, 111, 183n26; Yasuda Tower rally, *84*. *See also* barricades, student-run

URA (United Red Army) purge, 126–28, 154–56, 161
U.S. Foreign Operations Administration, 66–67
U.S.-Japan Security Treaty, 30–31, 53. *See also* Anpo struggle

Vietnam War, 2, 55, 57, 59–60, 68, 81–82, 113
violence: and eroticism, 114; gender and, 17–18, 143; intersectarian (*uchigeba*), 59, 108–9, 124–29; state, 18, 24–25, 30–31, 36, 105, 123, 131, 160; street fighting, 105, 132, 141
voice: gender and, 18
vulnerability: gender and, 17–18, 22, 36, 48, 159–60; New Left and, 105; postwar family and, 71–73

Wakamatsu Kōji, 160, 187n58
Waseda University, 94–95, 106–7
Watanabe Hitomi, 92
Weather Underground (U.S.), 155
Weil, Simone, 60, 139
"When the Acacia Rains Stop" (Nishida), 21
women: as bourgeois, 16; conceptions of, 4; as educators, 177n75; in industrial work-force, 10–11; in masculine positions, 151, 188n51; and naive politics, 23–26; and nurturing, 51; and oppression, 63; and social movements (1940s and 1950s), 23; U.S. ideas about, 24, 25, 171n5. *See also* female student activists
women, Japanese: and imperialism and milita-rism, 63–64; and politics of purity, 24–25; as moderate, 23–24; participation in soci-ety, 71–73, 76, 158–59; and peace, 25, 62
womenomics, 165
Women's Democratic Club (Fujin minshu kurabu), 25, 161
women's history, 62–64, 74–75
Women's History (Takamure), 63–64
women's liberation movement, 8–10, 12, 16–17, 60, 108–9, 151, 155. *See also* feminism

women's logic (nurturing), 18–19, 50–53, 59–65, 74, 77, 102, 159–60, 162
women's suffrage (Japan), 23–25, 159–60
World War II, 24, 60–61

yakuza, 45, 107
Yamada Masahiro, 115
Yamaguchi Yoshiko, 156, 188n63
Yamamoto Chie, 39, 75
Yamamoto Kiyokatsu, 124
Yamamoto Yoshitaka, 54–55, 58, 82–83, 87–88, 141, 161
Yamazaki Hiroaki, 81–82, 122
Yangu redi, 135
Yomiuri shimbun, 140, 141
Yoneyama, Lisa, 23, 62
Yonezu Tomoko, 96, 109
Young Lady, 152
youth crime, 71
Yūkan fuji, 135–36

Zengakuren (Zen Nihon gakusei jichikai sōrengō; All-Japan General Alliance of Student Self-Governing Associations): in Anpo, 30–32, 44; dissolution of, 53; fac-tions within, 58; founding of, 27–28; under JCP, 28–29, 172n22; under New Left groups, 29; under Sanpa, 58; Tokoro's influence on, 54. *See also* Bund; Haneda Airport protests
Zenkyōtō (Zengaku kyōtō kaigi; All-Campus Joint Struggle Committees): authenticity, 90; diversity in, 85; founding/growth of, 58–59, 78–79, 82–83, 85, 87–90; and gender, 93, 100, 106, 161–62; and New Left, 6; of Ni-hon University, 59, 85, 87–89, 180n30; partic-ipatory democratic structure of, 93–94; ral-lies by, 83, *84*; on revolutionary subjectivity, 60; as "shattering jewel" (patriotic suicide), 137; and Tokoro, 54, 57–65; women and, 97. *See also* Gewalt Rosas (Violent Rosas); Uni-versity of Tokyo Zenkyōtō

www.ingramcontent.com/pod-product-compliance
Lightning Source LLC
Chambersburg PA
CBHW071740270326
41928CB00013B/2744